Living is an unending mystery to be experienced,
not a problem to be solved nor a dogma to be believed.

BORN AGAIN TOO SOON

A Journey from Certainty to Mystery

By Harles Cone, PhD

Cone Resource Group

Published in the United States by Cone Resource Group,

Chapel Hill, North Carolina.

Cover and interior design by Granger Eltringham

First edition: March 2026

Library of Congress Cataloging-in-Publication Data LCCN 9798994206409

Includes bibliographical reference and index.

ISBN paperback 979-8-9942064-4-7

Printed in the United States of America

To my teachers and professors – from first grade when I was five years old through completing two master's degrees and a doctorate in 1976.

To the accomplished psychologists – who mentored me as I started learning the art and science of being a counselor and therapist.

To the numerous friends – who gave a part of themselves to me.

To my parents – who built a family of five children at the end of the Great Depression in a small rural town in Texas. They loved me and gave their best.

To my family – our children and grandchildren.

To my grandson, Granger Eltringham – who designed the cover and laid out the book.

and

Above all else to my wife, Judith, my soulmate, who has shared in the building of a triangular relationship that includes a her, a me, and an us. As the vicissitudes of life come our way, we seek to agree to whose wants/needs shall have 'the edge' in guiding us to our next decision.

CONTENTS

PART I

Chapter 1

STORIES

That it has always been much easier for me to hear, speak, or
read words than it has been to write them perplexes me. I am
forever indebted to the University of Missouri, Kansas City,
for a simple rule they held in conjunction with the awarding of
a doctoral degree. From the acceptance of a topic worthy of
dissertation research to the submission of the final document
and its oral defense, there was an absolute five-year time limit for
completion. I managed to submit my own work to the university
within that span—with only six weeks to spare! I was in awe of
those who could complete the process within eighteen months
to two years. The research portion of the work did not consume
much time. It was the writing of findings, with implications and
personal observations, that took the majority of that time.

Throughout my career and my personal life, words were
and continue to be of particular interest to me. I discovered as
I got deeper into this writing that it became progressively more
difficult to find the right words to tell my story. Why, when I have
made my living from helping people understand the dynamics of
words, were they so reluctant to flow from me in print? Perhaps
because the words I wanted to put down that would tell my story
were too revelatory of the essence of me and my journey from

certainty to mystery. Or perhaps as Flannery O'Connor said, "I write because I don't know what I think until I read what I say."

Going backward from my most recent to the earliest days, I have worked professionally as an executive coach, management consultant, leadership trainer, counseling therapist, college professor and administrator, and a thirteen-year stint as a young minister. My educational journey for all of this started as a 17-year-old who entered college for a bachelor of arts degree, progressed to getting a bachelor of divinity from a seminary, a master's degree in counseling and testing, and finally a doctorate. Psychology, interpersonal skills, group dynamics, history, philosophy, and brain science have been my intellectual foci. Careful parsing of words is critical to each of these fields.

I bring that part of my life to this present moment, because for nearly twelve years I have been playing with the central theme of the ideas which follow: I had been **born again too soon.** In the mid 1980s, at the age of fifty, these four words seemed to appear in my head from out of nowhere. I first heard born again as a child, relating to instructions on what it takes to become a Christian. Adding in too soon makes the phrase represent the struggle I have had in unlearning the certainty I had in what I was taught from birth as I started to study ideas that went beyond confirming the principles of the indoctrination of my youth. I started my journey in finding my own understanding of life and living. But those words—**born again too soon**—at that mid-century mark were riveting, compelling, and revealing. They still are.

It was the persistent, lingering impact of those words that led to the original desire to write about why they seem to hold onto me so tightly. Or was it just the opposite, me holding onto them? I can't seem to tell the difference anymore. But whatever the case, it is the actual writing that has proved the greatest challenge of all.

Why the challenge? I discovered, for me, that putting in print what I considered to be my conscious memories of important life events, my stories, were just that, stories. They were not nearly as complete nor accurate as I had felt them to be—as I had assumed them to be. Writing the words so that they became visible for my eyes rather than held solely in my thoughts, triggered other related words, quick flashes of thoughts, tangentially related to the first ones, yet different. Sometimes the peripheral thoughts were only slightly different, but in a few cases, they became the doorway to profound shifts in the core line of the original story.

Twelve years ago, when I first began this writing, I was feeling hurt and angry, even betrayed. The major culprits were my parents, my church, my culture, especially the messages surrounding my religion, my gender, and my race. So certain was I of those feelings and the justification behind them that the first words literally gushed out. Pages and pages flowed with ease. I felt relieved. After a few weeks of heavy writing the gushing tapered, the words became increasingly slow in coming, even hesitant. Yet, the original roiling I had experienced refused to be abated. The words shifted. They became less like blaring trumpets and more like the low vibrations of bassoons. Somehow, my own words, when out before me in print, seemed less me, less personal. And that, remarkably, freed me to look at them with less passion and certainty.

What slowly emerged was a sense of my own complicity throughout my entire enculturation and learning processes. Obviously, the cultural shaping of a child's first experiences, perceptions, attitudes, and beliefs is profoundly one sided: parents and siblings to infants, clans to families, institutions to individuals. And in many, if not most, cases, those first learnings have remained tightly and powerfully in place throughout my entire life, to both my disadvantage and advantage, my hurt as well as my joy and pleasure.

Now, a powerful but recognizable tension, a yin-yang, has surfaced. The yin of wanting to understand as much as possible about what may have gone on in the world beyond the narrowness of what I was taught first engaged me. Information, different from what I was taught was everywhere. My appetite for listening and reading has seemed insatiable, limited only by time and energy. The yang of wanting to be understood, to be more fully known, more open and honest with both myself and others, has evolved much more slowly. Yet this new force has been no less powerful.

Writing my stories—seeing the stories that I had written laid out before me, out of the closet of my mind and into a public arena—altered in some significant ways my sense of their power over me. To be clear, the enlarged view did not alter the relevance of a story. It did, however, profoundly soften the connected passion, hurt, and anger. A sense of my own role, responsibility, and accountability began to show its frighteningly ugly head! In the stories that follow, I have tried my best to present them with as much balance and fairness as possible. And, while doing so, I am fully aware that anyone who was a part of any of my stories would have his or her own variation in the telling of the same event. They see the world the way they are just as I see it the way I am.

Story - Poochie

For instance, I see little or no alterations in the life impact of one of my stories as a five-year-old child. The image of my mother fiercely beating our dog, Poochie, with a broom while, exclaiming in sharp tones, "Bad Dog!" is still strong. Mom had a red and taut expression on her face like I had never experienced before. In that moment, my mother seemed literally beside herself. This has remained a powerful, lifelong memory. As an adult, I understand what was going on and why she behaved as she did, but as a five-year-old, dependent on this woman for love, support, and survival, my basic senses were triggered. I would never want her to react toward me like that!

I learned in my adolescent years that Poochie was only doing what male dogs do when in the presence of a female dog in heat. In those moments following the reproductive act, dogs are often physically unable to separate, and I assume that is what had happened.

What would remain is a powerful, lifelong memory of my mother's behavior. I can only assume she saw the dogs from our kitchen window, with my two-year-old brother and me making a fascinated audience, grabbed her broom, and rushed to the yard. The fierceness of the beating, the voice tone, and facial expression was all pointed toward Poochie. To my memory, no whacks were given to the other dog. What was clear in the extreme was that our dog, whom I had never seen treated poorly, had done something so bad he was getting a punishment harsher than anything I had ever witnessed and from a part of my mother I had never seen. Separating himself and running under our house with his tail between his legs probably saved him.

~ ~ ~

Reflecting on this story and my reaction at the time, I think I was both fascinated and terrified. Having my mother's good will and approval became a major shaper of my early life. Did I, at some sub-rational, preconscious level, sense that living within my mother's boundaries was important to my well-being and safety? Did I ever broach the topic of this story with her as I grew older? No. I wish I had, for both our sakes.

In a manner that is still very much a part of my current life, I have cautiously come to this conclusion: My life stories seem to have served at least two functions. One, and the most obvious, was to keep alive the sense of self to which I had come and was becoming. As far as I knew, my stories were true. They represented the real me. They were my way of explaining myself to me, as well as to others. What has emerged is an uncovering of another reason for their retention and telling! The second reason is that they not only explained me (and to me), but they also told of the protection I needed as a child and young person. At my core, I sensed at a most profound level that coloring outside the lines was not to be tolerated. If I was to be loved and accepted, I needed to be a good boy, do as my parents said, follow the societal norms of my small East Texas town and the fundamentalist religious norms of my Southern Baptist churches. The need to fit in, to have people think well of me, had an iron grip on me. I wanted to survive. I wanted to be part of the village that was raising me.

What I have now come to understand about my stories and other's stories and the way the brain works is best stated by Albert Einstein: "Reality is merely an illusion, although a very persistent one. We do not see the world the way it is, we see the world the way we are." My story reflects my being, it is who I am, I am the story.

Here is the first of what I am calling Spoiler Alerts. As with films, my spoiler alerts are warnings that an important detail of the plot development is about to be revealed. In this case, together, these spoiler alerts call attention to perhaps the most powerful single factor of my story that I only came slowly to understand as I wrote this. My formal education in history, religion, and psychology has been enhanced over the years by my own curiosity. I have studied a wide range of topics—mainly the Civil War and neuroscience. As I wrote this story, I studied the history of the Southern Baptists which led me to a bombshell of a discovery as it relates to me, my heritage, and the views held by me today. These spoiler alerts point to that revelation.

Spoiler Alert 1 - The Broader Cultural Influence

Some of my most powerful stories, I belatedly discovered, had come to me via the larger culture of which my family, my clan, my religious community were but a very small part. The larger, less-aware-to-me, world consisted of my town, my state, my region, my country, and my hemisphere. Within these larger dimensions, I would also include my gender, my ethnicity, and the period of historical time in which my experiences occurred. In a Biblical statement paraphrased: I had eyes and could not see, ears and could not hear. This is an accounting of the life and living of a human being from conception to his current existence in the last half of his ninth decade on this planet. It has been a trip, a journey, and a seemingly long and bumpy one at that. Its two touchstones are opposites. On the starting end was a profound confidence in the rightness and accuracy of the beliefs that guided my thoughts and behaviors, a certainty, if you will. On the other is an equally profound confidence in the idea that there is hardly anything that I know for certain. Instead, there is a sense that with each thought of what I might know, there is profound awareness of the vastness of what lies beyond, what I do not yet know—a mystery. My family and friends have heard me often say: "There are things I know, and I know that I know that I know them." I have demonstrable evidence to prove it. "There are things that I don't know, and I know that I don't know them." These can also be demonstrated. "There are things that I don't know, and I don't know that I don't know them." And that arena is where the mysteries of life and living exist.

Chapter 2

MY VILLAGE

The African proverb—It takes a village to raise a child—is a common saying. I think of the village that helped raise me and helped me interpret the world. There were several sub-groups, each holding common beliefs.

The broader culture that surrounded me included my being a White male child in the middle of five—two older brothers and a younger brother and sister, each of us separated by two to three years. We were born between 1930 and 1940, the decade of the Great Depression and the run-up to World War II. We lived under modest circumstances in two small towns in eastern Texas when segregation of the White and Black races was the law. Our grandparents, and their parents, had migrated to East Texas from other southern states—Louisiana, Alabama, and Georgia. We were White, living in the southern region of the United States, in the Western Hemisphere, in the middle of the twentieth century AD.

The primary influencers of my religious life were family, church, college, and seminary. Collectively they formed the village in which I was reared, in a particular religion practiced by Southern Baptist evangelical fundamentalists. As far as I could see at the time, there was a oneness, a sameness of ideas from group to group. In hindsight, it was only a small village within a much larger world; but for me it was the world.

Their role was to teach. My role was to learn, believe, trust, and obey. The impact of my larger culture in which this all took place (small Southern towns, modest socio-economic status, and limited educational exposure) was generally hidden from me for another three decades. Differences were there. I could not see them.

Religious Fundamentalists

One of the most distorting and lasting impacts on me and my stories came from being a part of a family and a church set in a town and region where many adhered to the principles of religious fundamentalism. This village had stringent rules and was certain that they were the only true way to God.

Being a Christian fundamentalist implied a person held tightly to five basic tenets:

• The inerrancy of the Bible—the Bible is true and accurate in all its declarations.

• The literal nature of the Biblical accounts—especially regarding Jesus's miracles and the Creation account in Genesis.

• The Virgin Birth of Jesus and his all-wise and sinless living.

• The Bodily Resurrection of Jesus three days after he was crucified.

• The physical return of Jesus, his Second Coming, and the substitutionary atonement of Christ on the cross. He died for the sins of all humanity. Those who believed would spend eternity in heaven. Those who did not would spend eternity in hell. (A more extensive discussion of the origin of these five basic ideas for the Southern Baptist Convention is in Chapter 12.)

I was living under an umbrella of religious fundamentalism with little awareness. Distinctions like liberal, moderate, conservative did not exist in my world. To me it was simple. It wasn't just my Christian faith; it was THE Christian faith.

The rules of society and behavior were interpreted to me and those in our fundamentalist Christian churches by preachers. They had studied the rule book, the playbook for life, and then put it into practical dos and don'ts. The Bible was the infallible, literal word of God—the Sword of the Lord. End of story. No questions asked.

Bible verses I was taught for living a Godly and fulfilling life included:

• "Train up a child in the way that he should go. And when he is old, he will not depart from it." (Proverbs 22:6 [KJV]). King Solomon, circa 1000-900 BC.

• "Marvel not that I saith unto you, Ye must be born again." (John 3:7 [KJV]). Circa AD 50-100.

• "Jesus saith unto him, I am the way, the truth, and the life: no man cometh unto the Father, but by me." (John 14:6, [KJV]). Circa AD 50-100

• "And you shall know the truth, and the truth shall set you free." (John 8:32, [KJV]). Circa AD 50-100

Born Again—Too Soon

Being born again in the Christian vernacular means a rebirth by accepting that Jesus is the Son of God and that you dedicate yourself to this concept and to serving the Trinity—God, the Son, and the Holy Ghost. The commonly used phrase is accepting Jesus as your personal Lord and Savior.

I was born again—but too soon. I was made free from sin not only before I knew what sin was, but also before any experiential knowledge of being trapped, imprisoned, or enslaved by anyone or anything. I was given answers to eternal verities before I had any clue as to what life's essential questions might be and before I could appreciate the distinctive beauty of a well-framed question. I was taught, and believed, the ends before any comprehension of beginnings or the place of paths and processes. I learned what to think before there was any understanding of the why, the how, or the wonder of thinking itself. What thinking I did was focused on how important it seemed to believe what I was being taught. And the teaching was done by people who loved and cared for me and my wellbeing.

My first birth occurred on December 14, 1935, in our home on West Larissa St. in Jacksonville, Texas, Dr. J. M. Travis presiding. My second birth, and first formal act of my religious journey, occurred nine years later.

With some prompting I confessed that Jesus was my Savior at the First Baptist Church in Lufkin, Texas. Lufkin, 60 miles south of Jacksonville, had been our new home for two years. To my knowledge this confession of sin was the first outward step I took that reflected my inward state—the beginnings of my conscious grappling with being a person wanting to relate to the world. I was fulfilling my mother's greatest wish—that I not suffer eternal damnation for failing to accept Jesus Christ as my Lord and Savior. It was the most central point of concern in her faith.

My sensitivity to the wants and needs of others, especially my mother, was a consuming force.

I remember very little about the event itself. I went forward to make my confession at the end of a Sunday morning sermon by our pastor, Dr. Bradford. I was duly voted on by the congregation as eligible for membership in the church, and at the end of evening worship service, I was immersed in baptism by the pastor, "In the name of the Father, the Son, and the Holy Ghost." My mother was happy. My Sunday school teacher was happy. The pastor was happy. All this made me happy. Sensing and doing what people I cared about wanted from me was a big part of my life. I was good at it. It was paying off. I would get even better.

Growing Up

The first years of my religious upbringing were uneventful. I passed through the elementary and junior high school years like most of my friends. We enjoyed activities, sports, games, and girls. Playing "Spin the Bottle" at parties to see which girl you got to hold hands and go for a walk with was especially fun. I don't remember clearly how we could almost always manage to get the bottle to point toward the right girl—the one we liked, plus the one we knew would be willing to take the walk.

Going to school made these fun things possible, and church supplemented these activities. There were Vacation Bible Schools in the summer and youth groups on Sundays as well as throughout the week. The Boy Scout Troop, of which I was a part, was also under the auspices of my church. The youth group Royal Ambassadors (RAs) and Boy Scouts of America Troup 123 (BSA) were especially important. Everything pointed toward being a good boy, a good citizen, and a good Christian.

I knew the Boy Scout laws: A scout is trustworthy, loyal, helpful, friendly, courteous, kind, obedient, cheerful, thrifty, brave, clean, and reverent. These laws were important to me. In my heart, I honored them all.

I spent three years in scouting, rarely missing a meeting, troop campout, or the annual regional summer week outing at Camp Tonkawa. After all those years, my rank peaked at Second Class, one step above the entry level, Tenderfoot. My older brother, Bob, over the same span, attained the rank of Eagle Scout, the highest! I liked the activities associated with the meetings, the games, and the contests. I also enjoyed being with friends I liked and those who liked me. I was pretty skilled athletically, so people wanted me on their team and in their group. Looking back and trying to remember, it is not altogether clear why I didn't do the individual work for badges that would move me up in the ranks. I am mindful that one of the constant messages from my mother was: "Don't get too big for your breeches." If I got too big for my breeches, people wouldn't like me.

The friends at church and school were almost always the same. I was only vaguely aware that there were others who were members of other churches, or none at all, but in my mind, they seemed no different from me. We were all "good" boys and girls. If our parents saw things differently, I didn't know it. I learned later that what one believed, when compared with the beliefs of another, could be viewed as critically important.

The summer following my eighth grade in Lufkin, our family returned to live in Jacksonville. High school days were passed in essentially the same way as elementary and junior high, just a bit more advanced. Activities, athletics, and parties were geared to follow the calendar of the school and church. Dating was new and serious business. Spinning the bottle to hold hands and go walking was replaced with dances, going steady, parking, and sexual explorations. I was popular.

Life-Changing Events

Two pivotal life-turning-points occurred in the summer that
followed my senior year in high school in 1953. I was seventeen
years old.

Key Moment 1—Rededicated Myself. Our church, Sunset
Avenue Baptist, held a week-long Youth-Led Revival, a series
of church services led by single young people. The evangelist,
Jimmy Draper, from Houston, was my age. He had lived in
Jacksonville during my ninth and tenth grade years. His father
had been the pastor of Central Baptist Church, the town's largest
church of any denomination. We had been friends and had
played basketball together.

Jimmy was now himself a preacher, a youth evangelist—
at eighteen years old. I was impressed. He was handsome,
charming, and passionate about his beliefs. His sermons were
filled with powerful stories and Biblical references regarding
good and evil, right and wrong, saved and lost, good Christians
and weak Christians. He was a fundamentalist Christian. I was
touched. It was clear to me that I had not nearly been as good
a Christian as I could have been, should have been. At the end
of one of his sermons, I went forward for the second time in my
life. This time it was to rededicate my life to Jesus. I was sorry
for my sins and my careless way of living, especially for my deep
involvement in the things of this world. All this constituted a new
way of thinking, feeling, and acting for me. There was more to
come, more serious and more formal.

Key Moment 2—Decided to Become a Preacher. A few
weeks later, Jimmy invited me to be a guest in the Houston
home of his parents. He was going to conduct another Youth-
Led Revival in a church in that city, and he wondered if I might
want to participate. I did. In the course of the week, I also went
forward for a third, and what would be, the final time of my
life. This time I was surrendering to God's call for me to be a
preacher. Like my friend, I, too, had now been called by God to
preach. I felt strongly that this was God's Will for my life.
I promised to live life, as much as possible, as Jesus would
want me to, up to and including being a preacher on behalf
of this religion. Primarily, this entailed two things—one
private in nature, the other more public. On the private side
was a more regular and disciplined approach to reading and
studying the Bible, along with accompanying prayers to God for
understanding and guidance. Making this a daily practice was my
goal. On the public side, it meant I would stop doing
un-Christian things—smoking and drinking, neither of which
I was doing anyway because of my commitment to athletics;
gambling, which I wasn't doing much of unless it was for match
sticks or other items that could be won or lost with no tangible
value attached; dancing, which I was doing and knew from
personal experience where it could lead, because it had led me
there; profanity and cursing, which I didn't do already because it
was absolutely forbidden in my home; doing un-Christian things
on Sunday, the Lord's Day; and listening to music that was not
produced by Christians.

The last two were new areas of focus for me. Until the
revivals, I would not have considered eating out (forcing others
to have to work on Sunday rather than being free to attend
church), playing ball, or going to movies on Sunday afternoon
un-Christian things to do. Adhering to these new rules was a
measure of the depth of my commitment to living a Christian

life—"Remember the Sabbath day to keep it holy." By turning away from non-Christian music, music that was being performed by those not promoting the Christian faith, was refusing to give any support for what they were doing.

For all practical purposes, I now had as many as a half dozen models to help further my understanding of what being born again entailed in life and living. Two were from the Bible. They were the conversation between Jesus and Nicodemus recorded in the third chapter of The Gospel According to John and the conversion of Saul of Tarsus to Paul the Apostle recorded in the ninth chapter of the New Testament book Acts of the Apostles. The other models were modern day—my friend Jimmy and a few of his counterparts.

The Evangelist Billy Graham was heralded as the most outstanding of them all. Billy Graham Evangelistic Crusades were being presented around the United States and numerous foreign countries. I shared that view of Billy Graham and heard him in person in June 1953, in Tyler, Texas, 26 miles north of my hometown of Jacksonville. To a crowd of 20,000 people in Rose Stadium, he preached a sermon highlighting the heart of the fundamentalist Christian gospel—the substitutionary death of God's Son, Jesus, to save all humankind from sin and eternal damnation. I saw and heard the musical skills of Cliff Barrows as well as the magnificent voice of George Beverly Shea singing solo the inspiring song "How Great Thou Art." It seemed obvious to me that God's hand was directly guiding the work of Graham and the Crusades. What other explanation could there possibly be?

Two other lesser lights, Evangelist Freddie Gage and Evangelist Angel Martinez, would also help shape my image of what preaching and evangelism could be like, but I had little personal contact with either. Gage had the most dramatic conversion story (testimony) I ever heard. As told, it dealt directly with the bad and evil to which humans could sink—and yet still be saved, born again. Many times, he would tell the story of a ghetto life in Houston of drugs, sex, lying, stealing, and gangs. Being born again had saved him from it all.

Being Pure

I had no understanding of two long-standing and conflicting views of God and the corresponding expectations of His believers. One view exalted the purity and holiness of God, while the other held high the loving kindness of God. These were based on the rules in the Bible, interpreted through the lens of fundamentalist Christians. At this age as a high schooler, I had no understanding of such concepts as fundamentalism. God was God, and my parents and my church told me all about what to think, feel, and do.

This passage, "Be ye holy as I the Lord your God am holy." (Leviticus 19:2), along with many of the chapters in Leviticus and other books of the Old Testament, spelled out holiness as being separated from any and everything unclean. The good were to have no contact with the bad. The Bible states: "Wherefore come out from among them, and be ye separate, saith the Lord, and touch not the unclean thing; and I will receive you."
(II Corinthians 6:17).

This proved to be the earliest guiding view of God for me. Bad was everywhere. Good was keeping my distance from it. It took me another sixty years before I would understand the extent to which the concept of being good as a matter of not doing bad could be taken. In 2014, I came across a partial listing of wrongdoings proclaimed by John Roach Straton, a minister in the first half of the twentieth century. The list of sins to be avoided in his day, according to him, included cocktail drinking, card playing, poodle dogs, jazz music, the theatre, low-cut dresses, divorce, novels, stuffy rooms, Clarence Darrow, overeating, the Museum of Natural History, evolution, the Standard Oil influence in the Baptist Church, prize fighting, the private lives of actors, nude art, playing bridge, modernism, and greyhound racing. His list put to shame anything I might have ever created on my own!

As to the other long-standing view of God, one that held high His loving kindness, I was a slow-learning student. Avoiding evil seemed clear to me. No drinking, no gambling, no cursing were my family extensions to no lying, no killing, no stealing, and no adultery. Loving and caring actively for those in need, particularly the poor and outcast, seeking justice for others, and viewing all people as God's children were not so obvious.

I learned later that, according to some, Jesus supplemented and expanded the emphasis on purity with an emphasis on compassion—"Be ye merciful, as your Father in heaven is merciful. He who saith he loveth God, but hateth his brother the truth is not in him for God is love. He that loveth not, knoweth not God for God is love" (Luke 6:36, I John 4:8, I John 4:20). It was this distinctiveness, according to popular belief, that brought Jesus into his sharpest conflicts with the religions of His day. The Bible stories portrayed Jesus as one who associated with all forms of uncleanness—women, tax collectors, poor, sick, Samaritans, drinkers, and such. The idea of compassion and concern for others as the pivotal pillar of faith did not come my way for years. For now, holiness was king, and I was separating myself from all things unclean. The emphasis on purity, however, had little or no impact on the way my girlfriend and I expressed our affection to each other. We were still going steady and eventually planned to marry.

Becoming a Preacher Boy

Like my nine-year-old experience, everyone was happy with the summer decisions I had made—Jimmy, my preacher friend, my home-town pastor, Donald Grolliman, when he was told of the commitment I made in Houston, and my parents. I wasn't as sure about my friends. What I had come to over the summer had separated me from them more than a little. I was now a bit more dedicated than they, more serious regarding matters of faith and religion. Fortunately, or unfortunately for me, I did not have many dealings with those friends. Our high school connections were over, and under the guidance of my pastor, I was formally ordained to preach the Gospel by my church. It included the laying on of hands by the deacons of the church along with the gift of a beautiful, leatherbound Bible.

I soon became a student at one of my denomination's liberal arts colleges, East Texas Baptist College. The process of educating a young ministerial student was officially beginning. I said no to the offer of a partial basketball scholarship to my hometown Lon Morris College.

Years later during my friend Jimmy's adult ministry, he became highly regarded by the fundamentalists of the Southern Baptist Convention. He was recognized for his evangelistic fervor as well as the numbers of persons being baptized annually in churches where he served as pastor. At one point, he was elected the president of the Southern Baptist Convention. He also played a large role in what became known as the fundamentalist takeover of the Southern Baptist Convention's schools and agencies in the 1960s-70s.

Having Faith

In hindsight, I can see that I started my religious journey with a lot of beliefs—but very little faith. I inherited, literally, the faith of my fathers, though, in my case, the mediator was primarily my mother. It was not so much being educated in a religion that required having faith at its core as it was being indoctrinated into a view about it—a lot like eating food that had already been well chewed by others. For the next several years, I ate a lot of food that had already been masticated.

In my youthful exuberance, it seemed vitally important to hold the correct beliefs, the right ones versus those that were wrong—and to convince others of the correctness of those beliefs. Believing in Jesus was crucial, central to all else. The phrase believing in Jesus meant primarily believing things about Jesus, specific things about His birth, life, baptism, death, resurrection, and final return, and the Bible, in which these stories were told, and that He (God/Jesus) had a specific plan for my life. The ultimate driving force behind Bible study and prayer was to find and follow the Will of God for my life.

Believing things about Jesus and the Bible was easy then. It was what I was taught. There were no objections, no questions, no concerns, no challenges raised in my earlier training, none. There were only confident declarations. The more I believed them, the happier were some of my teachers. I felt proud. Most of my relationships were with people who were reared and taught as I. From the broadest of views, I was a fundamentalist Christian. That other views existed—conservative, moderate, liberal, skeptic, atheist—was unknown to me and would have been unthinkable. After all, what I had been taught about Christianity was either true or it wasn't. I believed it to be true. Although the expression religious supremacy was never used,

I believed that my religion was the only authentic one for the entire history of human experience!

The religious doctrine I inherited was the complete package, soup to nuts. And a part of the package included a prohibition regarding questioning the package itself. To do so was construed as an act of unbelief, a lack of faith, the work of the devil, and worthy of the greatest of punishments. Here is one of the favorite hymns we sang.

This hymn for me, like none other in the entire Baptist Hymnal, reflects every aspect of Christian doctrine singled out at the end of each of the four stanzas. No questions. No curiosities. No doubts allowed.

Hymn: *Trust and Obey,* John H. Sammis, 1846-1919

1. When we walk with the Lord
in the light of his word,
what a glory he sheds on our way!
While we do his good will,
he abides with us still,
and with all who will trust and obey.
Refrain:
Trust and obey, for there's no other way
to be happy in Jesus, but to trust and obey.
2. Not a burden we bear,
not a sorrow we share,
but our toil he doth richly repay;
not a grief or a loss,
not a frown or a cross,
but is blest if we trust and obey.
(Refrain)
3. But we never can prove
the delights of his love

until all on the altar we lay;
for the favor he shows,
for the joy he bestows,
are for them who will trust and obey.
(Refrain)
4. Then in fellowship sweet
we will sit at his feet,
or we'll walk by his side in the way;
what he says we will do,
where he sends, we will go;
never fear, only trust and obey.

Religious Cocoon of Certainty

As my religious life unfolded, it was the outer packaging in which the religion was housed that presented the greatest personal reassurances—and most serious challenges. Like the shell of a cocoon, without its breakage, there could be no light or movement to the outer world. My religious packaging was presented in such a manner as to minimize, discourage, or eliminate any serious looking at the outside. The incasement was a part of the religious beliefs, and it was to be taken together as a whole. It was made up of certainty, no questioning needed.

The cocoon consisted of several key ingredients. One was absolute belief, confidence, and trust in the veracity of the Bible, from which all core concepts were drawn. To doubt or question any of its aspects was viewed as a sign of spiritual immaturity, weakness, doubt, or worst of all, sin. Great value was placed on child-like faith. Proverbs 9:10 states, "Fear of God is the beginning of wisdom." In Matthew 18:3, Jesus is quoted as saying, "Verily I say unto you, except ye be converted, and become as little children, ye shall not enter into the kingdom of heaven." And in Matthew 19:26, "And looking at them Jesus said to them, 'With man this is impossible, but with God all things are possible.'" 1 Corinthians 3:19 states, "For the wisdom of this world is foolishness to God." And to behave or think or question in a way that might cause other people to stumble or doubt was worthy of the most extreme punishment. Luke 17:2 states, "It were better for him that a millstone were hanged about his neck and be cast into the sea, than that he should offend one of these little ones." The value and authenticity of the core was unassailable and unquestionable. The paralysis of thought associated with such a limited arena in which to live would prove to be profound.

This first ingredient, the importance of a childlike faith, had enormous impact on what I would do with miracles cited in the Bible. Did Jesus forgive sin, walk on water, heal the sick, raise the dead, calm the seas, change water to wine, feed the five thousand, rise from the dead? Of course he did! Our faith in God and the veracity of the Bible confirms them all. For the truly childlike faithful believer, once I started down the path of believing in miracles, there was no turning back. Old Testament miracles, God speaking the earth into existence in seven days, Noah building an Ark and securing a pair of every living creature on Earth to survive a universal flood, Jonah swallowed by and living in the belly of a whale, the parting of the Red Sea, unconsumed flaming bushes to guide, the walls of Jericho collapsing at the sound of trumpets, Elisha caught up by a flaming chariot into heaven, Elijah bringing the Priests of Baal to ridicule, axe heads swimming in water along with countless others were all part of acceptance by having faith. After all, if they were not true, God would not have placed these accounts in the Bible. The strongest of Christians believed and trusted in them all. Childlike faith was the key. The greater one's faith, the more one could believe. Faith and questioning in any form were incompatible. I wanted to be counted among the strong. Later in my life, this way of thinking became the context for my reaction to hearing the word devout when used to describe the degree of commitment someone had regarding his or her religious doctrines and beliefs. The word was typically reserved for those who were completely accepting and committed to every item of dogma they had been taught.

Another important ingredient in the religious packaging had to do with the response of others to my beliefs. In the case of non-believing outsiders, if I was questioned or teased, or, God forbid, punished for the faith that I espoused, it was to be expected, even celebrated! After all, was that not what had happened to Jesus? Was he not ridiculed and marginalized by some? Yes! Was he not treated poorly? Yes! Was he not crucified for what he believed and taught? Yes! As a true believer, I should expect no less. In fact, to be questioned or teased or ridiculed was to be seen as an indicator that I was on the right path. Raising questions, showing doubts, was evil and associated with the work of Satan. Holding firm and unwavering was the work of God. In other words, having my belief system called into question was not a time for rethinking, exploring, or reconsidering, but rather a time to reassert, reaffirm, and continue forward! In Matthew 5:11-12 Jesus is quoted as saying, "Blessed are ye, when men shall revile you, and persecute you, and shall say all manner of evil against you falsely, for my sake. Rejoice, and be exceeding glad: for great is your reward in heaven: for so persecuted they the prophets which were before you."

The same idea is repeated in Luke 6:22-23, "Blessed are you when men hate you, when they exclude you and insult you and reject your name as evil, because of the Son of Man. Rejoice in that day and leap for joy, because great is your reward in heaven. For that is how their fathers treated the prophets." The value and authenticity of the core was unassailable and unquestionable. Anyone who could not see this was in great need, and if they were to ridicule or abuse me for the beliefs, I held it as a sign that I was on the right path. Said another way, I learned how to double down before I could examine the bet itself! What a self-fulfilling, thought-limiting cocoon that proved to be.

The third ingredient was regarding fellow believers who may have come to different conclusions than I about the good-bad, right-wrong issues of faith and living; they needed to be corrected. Statements made in the Bible were to be used as my basic guide.

A final element of the religious packaging would handily serve the first three. What does one do with obvious contradictions and inconsistencies that arise around complex issues within the religion itself or between one Bible statement and another? What really happened on the morning of Jesus's Resurrection? The Gospels of Matthew, Mark, and Luke each tell a different story. How can God give the commandment, "Thou shalt not kill," as His people are leaving Egypt and order "every living creature, including men, women and children" be put to death when those same people are entering the city of Jericho? Why do bad things happen to good people? If God is omnipresent, omniscient, and omnipotent, why is there such suffering, war, poverty, and cruelty? If God hears and answers prayer, why do so many prayers seem to go unanswered? If believers have been saved from sin, why do such sinful temptations and behaviors persist?

The answer to these and dozens of other similar inquiries: It is all a part of God's overall plan! It is a mystery to us human beings for the present, but it will eventually be made known to us in good time, after death, when we are living with God in our next life, in Heaven. God moves in mysterious ways his wonders to perform. In the meantime, we must cling confidently to our faith in God as it has been laid out by those older and wiser than we. Any contradictions, inconsistencies, irrationalities that might occur in the living out of one's life were but a part of God's mysterious plan and all would be made clear in our next life with Him. All I had to do was trust and obey, as the hymn that I sang so often admonishes.

This part of the cocoon provides a partial explanation for how genuinely caring people who, when others are facing personal distress and tragedy, inadvertently can make the cruelest of comments. In crises, caring people schooled as I was, want to show their care. They want to bring comfort to their loved ones and their friends. Expressing their care in the midst of contradictions and complexities becomes a challenge. "He's in a better place now." "Just have faith, God knows what He's doing." "It'll all work out, God is still with us," were some of the comments my brother suffered through at the funeral of a son who died of cystic fibrosis in his early 30s shortly after a lung transplant. Trust and obey are at work.

In the meantime, the early basic elements of my religious training, plus the outer packaging, provided the parameters for dealing well with those outside the religion. They also worked well for promoting a great sense of belonging, appreciation, and respect from those on the inside. I had absolutely no awareness that the regard was coming only from a very limited and narrow group within a much larger body. However, as my life unfolded, the packaging proved woefully inadequate, even crippling, for dealing with those within the religion when differences of opinions arose—when conflict emerged among those in places of authority. It was twenty plus years before I could begin to understand that believing not thinking is part of the price of admission for anyone who wants to be a part of a fundamentalist religious group, tribe, or sect! And it is not so much being true to God as it is being true to what other human beings who have come before you had to say about God. Breaks in my cocoon's shell were coming. I was becoming a fraction less certain.

Chapter 3

CRACKS IN THE COCOON

"He's got a hand, ain't he?" was all Harold E. said. But in that moment, in that phrase, my heart immediately began to pound. I could barely breathe.

It was mid-day, mid-July 1954. I was eighteen. It was lunch break time. The four of us were sitting under an oak tree, which itself was something of an oddity. We were in the section of East Texas known as the Piney Woods. Any trees beyond the pines were few in number. The big oak tree stood out from the rest. We were on the side of a dirt road that was in the process of being shaped and paved to become one of East Texas's farm-to-market, asphalt-topped roads. The Heidelberg Construction Company of Jacksonville, Texas, was busily at work.

We few were root grabbers, the lowest rung on the ladder of jobs required to build a road such as this. The bulldozers, maintainers/road graders, and dragline had already done their jobs. They knocked over trees, pushed them to the shoulders of the road-to-be into piles to be burned later, and shaped the ground with a slight crown in the middle for water drainage. Invariably, root systems of the trees would remain at, and just below, the surface of the road. A grabber's job was, with axes, saws, and shovels, to remove as many of these remaining root systems as possible. If not removed, over time, the roots would deteriorate, rot, and create holes beneath the surface, causing bumps and potential potholes in the road. The job was an important one. It just did not require much from the persons doing it beyond good eyesight, and strong hands, arms, legs, and back.

As a group, we tended to eat separately from the more skilled employees, not only a reflection of our status on the job, but on the quality of the food we were about to eat. At $1.10 an hour (minimum wage was 75 cents), living on the road from Sunday evening until Friday afternoon and sharing the cost of a cheap hotel room for four nights did not leave much to invest in brown bag lunches prepared by a small cafe near the hotel. The operators of the heavy earth moving equipment, the bulldozers, maintainers, earth movers, and above all, the dragline operator, made multiples of what we did. They could afford a much more appetizing range of food options for lunch and breaks. Rather than subjecting ourselves to good-natured ridicule or envy, we just ate apart from them.

It was a summer job for me. Harold E. and the other two were full-time employees. Mr. Heidelberg had always been willing to provide me with summer work. He thought of me as a good hand. It was my second summer to work for him, the first on the road.

I had just finished my freshman year at East Texas Baptist College—I was a college man. I worked on a road crew where a high school diploma was often unusual, if not suspicious. These were men who lived by their wits and their work skills. For them, it was enough to be able to read, write, and do your numbers. I was different. My fellow root grabbers were fascinated and curious about that difference.

Not only was I a college student, but I was also a ministerial student. I was a preacher boy. At this point, I had not only been licensed to preach by my home church, I also had been ordained to preach by the Board of Deacons of the same church. After all, I was now the weekend pastor of a small rural church. So, in the eyes of my working buddies, I was a preacher boy, a pastor, and a rootgrabber. I was a frequent topic of lunch break conversations.

Harold E. was an unschooled Black man. To me he was handsome, smart, strong, and ageless. As I write this, I am curious as to what his age was. He was my friend. We had hit it off from the first day I had come to work for the Heidelberg Construction Company one year earlier. Shortly after I was hired that first summer, Harold E. let me know that two other guys had been fired immediately. They were not particularly good workers, nor could they be counted on to come to work every day. Harold E. shared Mr. Heidelberg's view that I was a good hand. He was glad I had come to work with him.

From the beginning, Harold E. took me under his wing. He taught me how to shoulder seventy-four-pound sacks of cement. One of our first jobs was to unload a railroad boxcar filled with sacks of cement. We would pick up a sack in the boxcar, walk up a pair of strong two-foot-wide boards stretching from the boxcar into a storage barn adjacent to the railroad, and drop the bag in an orderly pile. Harold E. showed me how to plant my feet and hoist the sack to my shoulder in one quick move. He also showed me how to distribute its weight on my shoulder to make walking easier and safer, while protecting my back from unnecessary strain. The storage barn also housed various types of construction-related vehicles and equipment. Mr. Heidelberg was building a cement mixing plant.

There was a rhythm to everything Harold E. did. He got a kick out of teaching the young White boy the lessons he had learned. He made jobs look easy and effortless, when in fact, the work was hot and difficult. The rhythms he taught me, though, allowed us to work and talk. Harold E. liked to talk. I did too. Those first summer days passed easily and quickly in his company. Many years would pass before I could appreciate that Harold E.'s willingness to teach and my eagerness to please, and be thought well of, would make his workdays much, much easier than they might have been otherwise. He never made a comment about the two boys fired being Black. I was not too unlike the Tom Sawyer friend who found pleasure in getting to share the painting of the fence.

On occasion, he would bring up subjects that I am certain were for his pleasure only. Almost always they were of a highly personal nature. "Cone, did you ever stump a cow?" was the most outrageous example. By the time I could comprehend what he was asking, he was doubled over with laughter. No inquiry seemed to be off limits. He had a lot of life about him, and he didn't seem to mind making comments or raising questions as they would come and go in his head.

The cement-mixing plant was long finished, so we were now on the road, working together to build a farm-to-market road. The other two grabbers, White boys who dropped out of public school early, had learned quickly that Harold E. was a reliable source of helpful information and constantly sought his opinion and help. This day was no exception. It was the subject that was different. While working, the four of us were never too separated from each other. It was possible to carry on an extended conversation on any topic. One just had to be prepared for gaps of one, five, ten, twenty minutes between some of the comments. The three of them had occupied themselves with speculation regarding what it must be like to be a preacher and still be a male. What do preachers do? How do they act? What do they think? What do they say? They were always careful to carry on the conversations in such a manner and time that I could hear them. They were the talkers. I was both subject and audience. The topic of girls, dating, and sex was hot and heavy when we broke for lunch this day.

A hammer-like blow fell upon me soon after we sat down. "Harold E., do preachers jack off?" was the question. It was asked in jest. My heart pounded. I could hardly breathe. What do I say if they ask me directly? Do I lie? Do I tell the truth? What will they think? Will they want to know more? Will they ask about my girlfriend? I was paralyzed with a combination of fear, guilt, embarrassment, and shame. What breathing I could manage was high in my chest. Everything happened in an instant, though, for me, it was a long and painful moment.

Harold E. seemed to brush the question away as he might a fly that circled his lunch sack. It was no big deal. It was silly. The answer was obvious. Harles is a young man, ain't he? He's normal, ain't he? What do young men do in their teens when they are discovering sex and sexuality? They jack off. They masturbate. What's the big deal? He never looked up from rummaging in his lunch sack. "He's got a hand, ain't he?" was all he said. End of discussion.

~ ~ ~

More than fifty years ago, and still the memory of this story's origin is strong. My breathing is still a bit shallow when I think about it. It was a wonderful moment. Here was a man, a Black man, understanding and comfortable with the rhythms of life and a young preacher, a White boy, who knew everything but was not comfortable about anything.

In that moment lay an opportunity for me to learn about life and living, about openness and trust, about normal and hypocritical. But I learned nothing. I merely managed to dodge a very awkward topic of conversation. Had I spoken, I am confident it would have been some form of denial of anything about my involvement in sex and sexuality. Of all the sins of adolescence, none received more negative attention than sex.

There was no way I could have entered an honest conversation with these men on this topic. I had been born again. I knew unmarried sex was evil. Harold E. had spoken. The subject was closed. Thank God.

The Role and Place of Our Personal Stories

I had no way of knowing how this East Texas, farm-road, brown-bag-under-a-tree-lunch in mid-summer of my eighteenth-year conversation would linger in my mind. It did so, however, for the next four-plus decades. Over that stretch of time, it would increasingly become a defining moment for showing how an uncluttered mind responds to a simple question. Clear, simple questions, "Do preachers jack off?" have clear, simple answers, "He's got a hand ain't he?" How could it be otherwise? And when it is otherwise, what happened to make it so? How does simple become complex, awkward, convoluted, embarrassing? That's a significant question and has enormous ramifications for teaching, parenting, befriending, and relating.

It took years before I could consider, much less accept, the normalcy of all things sexual. For me at eighteen, believing was more important than thinking or reasoning. Those in the know—my parents, ministers, church, and schoolteachers—had taught me the truths of life. Did my parents have sex before they married … with each other … with others? How about the ministers in my life, my teachers? These questions were so foreign to my way of thinking they could never have been formulated, even for the briefest of moments. My task had been to believe and faithfully execute the teachings. The fact that I had masturbated when alone since I was thirteen and that I had sex with my high school girlfriend did not cause the slightest questioning of the beliefs. Masturbation, sexual fondling, and intercourse, while pleasurable, were still the deep secrets of my life. Though at times, I was caught up short by thoughts of guilt, shame or hypocrisy, they were never frequent enough or strong enough to appreciably alter the behaviors.

Spoiler Alert 2 - A Black Man and a White Boy

A few years later it occurred to me that the fact that he was Black and I was White was never broached. Working side by side was one of the few things that a Black man and a White boy could successfully do together. I have no explanation for how such an obvious matter could have been so neglected by me at that time, but perhaps the answer lies in a recognition he had of me that was well beyond anything with which I had even remote contact. He made it a nonissue.

I am embarrassed that I have no memory of where Harold E. spent his nights when we were on the road working. I am confident that it was not in the hotel where the rest of us stayed. Wherever he stayed, though, I knew he had a roommate, the dragline operator, another Black man. Successful operation of the dragline was considered the single most difficult job in road building and as a result his salary was the highest of all. Mr. Heidelberg paid for skill, not for skin color. Wherever they were, the highest and lowest paid workers were spending their work weeknights under a common roof.

~ ~ ~

My unique memories of the Harold E. episode became a story, my story. I say unique because my confidence level is high that no one else in the group had my experiences and, consequently, could not have had my responses. The culmination of eighteen years of my family's national, regional, local, gender, social, and religious values, and this, a middle son's response to them, came to bear in the moment of the question. I would not be surprised now by such a question. At that instant, though, a story was born, for me, one with some power.

I have since come to realize that my stories occurred and remained with me in stages:

• Part of me. As an event, typically highly charged for any one of many reasons, that is remembered and perpetuated in story form (like the Poochie episode). The story becomes a part of my being, it is who I am, I am the story.

• Blame. Sharing/telling or confessing a story is a part of me, but something outside of me (parents, culture, society) is to blame for the way I remember and tell it.

• About others. Telling this story, in its earliest stages, was not so much about me as it was about Harold E. and the other boys in the work group.

• About me. Discovering the story is all about me. How I remember and tell it is revelatory about me and how my brain and mind worked at that time. The elements of the story are invented so that I can be me. Blaming others for what I thought and felt was an extremely difficult hurdle to get over.

• Personal accountability. Coming to understand the me-ness of the story, and accepting it as just that, a story to help me cope. Harold E. was a part of me, a part that was too fearful and self-conscious to show itself except in third person story form.

• Acceptance. The story, upon a fuller and more complete understanding, began to lose its hold, its force. It goes away for the most part because there is no longer a need to prop up an imagined me.

In summary, I have learned that remembering and telling the stories of my past, especially the ones that are emotive loaded, remain with me until a fuller understanding of the stories, and my complicit role in them breaks through to my conscious awareness. When that occurs, the need for remembering or retelling begins to fade away. It is as if the story, when more fully understood, turns loose of me more than me turning loose of the story. There would be a few more stories coming in need of the same kind of unraveling. It was the writing down of the words—seeing of them laid out before me—that enabled much of the fullness of their role and place in my memory to be understood. The most challenging/frightening/life-altering stories to be examined turned out to be those associated with the unquestioned rightness and supremacy of my religious experience and views—and the cost.

For now, I enjoy the thought that by nightfall on this root grabber's summer day, the episode was likely gone from everyone's mind but mine. It would stay with me for years. Currently, it just brings a smile.

Story - "You Don't REALLY Believe That, Do You?"

One experience, another story, in my earliest years as a youth evangelist gave me pause regarding an important piece of the packaging of my religion. It became even more instructive in about twenty years. In fifty years, I came to regard this experience as my very first overt act of trusting my own reaction, my own judgment! It was a passive act to be sure, but for me, it was an act, a small step into a new and different world. In that sense, this story emerged, as far as personal learning regarding religion was concerned, as perhaps the most significant story and moment of them all.

The incident occurred in a suburb of Houston during the summer of 1956. During a Youth-Led Revival, I had come to know two young women from Atlanta. As I recall they had just graduated from high school, and I had just finished my junior year in college. One of the girls was the niece of a deacon in the revival's host church, and the other, a close friend of the niece. The girls, with the niece's uncle and aunt, attended every revival service. The entire family struck me as bright, thoughtful, and fun loving. I enjoyed being in their collective company.

Key Moment 3—A Straight-Forward Question. Following one of my sermons toward the end of the week, I was walking down a church hallway on my way to the fellowship hour, a period each night following the worship service, where the youth of the church would gather to sing and play group games. The hallway was crowded, but from in front of me I clearly heard the friend exclaim, "You don't really believe all that stuff, do you?" All that stuff would have been referencing the heart of my revival sermons—born in sin, damned in God's eyes, sent his son Jesus to rescue us from damned state, belief in that story constituted forgiveness of all sins and, following death, eternal life of happiness in heaven with God, Jesus, and other believers. "Really?"

There was something about her tone and manner that stopped me short. She seemed genuinely incredulous that anyone could believe such things. I did not hear the response from the niece, and neither would know that I had overheard the question. I was stunned, hurt even. I dropped further back and said nothing to anyone. I didn't feel attacked or ridiculed, just stunned. How could anyone not be caught up in the issues of heaven and hell, sin and salvation, saved and lost? After all, it came from God's Word, God's Holy Word!

~ ~ ~

A different story for me was born. I was in no way prepared for what seemed like an honest inquiry on the part of a thoughtful person regarding the basic tenets of my religion. In hindsight, I am willing to believe this simple event to be the first brush with a part of me never heard from before. Could there possibly be more to right and wrong, good and bad, life, living, and death than what I was taught, what I believed, what I preached? Did I really believe what I was preaching?

In that moment, I did not stand up for God as I had come to understand Him! What did I do? I backed away! I was prepared to have my faith doubted, challenged, even attacked. Previously on the few occasions when I had been challenged, I had stood up for my beliefs. But evidently, I was not prepared for a genuine, heartfelt, observation about its basic credulity. Of course I believed what I taught! I would continue believing it through the remainder of my college and seminary years. I still marvel at the fact that I simply backed away from her query. Any sense of a need for a reexamination of my foundational beliefs simply flared up and quickly receded from my consciousness. But the hairline

crack that was formed in my cocoon would lie in wait for another
opportunity to expand it.

Being a Preacher

I was married on September 3, 1957, following my second
summer of preaching in week-long Youth-Led Revivals, ten
in total. My spouse, the former Mary Boyd, and I moved
immediately to Fort Worth where I continued my ministerial
education at Southwestern Seminary. Toward the end of my
first year there and lasting into most of the second, I served
as the pastor of the Purley Baptist Church. Purley was a small
unincorporated community in northeast Texas. During the
school terms, we would commute from Fort Worth to Purley on
Friday afternoon until Monday afternoon. The seminary had no
Monday classes in order to support the many students, ministers,
and musicians who were doing as I was, serving churches in the
area and around the state. On the weekends, and during holidays
and summers, my spouse and I lived on site in the parsonage
provided by the Church.

**Key Moment 4—The Rules are Crucial for Maintaining
the Cocoon.** Toward the end of my first year as pastor, a young
couple with two children moved into the neighborhood of the
church. The wife and children immediately began attending our
Sunday School and morning worship services. After a few weeks,
she expressed an interest in having a conversation regarding
her becoming a member of the church. During a home visit,
I learned that she had accepted Christ as her Savior several
years earlier, been Born Again in Christ, had been baptized,
and immersed—but not in a Baptist church. I enjoyed the visit.
Her comments seemed genuine, the interest in becoming a
member of our church sincere. I liked her and her family. Any

awkwardness between us existed only in me. As a young pastor, I was now confronted with my first church polity decision.

Until this moment, I had only known of two ways an individual could rightly become a member of one of our Southern Baptist congregations. One, she could publicly confess her faith and accept Jesus as her Savior and be baptized into the church membership, the course I had followed as a nine-year-old child. Two, she could present herself as a candidate for membership by declaring she had already had the previous religious experience, been baptized in another Baptist church and, because of a move from one area of the country to another, simply wished her membership transferred. Within Baptist circles this was known as becoming a member on the promise of a letter. The new church would contact the former church seeking confirmation of the applicant's claim. It was a simple and common process.

In this case, the woman's religious experience had occurred in a church that was not Southern Baptist. Somewhere along my ministerial student way, I had heard comments suggesting baptism by immersion in any denomination other than ours was not acceptable, not God's Will. Although, in my mind and heart, I felt her comments regarding her religious experience seemed as authentic as my own. Yet, I could not bring myself to suggest that she would be completely welcomed into our congregation. I deferred the decision and indicated that we would talk again next week.

I chose not to talk to anyone in the church about the conversation. I felt as the pastor I should know what course of action was best to take, the right thing to do. Instead, upon my return to the seminary, I sought out a professor to discuss my concerns. He confirmed my earlier impression regarding polity. "She would need to be baptized again."

Conveying that conclusion to the young mother when I returned to Purley remains embarrassing and painful to this day. She was surprised, disappointed, and hurt. Neither was she willing to turn her back on her own experience as if it were somehow invalid and incomplete. I can see now that she had more confidence in her experience and independent judgment than I did in mine. She and her children never attended our church again.

Although, in my mind, I had done what was right by the church, in my gut it did not feel like what I had done was a good thing. Being a fundamentalist Baptist, as opposed to being a more open-minded and liberal Baptist, won the day.

Tiny Crack in the Cocoon

How did I know what was right? A person in authority had told me. I had trusted and obeyed. My personal discomfort with that rule was not to be trusted. The authority knew. Unlike the Houston experience of overhearing one person asking another about what was really believed, I could not just walk away from personal discomfort. In this case, action was required, and I acted. The action taken turned out to be a lingering and personally painful story. I never asked how the seminary professor knew. There are no verses in the Bible that suggest only Southern Baptist immersions are real!

In later years, I wondered what course of action I would have taken if the seminary professor had advised me to, "Trust your own judgment, act accordingly, and live with the consequences." For then, right had a much stronger grip on all aspects of my life than any feeling good about myself I might have mustered. To trust my own judgment was foreign to me. The packaging, the outer shell of my religious beliefs, had been forcefully encouraged and accepted. Virtually no space to think for myself existed. That would have been exceeding the size of my britches on an enormous scale. In time, that would dramatically shift.

Story - Being Viewed as More Thoughtful Than I Viewed Myself

In the fall of 1961, I was engaged in my final semester of seminary training at Southwestern Baptist Theological Seminary in Fort Worth. In the spring of 1959, I had resigned as Purley Baptist's pastor and accepted a job with the Department of Student Work of the Baptist General Convention of Texas (BGCT). I became the Interim Baptist Student Union (BSU) Director of Arlington State Teacher's College in Arlington, Texas. From Arlington, a year later, I was promoted to be the full-time BSU Director at the University of Houston. My spouse, pregnant with our daughter, was in Houston. As in the Purley pastor days, I was commuting to the seminary from Monday afternoon to Friday afternoon.

In that last semester, one of my final courses, Philosophy of Religion, took on a very special meaning for me on two fronts. One immediate, in the classroom, and one that came to fruition some five years down the road. The immediate challenge had to do with the professor, John Newport. He was well known, well trained with two master's degrees and two doctoral degrees culminating with a PhD in Philosophy of Religion from the University of Edinburgh. I had seen him many times off and on around the campus since coming there three years earlier. I had simply not chosen to take any courses in philosophy. This was my first direct contact with him.

The students who made up this class (it was elective not required) were noticeably different to me than others I had been in class with. They were older, more thoughtful, more oriented toward discussions than affirmations. There was generally more curiosity and thoughtfulness than certainty in the exchanges. However, it was Dr. Newport's teaching manner that commanded my greatest attention.

At the front of the classroom, between students and a large chalkboard, was a three-foot by six-foot table with a small portable lectern on one end and a straight-backed chair. Dr. Newport would enter class carrying two large, bulging-with-books briefcases. One case was noticeably more worn than the other. I learned later that as the older case deteriorated, it would be replaced by a new one, keeping alive the image of one old and one new case. I could not fathom the amount of case usage, openings and closings, required for a case to deteriorate to the point of being retired from service.

He was tall and fit with what struck me as a calm, thoughtful, and engaged manner. Upon entering the room, he would stride to the table and proceed to open each briefcase and stack its contents on the table before him. These were mostly books—maybe six to ten—but occasionally magazines or journals were laid out.

I was seated near the front of the classroom, and the first time I saw this procedure, I was amazed. After all, as in most prior classes, there was an identified course text—only one. I had already purchased it and was prepared for him to begin taking us through it. Why would all these other books and materials even be around, much less unpacked and displayed for all to see? I learned that the books and magazines were representative of Newport's current reading materials. He was known as a voracious reader. He was often seen driving in and around the seminary neighborhood with a book propped on the steering column of his car for reading while driving.

I was aware for the first time that I was seeing a genuinely curious man chasing answers, insights, and understandings. And he was clearly reading to learn and understand more than reading to find confirmation and support for already existing beliefs. Even now, to think of my first experiences with him brings a tightness in my chest. How could anyone seem to know so much, yet be completely caught up in the mysteries of life and living that were still beyond him?

The book display ritual, however, was not the only sledgehammer that would land on my personal comfort. It was in his lecture method. From the very outset, he made general assumptions about the students before him that were profoundly untrue for me. And one large assumption was that if we had been out of high school this long, that is, with at least one college degree, at least two years of seminary training, and perhaps additional studies, we all would have some general knowledge and appreciation for the major philosophers of the West (Plato, Aristotle, Aquinas, Descartes, Nietzsche, Kant, Sartre, Hume, Spinoza, Hegel, and others) and at least some appreciation of their impact on religious thought, hence the course title, "Philosophy of Religion." In the course of his lectures, he would often make a reference to one of these philosophers, or others, and start to make some point but would instead say, "But of course you gentlemen already know that, or you wouldn't be in this class," and continue down another path.

Key Moment 5—Tell Me What I Need to Know. I was jolted, shocked. Already know that. Not me! I didn't know. I took the class looking for things I might want or need to know. And if it's important, why are you not telling us so? I would often mutter to myself and think, am I the only one who doesn't know? Why isn't someone, anyone speaking up to challenge this assumption? Yet more importantly, Why wasn't I speaking up? Was I the only one making margin notes to check in the library to get some modicum of general understanding of these men, these philosophers? Was I the only one in the class who had never once had a class in philosophy? There had been no place for philosophical, speculative thinking in any of my past schooling. Neither was there any room in my desire to be known by others to acknowledge there might be limitations within my educational background. I never told anyone. And furthermore, I felt I knew what the Christian rebuttal was to a lot of the philosophical speculations raised by the writers.

~ ~ ~

While these classroom experiences were taking their toll, the full extent of a new realization would not actually occur to me until near the course end. It had nothing to do with the course per se, but rather with me—an insight, an "aha"—a stunning understanding. I realized that I had put the extent of my learning, my education, in the hands of others! If something was worthy of knowing, my teachers would tell me. Just as my childhood confession of faith was completely guided by those in authority whom I trusted, I had unknowingly and inadvertently placed the extent of my knowledge in the hands of teachers, not in my own hands as a student with aspirations for learning! It was the role of teachers to teach, coaches to coach, ministers to preach, doctors to heal, parents to parent. My role as student, athlete, congregant, patient, and child was three-fold—listen and learn, trust and obey, and be respectful in the process.

It was a profound realization, sobering, and frightening. This crack in the cocoon allowed slivers of light into the gloam. Up to that moment, I had surrendered the extent of my learning to the teachers in my life! I was the embodiment of a passive learner, yet I felt myself simply being respectful of authority. To question authorities, in person or in books, had been unthinkable, even potentially sinful, in the world as I had come to see it. Several years passed before I grasped just how severely limited was the scope and background of many of the teachers that made up my earliest educational experiences.

To this point in my education, the basic structures had been in place. As observed earlier, God was the ultimate authority, the Bible was where the authority was made known, those who spoke on God's behalf (ministers, teachers, and parents) were the agents of learning. I had been born again. My job, as so well expressed in the hymn of my denomination was to simply trust and obey. I had virtually no recognition of how narrowly focused, how limited, and limiting, my life experiences, education, and training had been. The voice of my parents, the family church, the small town of my childhood, in which I took such pleasure, the college, and seminary of my Southern Baptist religion had essentially all spoken with one voice. The truth was known. I was to believe it and trust it—and I did. To question it would have been unthinkable, unfaithful, disrespectful, and ungodly.

Though this experience with Dr. Newport was strangely moving, even exciting, its immediate value was quickly lost; not gone, as it turned out, just tabled. At the end of the semester, with seminary graduation now behind me, my schooling finished, father of a newborn daughter, I became completely absorbed in my new job as director of the Baptist Student Union at the University of Houston. I was for the first time living and working as an adult in a full-time job. Student days were over. It was a world unto itself, a new one for me.

It was now time for the young minister to demonstrate the value of his four years of college and three years of seminary training as a practicing professional. It was a role in which there was very little need for any of my preaching skills.

Chapter 4

OUTSIDE THE VILLAGE

I had been an employee of the Baptist General Convention of Texas for three years, the first two years as the Baptist Student Union (BSU) Director at the University of Houston and now, for one year, as the Assistant Director of Student Work in the Division of Christian Education. I had been flattered and felt blessed to be invited to do both jobs.

Being invited to do a job had been, and would be, the pattern of my employment for fifteen years. An invitation would come, I would accept. Sitting down to thoughtfully examine likes, dislikes, preferences, expectations, dreams, and skills with a view toward seeking a lifestyle of my own crafting and conscious choosing was alien. Whatever was going to happen to me, and my life, would have to come to me. It would all be a part of God's Will. I had faith. Like turning to teachers for what I would learn, I turned to employers for whatever career I would have.

As mentioned earlier, toward the end of my three years in the seminary, I had been asked by Dr. W. F. Howard, Director of Baptist Student Work in Texas, to serve as the BSU Director in Houston. In my mind, it was an honor. It was a full-time job following years of schooling. It was also God's Will. Why else would I have been considered for such an assignment if God's

Hand had not been at work? After all, one's future was in His Hands. He guided lives as He guided the stars.

As a chaplain for students representing my denomination, my responsibilities fell into several categories. One, I was the manager and overseer of a student center. It was a stand-alone building, a renovated house located across the street from the university's main campus. My chaplain status entitled me to a small cubicle in the university's student center where chaplains of other faiths were also housed (Catholic, Lutheran, and Methodist)—all gentlemen I would come to know. The cubicles could accommodate three to five people at one time with the door closed. The BSU Center on the other hand included study areas, two offices, a game room, a kitchen, a large living room for group gatherings, and a garage apartment in the rear. The apartment housed three male students who tended the lawn and kept the center clean in lieu of rent.

One of the students was already in the apartment when I arrived. He was a holdover from the BSU Director who had preceded me. He was a young man from Mexico, Jose Avila. I learned there had been a plan in place, when it was possible, to have the Student Center apartment housed with international students. It seemed a way to expose foreign students to their Christian student counterparts and vice versa. I recruited two other young men. One from Tokyo, Arihiko Nachigami, a Shinto. The other was from Baghdad, Adil Al-Attar, a Muslim. They were individually and collectively the source and cause of numerous conversations not only with them but about them as well. On more than one occasion, after The Center had closed for the evening, and since my home was next door, I would be asked to help clarify and settle differences in expectations and work assignments. Typically, these conversations occurred after one or more had lapsed into expressions voiced in his native tongue—Spanish, Japanese, or Farsi!

Another important responsibility in Houston was to my
employer, Dr. Howard and the Department of Student Work in
Dallas, which he led. Together we supported several statewide
student initiatives: an annual convention of Baptist students
from all the state's colleges and universities, a spring leadership
training conference for the student officers of BSU Centers
such as mine, an annual international student conference, and a
special summer week for college students—national in scope—at
one of the denomination's two assembly centers, Ridgecrest,
North Carolina, or Glorieta, New Mexico. There was also a
statewide program for students who sought to serve as summer
missionaries in a variety of roles and in numerous countries
around the world.

Story - Taking International Students to a Museum

The University of Houston was like a magnet for undergraduate
and graduate students from countries outside the United States.
The combination of the school's orientation toward research, its
departments of science and engineering, its professional schools
of law and pharmacy, plus its focus on the social sciences drew
large numbers of foreign applicants each year. A majority of
those candidates came from the Middle East (we called it Arabia),
Asia (we called it the Far East), and South America. Many were
married when they came.

The International Student Conference sponsored by the
Texas Baptist Student Department scheduled for fall of 1962
became noteworthy for me. The meeting's agenda included
scheduled events beginning on a Friday evening and running
through Sunday morning. The meeting site was a large Southern
Baptist Church in Austin.

In announcing and promoting the event through our BSU
Student Center, we promised participants a tour of the Texas
State Capitol building as well as a tour of the Sam Houston
Memorial Museum in Huntsville. In addition, all expenses such
as transportation, accommodations, and meals were paid. The
Women's Missionary Union (WMU) of many of our Houston
churches had provided scholarships for any foreign students who
opted to attend. The WMU groups were happy to support a
foreign mission's activity so close to home.

A chartered bus with 50 seats was a sellout. While many of
the students were already known to me, most were not. And
many of the unknowns were married couples. It was fun to meet
them. There was a lot of excitement around the Center as we
gathered to board the bus and begin our weekend adventure.
First stop was to be the Sam Houston, Father of Texas, Museum
in Huntsville, seventy miles north of Houston.

As the bus approached the museum, I asked the students
to remain seated a few more minutes while I checked with the
museum staff to verify that their guides were ready to receive us
as a group. It was my first trip to the museum. As I crossed the
atrium toward the registration desk, I froze. There on a side wall
for all to see were drinking fountains. A sign above one read "For
Whites Only;" the other simply read "Colored."

I was stunned and my heart raced, not because such signs
were new to me, but because it never occurred to me to even
consider the possibility of their prominence in the museum. I was
also aware that there were no more than six white faces on the
entire bus.

By the time I reached the museum director, there were three
things I felt compelled to say, excitedly to be sure. We were
essentially a church–sponsored tour group even though we were
coming from a university. Huntsville was our first stop on the way
to Austin. There was no way I could bring students from India,

Japan, the Middle East, and South America to see such signs. It would have been too embarrassing for me, my denomination, my state, and my country and might have put in jeopardy the value of our entire trip.

I was immediately reassured. "Don't you worry, it will be taken care of." It was. In the few anxious minutes it took to return to the bus and invite the students to enter, the signs had been removed. In their place were hanging small works of art.

I was barely breathing as I got back on the bus. This event was a powerful glimpse at the limitations of my childhood culture on any ability or comfort I might find when surrounded by young men and women from markedly different cultures than mine. Another story was born and rift created.

~ ~ ~

Spoiler Alert 3 - Drinking Fountain for Whites Only

While to this day, I remember nothing else about that entire weekend, the feeling of panic I had in the atrium still remains. At the time, being stunned by the incongruities associated with the signage of childhood directing the behaviors of White and Colored played out on a larger stage were beyond my capacity to absorb. What had seemed in my childhood mindset as no big deal or that's just the way it is was instantly brought into sharp relief on a world stage. I also recall, after our group had exited the building, while thanking the director for help, seeing the artwork being removed and original signage returned! White Supremacy was strong medicine in my home state.

~ ~ ~

A Shift in Thinking

Finally, in addition to the responsibilities cited above, I had been the director of our own on-campus organization and its activities. We sponsored local mission programs, weekly luncheons and discussions, Bible study and prayer activities, occasional student social gatherings, and one-on-one counseling discussions. The weekly Wednesday free luncheon, followed by a brief discussion, was especially popular. Women's groups from local churches would take turns providing and serving food to the students. To honor class schedules, the meal was served promptly at noon. Discussions, usually of a faith-based nature, were typically led by me, local clergy, or a faculty or staff member of the University and ended promptly at 1:00 p.m.

I was also expected to be a part of my denomination's activities within the city of Houston. Because of this last role, I was often invited by local ministers to be a guest speaker in their churches, especially when one would be away from his congregation on some business or vacation period.

Regardless of the preaching assignments and with limited awareness on my part, a change was occurring in me. I was shifting from preaching to counseling and listening, from believing I knew the truth toward respect for the confusing and unknown. The preacher was being called upon more and more to be a listener, an encourager, and one who understands. Proclaiming and telling people what the truth was, was becoming increasingly uncomfortable. Most of the students who made their way to my office were looking not so much for someone who would tell them what to think or do as for someone who would let them talk about their fears, pains, problems, and challenges. A caring listener I was—though awkward and unskilled at exactly how to do that, for sure.

A common experience on a typical day was being drawn
into a conversation with a student or faculty or staff person of
the university that began on one topic at one level and quickly
changed into a more personal topic on a more serious level. I
was engaged in conversations with people from backgrounds and
situations markedly different from mine. The simpler answers
of my religion, the ones so meaningful to me, now seemed
of limited value. I felt the need for something more than rote
answers to perplexing problems.

Looking back, I can see that while many were turning to
me for help and guidance, I was the one whose horizons were
being broadened and education about life being expanded,
if not transformed. I was particularly impacted by the two
years of conversations that arose between me and the three
young international students who lived in the center's garage
apartment—three young men, each from a distinctively different
culture, each aspiring to a common end—the successful
completion of a degree from a university in the United States.
The lessons from Dr. Newport's class were beginning to show. I
was growingly curious about what I didn't know, what I didn't
understand.

Crack

The presidential election of 1960 had its impact as well. It
proved to be my first clear look at how leadership within
my Southern Baptist denomination could be divided, and in
outspokenly different ways. We were clearly not all of one mind.
The largest and loudest voices were adamantly opposed to a
Catholic in the White House. They seemed certain that it would
be the precursor to the Pope in Rome having undue influence on
our country, our constitution, and protestant Christians. A vote
for John F. Kennedy was a vote for the Pope and a weakening

of our role as a Christian nation. I was more influenced by the fears generated by this group than I was by the smaller group that thought the fears were without merit and that the young Kennedy represented a more hopeful future for the country. One of the less outspoken voices was my own pastor at the South Main Baptist Church. I cast my vote for Mr. Nixon without calling attention to it in any way.

I mention the 1960 election because it was my first direct and personal experience with how strongly religious people can differ over politics and their religious beliefs; how one side seemed to want to discuss concerns and issues in a reasonable and respectful manner and the other being so certain of the rightness, the supremacy of their view that any open discussion was tantamount to a betrayal of God and country. It was a great example of religious supremacists in conflict with views that differed from their own. For the most part, when the election was over, I quickly returned my attention to the duties of the BSU Director and Baptist Chaplain at the University of Houston. Perhaps the differences that existed within the Southern Baptist Convention were not that big a deal after all. I was mistaken.

As far as I could tell, the way I had handled each of these expectations at the University led to my next job offer. I was invited to be the assistant state director of the same college student ministries and ministers of which I had been a part. What I had been asked to work with on an individual campus, I was now being asked to support on a state level. I was also expected to direct the state convention's program for Youth-Led Evangelism, the program that had been so influential in my own life as a college-student minister.

I had spent the summer following my junior and senior years at East Texas Baptist College as a Youth Evangelist. I learned later that the 1940s and 1950s became known as the time of the Youth-Led Revival Movement within the Southern Baptist Convention.

Individual churches would request that the State Student Office send a Youth-Led Revival team to them for specified periods, usually one week in length. The state office would provide the team. A team was typically a college student preacher and a music minister. Very large churches might request two preachers and a music minister. The student ministers and musicians had been identified earlier on their various college campuses around the state. A weekend retreat for prayer, Bible study, instruction, and inspiration would be held for these young ministers at the beginning of each summer to help prepare them for what lay ahead. I was now responsible for the program that had meant so much to me.

Story - The Main Boss

It was early 1964. The intercom call was totally unexpected. The Executive Director of the Baptist General Convention of Texas, Dr. T. A. Patterson, wanted to talk with me. My office was down the hall from his. I was in the Christian Education Wing of the Baptist Building in Dallas, and he was in the administrative suite. The message was on my answering machine when I returned from lunch. Could I come by his office at 2:00 p.m.? I didn't have the faintest idea what had prompted the call.

As it turned out, it was my performance of these Youth-Led Revival leadership duties that occasioned the conference to which I had been summoned. Specifically, it had to do with speakers that I had invited to help lead retreat conferences for the young ministers who would be participating in the Youth-Led Revivals. Two speakers in particular, Dr. Cecil Sherman and Dr. Kenneth Chafin, were called into question.

They were men whom I had personally chosen to help lead these conferences. Importantly for me, they represented men whose ideas and energies had been the most positive for me as a BSU Director in Houston. One was a pastor, Dr. Sherman, who would soon be invited to be a staff member of the Department of Evangelism in the same state office of which I was now a part. The other, Dr. Chafin, was a seminary professor in the Department of Evangelism. As far as I knew, my regard for them was widely shared by others who had been in the same meetings and conferences as had I.

Dr. Patterson's message to me, while couched in the most cordial of language, was clear. He did not think it was good for the denomination in general, nor for the young ministers in particular, to be subjected to the attitudes and teachings of Drs. Sherman and Chafin. He suggested that I not use them again in such a manner!

As I had been in Huntsville with the international students, I was stunned, speechless. It was a shot at what was becoming part of my core thinking and at the heart of my most recent experiences. Mine had been a lifetime of total respect for those in authority, especially religious authority. The respect typically expressed itself in a powerful desire to please as well as one of willing obedience. And here I was being corrected, by someone in authority, for doing something that I felt so good about, so confident in my choices. So strong was my personal admiration and appreciation for the two men in question, I knew I could never comply with this request without forfeiting something important within me. (I had traveled a bit farther down a personal awareness and acceptance road since the summer of road work with Harold E. and my fellow rootgrabbers, as well as the young woman who wanted to become a member of the Purley Baptist Church.) I would not know for a few more years that the part of me at stake was a clear willingness to trust my own judgment, not only in some but in all matters of life and religion. For now, it was not much more than a deep sensing of what was coming.

Also at stake here was my personal faith, my personal beliefs, me. Some of the discomforts surrounding the Kennedy-Nixon election were returning. My naïve and childlike sense that all who shared my denomination's name also shared common views about the Bible, the church, and the world was eroding further and more sharply.

Crack

For the first time some of the differences that existed among Southern Baptists were coming into sharp focus. I knew differences existed between denominations and other religious groups. For the most part, I viewed those who differed from me as well meaning. They simply lacked a full understanding of the Bible and, if they had it, would essentially believe as I did. Part of my challenge as a young minister had been to help them toward this more complete understanding. I was unprepared to have two of my heroes of faith cast into the unacceptable pot.

As powerfully as this memory—story—remains a part of me, I do not clearly remember how I exited the director's office. However, I am one hundred percent confident that I did not overtly challenge anything he had said to me. Neither did I indicate that I would comply. Stunned is all I clearly remember.

A huge crack in the cocoon's shell had occurred. When I returned to my office, I went immediately to talk to my direct boss, W.F. Howard, and told him of my experience and how shocked I was. This being my first job working within a large organization, I had no appreciation for the organizational inappropriateness of Dr. Patterson's decision to talk directly to me rather than to go through my direct boss.

After all, there was a chain of command in place. I reported to my boss, the director of the Department of Student Work, and he reported to his boss, Dr. E. N. Jones, the head of the Christian Education Commission, who reported to his boss, the Executive Director of the Baptist State Convention, Dr. Patterson, who reported to his boss, the Board of Directors of the State Convention itself.

My boss's response was helpful, but the impact from the experience took its toll. He explained that the Executive and the two ministers in question had sharp differences in what theologians regard as church polity. The Executive had a much more restricted view of what constituted a true New Testament Church than did the two ministers in question. Dr. Howard suggested I need only be respectful of the executive. I need not adhere to his request. I should continue to trust my own judgment in the selection of program personnel for my conferences. He made no comment regarding why he or his boss had not been brought into any part of this communication.

~ ~ ~

As I write about this incident, I find myself wondering if Dr. Patterson had seen something in me, a deferential respect for him and his authority, that might not have been true of the two men who stood between him and me in the organization's pyramid. It is also clear to me that I lacked whatever personal characteristics were required to disagree with him directly and openly.

I learned a few years later that the Executive's commitment to fundamentalism was a powerful part of who he was and what he believed. His son, Paige, became one of two major players in the fundamentalists' takeover of the Southern Baptist Convention, the national organization of which I had been a part. Though I could not know it at the time, I was in the shallowest beginnings of what became a floodtide during the next twenty years in my denomination, the clash between fundamentalism and liberalism.

A First

Until this incident, I had never had a direct experience that demanded a choice of belief and behavior that went against something I had come to feel so strongly about, something and someone(s) who were important to me. For the first time, I held a viewpoint that was clearly different from one held by a notable authority. I was now knowingly behaving in a way that some in positions of authority approved, and others did not. The experience provoked considerable anxiety (dissonance) in me, though it was an anxiety that I kept largely to myself.

Chapter 5

CRUMBLING COCOON

It was the summer of 1965. I had been an assistant pastor of Park Cities Baptist Church for a year. My wife and I had been members of the church since we had first arrived in Dallas from Houston three years earlier. In the two years of membership, prior to this staff position, we were active and well-acquainted with the church's senior minister, Dr. Herbert Howard, and its two other assistant ministers, Dr. Brownlow Hastings and Dr. Harvey Whaley. Because of our interest in education, we also knew the staff members assigned to responsibilities for music and religious education. This group worked under the direction of the church administrator, Bob Feather. It was a large church and a large staff.

I had come to the position of assistant pastor following the four-year employment as BSU Director in Houston and W. F. Howard's assistant in the Department of Student Work of the state convention. It had been a year since the exchange with Dr. Patterson regarding Sherman and Chafin.

Changing jobs this time had not meant a change in residence, nor church membership. Once again, I had been invited to consider a job different from the one I had been doing. I was glad to move away from organized denominational responsibilities and happy to be a part of a local church and its ministries. My awareness of the cleavage between fundamentalists and liberals had been sharpened. I was twenty-nine years old and the father of two young daughters, Laurie, soon to be four and Lisa, two. The pastoral duties assigned by the senior minister Dr. Howard—ministering in general to the needs of the congregation through worship, counseling, and visitation of the sick—were expanded by Mr. Feather to include giving oversight to the Sunday School education of college students and the Single Adults. I oversaw these Sunday evening discussion sessions for the young adults.

Story - "What do you think Harles?"

It was a Sunday evening discussion group in Park Cities Baptist Church. By official name, the group was known as the Single Adults. They met weekly on early Sunday evenings for conversations around a wide range of topics. Most had never been married, but a few had, and were now divorced, and nearly all were college educated. Most lived alone in surrounding apartments and condos, but a few shared their living costs with friends or family. They ran the gamut of jobs and careers (medicine, law, education, business, both staff and ownership). It was a bright, energetic group. Ages ranged from mid-twenties to mid-forties, with slightly more females than males.

Friendships with members of this group had developed over the years, particularly following my appointment as the staff minister with whom they would have the greatest amount of contact. A kind of closeness with, and appreciation for, the group emerged. Genuine interest and support for and among members was commonplace. This was particularly evident when personal and professional setbacks would occur or when occasions for celebration were made known. It was a rare Sunday evening when some combination of the group would not extend the evening by going to dinner together at a local eatery or retire to someone's residence for more time together. I was often invited to join in but didn't. Although I was their age, there was one large distinguishable difference. They were single, I was married. I typically went home to be with my spouse and family.

I do not recall the book under consideration. Whatever the title, it would have been one that dealt with interests commonly held within the group: careers, relationships, families, political or social issues touching Dallas and our church. One of the participants, in the midst of a spirited give and take between several members, turned to me and said, "Harles, what do you think?"

That's all there was to it! It was not asked in a manner that was designed to bring clarity, nor to take sides, nor to redirect. It was as straightforward as the words suggest. He simply wanted to know what my thoughts were on the topic at hand.

To this day, I am surprised and filled with wonder over what transpired. I knew what I had been taught to think about the subject being considered. And I knew what I would be expected to say based on what I had learned from those I allowed to be my religious authorities. But I knew with equal clarity that the young man speaking to me wasn't asking for the results of my training. It was infinitely more personal than that. He simply wanted to know what I thought. In that moment, I acknowledged that I did have thoughts about the subject, not well formed to be sure, but thoughts that were different from what I had been taught. It was a new experience. I remember the subtle, yet thrilling feeling. I was being asked to fly on the wings of my own ideas, not just on those that had come from others. The recent experience with Dr. Patterson and his objections to my choices regarding program personnel had kindled an increased awareness of places where my thinking might deviate from that of others.

"What did I think?" What a concept. To this point, in matters of religion, I had few thoughts that I could claim as my own. My thoughts had been the products of my teachings. My task had been to believe, not to think. Others had thought—I believed. The thinking had already been done, and by people far wiser than I. My job had been to accept the teaching that had been passed down and encourage others to do likewise. The experiences with my Philosophy of Religion seminary professor, the counseling role at the University of Houston, and the encounter with the convention's executive director had coalesced. They were taking hold in a public manner.

Something else was new as well. I was with a group that provided a lot of latitude for individual thinking. For the most part, each member just wanted to know what the others thought. I had never been part of a group where this freedom was so evident. Most of my religious-based groups had leaders who would remind or expand on what we already believed. Occasionally, I would be in groups where leaders were speaking things I did not believe. My job there had been to challenge or disagree, sometimes out loud, though usually to myself. I was not comfortable speaking up directly for what I believed in settings where I felt others held views very different from mine. However, I could talk critically of the experience later, when I was back among those who shared my newer beliefs.

Also, I was aware that Park Cities was known as liberal. Liberal, in my mind, when we first joined as members, was construed more along social than theological lines. Now though, its liberal approach to issues more theological was increasingly a source of satisfaction and joy.

"Harles, what do you think?" had been the question. When my answer came, it was a new expression for me, and different. "Honestly, I don't know exactly what I do think!" is what I was finally able to say, which in turn provoked more give and take within the group. Then another interesting turn occurred. We were running out of our allotted meeting time and there was clear interest in continuing this discussion at our next gathering, the following Sunday. I blurted out, "Let me think about it this week, and I'll let you know what I come up with." They agreed and a pact between us was made. I would give the subject some careful and personal attention and share whatever conclusions might result. The entire process was exciting to me. I had a "give it some thought" assignment. It was heady. I did as promised. As time and circumstances permitted the week following, I thought about the topic, made notes, felt myself coming to conclusions—some tentative, some with firmness.

When we gathered again, I shared my thoughts and the conclusions to which I had come. To them, it was no big deal. My thoughts were similar to some that had already been voiced and different from others. To me, however, it was a bigger deal. The thoughts were personal. They were the ones I was currently living with. I was an individual thinker within a group of other individual thinkers. I had listened to them; they had listened to me. We were a group composed of individuals with a variety of opinions and experiences, and we were showing and telling. Yes, I liked it. It was exciting. I felt more me—more real.

Incidentally, before our group concluded its discussion of this particular book, there were a few other occasions when I felt compelled to play the "I don't know for sure how I really feel about that, let me think about it" card. It became a joke among us. "Harles is slow! He runs about a week behind the rest of us in our conversations." Their leader was patiently and kindly being led and supported by the group.

~ ~ ~

This episode became the widening of a walk down a path I could not completely acknowledge. The new path was wider. I just didn't understand that I was on it so fully. The straight and narrow path had been broadened considerably.

Though it didn't have the power for me then that it does now, I was being further exposed to how important respectful listening is to the formation and expression of one's ideas and feelings. The group's genuine interest in wanting to know what I thought, plus their respectful acceptance of those thoughts when I spoke them, was liberating for me. I was able to locate and identify more complete thoughts and feelings, because they were able and willing to tolerate and accommodate the thoughts and feelings that resulted. Their appreciative listening freed me to become more aware of my own thinking, to listen to myself. It was my first personal, clear exposure to the impact of listening to another for the sole purpose of understanding. What I had sensed as having value for the students and faculty of the University of Houston was now being provided for me. Learning to express my views and feelings to someone who might not be so accepting and supporting would prove an altogether different matter!

At a much deeper level, I was beginning to move even farther away from the role of a teacher to that of listener, to one who is trying to understand as well as one who wanted to be understood. I discovered to my great surprise that the harder I worked to understand another, the harder they would work to help me understand. Ironically, I had learned to listen more carefully to others before I could pay close attention to the range of thoughts I was having. More years went by, however, before this awareness would become a conscious and deliberate way of life for me. I also learned how difficult it can be to listen carefully and respectfully to others when I was preoccupied with my own concerns, attitudes, and beliefs. I was, and remain, a slow learner.

Being born again too soon had left me with too limited a set of responses.

There was another dynamic going on for me at Park Cities Baptist during this period. It is one I now feel must have been extremely important at the time, but for reasons that are difficult to grasp, I had completely forgotten until these writings.

Dr. Harvey Whaley, one of my counterparts on the church staff, served also as an assistant minister. What my role was for college-age students and young single adults, Dr. Whaley's was for the senior adult members of the congregation, a very large number of folks. He and his spouse, Catrina, were seniors themselves. They were living in a state of semi-retirement following Dr. Whaley's distinguished career as a minister of Baptist churches in the southeast region of the U.S. He held a doctoral degree in theology and philosophy of religion.

He was an avid reader of books, journals, periodicals, newspapers, and magazines. He would often engage me in conversations, or at least try to, prompted by something he had recently seen or heard. Many of these exchanges had occurred while I was still employed by the denomination's state office. They only increased when I became his colleague as a member of the church's ministerial staff. He felt strongly that I owed it to myself, as well as to the young men and women with whom I was working, to be more widely informed. Consequently, I begin to read, a lot, and broadly.

In all candor, I am confident that these first readings were more prompted by the desire to have this man think well of me than by a personal drive to broaden my own level of understanding. I regarded him highly. I wanted him to think well of me. I was also gradually becoming aware that masking my own desires behind the desire to please others was a way around the powerful dictum of my mother—"Don't get too big for your britches." Whom I wanted to impress, the kind of person or character I wanted to think well of me, was undergoing a change. As my personal idols changed, so was I also changing. This was an example of orthogonal learning which I discuss later.

In any case, the memory of this man was brought sharply back to me a few weeks ago while looking through some old personal files for reasons completely unrelated to what I am discussing here. I came across two reading lists. One was from 1965 and the other from 1966—the last two years I would have been associated with Dr. Whaley. Looking at the lists, I remembered committing myself to reading at least one book a week for a year! I had all but forgotten that I had kept the commitment for two years, fifty-two books in 1965 and fifty-three books in 1966.

As I write this, I have the lists before me, and, to use a modern expression, I am blown away by what they reveal. First, the readings were very broad-based, ranging on one end from popular novels of the day to current and historical writings of theologians, philosophers, sociologists, psychologists, and politicians. Second, they serve to document my growing curiosity for wanting to live in a world of broader and deeper understanding regarding life and living. (See Appendix B, Reading List).

PART II

Chapter 6

FROM WHERE DID 'I' COME?

"Go outside and play."

As mentioned earlier, I was born in December 1935 toward the end of The Great Depression the middle child of five. My oldest brother by five years, Ray Charles (Chadda), was conceived at its beginning. The next nearer to me, Bobby Gene (Bob), was born in the middle, I (Hoddy), at its end. A younger brother came three years later, James Ernest (Jamie), followed by a sister, Clara Nan (Nan), in five. The Great Depression loomed large in both my immediate and extended families. We were often admonished to "Clean your plate." "Remember the starving Chinese." "Make do with what you've got." "If it's too small, hand it down to someone else until it wears out." "Don't waste your money." "Be thankful for what you do have."

The houses of my childhood, ten in number, were rentals. My parents would not have a home of their own until we children were all out of the house, in the military, married, or soon to be, or in college. My parents would not own their home free and clear until they were in their mid-sixties.

The houses were, with two exceptions, not quite adequate for the size of our family. Space was precious and carefully used. Sharing a bed with a sibling was the norm. Noise control was always an issue, especially in the evenings when my father was home from work.

One of the larger houses proved to have impact on my entire childhood, especially on the image I would have of myself. This house was large enough to allow the sub-letting of a bedroom to a young woman who taught in a one-room rural schoolhouse in a small community, Cove Springs, about five miles from our home in Jacksonville. Having a mid-December birthday, and before kindergartens existed, I would not have been eligible for public school in our town until I was within four months of my seventh birthday. In those days one had to have reached his or her sixth birthday by September of the school year one intended to enter.

How the rural school got around the birthday rule, and exactly how my mother and our boarder worked it out, I am uncertain. What is clear is that the teacher thought me old enough and smart enough to join with her other first graders in formal schooling. I commuted with her each day for the school year to achieve just that. If my mother had any reservations about this arrangement, I am sure they were more than compensated by having only two preschoolers at home with her all day instead of three. Beginning with the second grade, I rejoined my neighborhood friends in the nearest public school in our area—Joe Wright Elementary. Forever after, as far as I knew, I would always be the youngest person in my class. It was a point in which I took some considerable pride. The price I would pay for the early pride went completely unnoticed until late puberty. Being the youngest also meant I was the latest to develop physically and was often the smallest boy in my class and the last to develop the manly signs of chin, underarm, and pubic hair. Little Hoddy Cone was not an uncommon nickname among my larger family and close friends throughout elementary and junior high school years.

Living in the South, and all we children essentially healthy, my mother's remedy for the small house and noise problem was simple and straightforward, "You children go outside and play." It was never a suggestion. It was a command. It was a way of life. If it was summertime, it was generally understood that we were not expected back until the next meal—dinner in the middle of the day and supper at the end. Snacks between meals did not exist.

Playing became a critically important part of my life and profoundly impacted my education and my attitude toward learning. Playing games, inside or out, was the most inexpensive way to find pleasure in living. Music was another, but without any instruments and no one seemingly inclined in that direction, except for listening and singing, music played a limited role in our family.

By local standards, I was a good athlete. As it turned out, nothing was more important in the shaping of my social life and my status with peers. I particularly enjoyed the team sports—the ball sports—football and basketball in the fall and winter and baseball in the spring and summer. I took up golf in college and tennis as a young adult. Playing golf with close friends is a joy to this day.

In the earliest years, primarily through elementary school, before the idea of organized school teams took on a great deal more significance, teams were selected at random. In the non-school months, or weekends, kids in the neighborhood would gather, often including older or younger siblings, teams would be chosen, and we would play until the sun went down or too many of us would be called home to eat. Recess period in elementary school followed a similar pattern. Those who wanted to play ball would rush to the gym or field, teams would be quickly chosen, and play would happen until the bell rang for us to return to class. Noon recess followed suit.

Being chosen merits a comment. By a variety of ways—coin flips, alternating hands going up the handle of a baseball bat, or the one who supplied the ball—two people would be designated choosers as well as the one who got to choose first. A lot of status was to be inferred by the order in which one was chosen. After all, both teams wanted to win, so it could be important to choose the perceived best player available at each turn of choice. It could be awkward to be chosen toward the last, for both the chooser and the chosen. I was always one of those who was chosen early, especially when the group was composed of similar-aged boys and often even when I was with my older brother's group.

Yes, playing outside was an important part of my growing up. But where and how did the importance, place, and role of education and schooling come in? To provide at least a partial answer requires a brief look at my parents and parenting as I experienced it.

Reading, writing, and doing your numbers was the sure sign of an adequately educated young man in my father's day in small towns in East Texas. This was especially true in those places where as many hands as possible were needed to help the family provide the basic necessities of life, and it was true for his family. He was the second oldest of eight children. Only the three youngest of his siblings would graduate from high school. None would attend college. All would marry, start to work, or join the military as early as possible.

It was a part of my family's lore that our dad had mastered the three educational essentials by the sixth grade. Therefore, he felt it was time to leave school and join his father and sister already working on behalf of the family. My grandmother was not so certain of this and insisted that he remain in school. Within a year, though, the key decision makers must have been happy with his progress because at some point in the seventh grade, my father was allowed to drop out of school and go to work.

I never heard any stories regarding my paternal grandfather and his experiences with school and schooling. He was killed the year before I was born when a boiler exploded in the laundry where he worked. At birth, I was given his name. His middle name of Edgbert would be changed to my Edwin. My grandmother became and would remain the head of her family until she died in 1969 at the age of 79.

I have no idea how, or to what extent, Dad was employed or employable during his teenage years. By the time he was married, and for the next forty years, he was employed by two companies specializing primarily in the making of peanut candies—the Jacksonville Candy Company and the Lufkin Candy Company. He was never without a place to work. Whatever challenges, difficulties, and embarrassments that may have come his way as a result of his limited formal schooling were never acknowledged or discussed; nor would any limitations in his reading, writing, or math obvious. He was good at basic math, took pride in writing neatly and legibly, and read those things of interest to him—the local newspaper, the Bible, and his Sunday School lesson.

Whatever else happened to him in those early years of working, though, one thing stuck with him. Staying in school and getting an education became one, if not the most important, message he would pass on to his children. The message would be stated with force. It was very clear to all.

Staying in school meant graduating from high school. In his mind, more schooling meant better job opportunities, a better life. Dropping out was not an option. He was willing to work his regular job and take on other odd jobs to earn extra money so that his children might be able to stay in school. Whatever was expected of us in terms of working was for after school, on weekends, and during the summer months. School came first, work came second. Getting an education came first. It was a simple, practical formula.

A Microcosm of My Father's Attitude

I was on the cusp of doing something that no one in his, or my mother's, family had ever done before. As noted earlier, at seventeen, in the fall of 1953 following my high school spring graduation, and having been called to preach, I was off to college! A family first!

The pastor of my home church, Rev. Donald Grolliman, had contacted East Texas Baptist College in Marshall, Texas, the nearest liberal arts college owned and operated by our denomination, and informed them of my decision to become a preacher. The College, in turn, seventy-five miles away, sent a recruiter in early summer to encourage my consideration of the school he represented. It seemed to me to be the Lord's Will that I should attend. After all, how else was I to explain so much interest in me, my calling, my life, and my well-being. A scholarship to play basketball at a hometown community college had to be ignored. It would have been selfish and worldly to have gone there. Saving money on college costs by playing basketball was of no concern if it interfered with pursuing God's calling.

Financially, if full payment was not possible, East Texas required a minimum down payment on the expenses anticipated at the beginning of each semester. Full payment was expected before semester's end. I had earned and saved enough money in a summer job to offset the minimum payment required. That, along with my denomination providing ministerial scholarships, a small percentage of total costs, for all aspiring young ministers like me, and I was more than able to get started. I had every confidence that I could find part time jobs as I went to school to offset the other expected costs. After all, being easily and quickly hired for a variety of jobs had been my work experience since age twelve.

I never gave a thought to the idea that perhaps my parents might offer financial assistance. Dad—and Mom, too, by this time, for she had joined Dad in working for the same candy company—had done their part. They had provided me with a high school education. Routine expenses for the remaining family's everyday living were too tight. No extra money was available, and none was expected. If anything, my going off to college on my own would afford them some relief. There would be one less mouth to feed at home. I felt good about that.

Then Dad acted! The day before I was to move into a dormitory in preparation for my first day at college, my father insisted that I take his only suit as my own. It was a double-breasted brown pin stripe, with accompanying white shirt and tie. He felt a college man should have a suit of his own. He didn't feel his son's one sports coat, that served all dress occasions, would now be adequate. No comments were made about what he would do for his own church-going clothes. He also presented me with $50 in cash, "Just in case." Again, no comments were made regarding where it had come from, nor was there any expectation of a repayment. What was perfectly clear, he had given me what he had to give! The rest was up to me—with his love, regard, and very best wishes.

Twenty-three years later, and two years before his death of lung cancer, he would give me another $50. This time we were celebrating the completion of my PhD. I would never know if he made the same connection between the two events as I did—the beginning and end of my post-high school formal education. My mother's role regarding her children, and their growth and development, was not so clear cut to me, and required years of thoughtful reflection to gain a modicum of appreciation for the impact she had on us all. And the most important insight of all would occur when she was ninety-four years old, and I was in my sixties! More on this topic is coming later.

Like my father, she came from what would be regarded now as a large family of very modest circumstances. She was the middle of five children and the only girl. My maternal grandfather was born in Georgia, my grandmother in Louisiana, where they would meet, marry, and move to Texas. All my memories of them were living as tenant farmers. Mom's father was a section foreman for a small railroad line, the Cotton Belt Railroad, in the eastern part of Texas. He was terminated from the railroad job after twenty-four years and six months of service. At the twenty-five-year mark, he would have been eligible for retirement benefits. Rather than make good on that commitment, the railroad generated an unchallengeable reason for his dismissal as an employee. For the remainder of his life, he would never miss an opportunity to cast a Democratic vote. The Democrats, in his experience, were the only party that supported the workman's right to form unions to protect themselves from the abuse of owners.

Spoiler Alert 4 - Racism & Politics: Southern Democrats Vs. Northern Republicans—the Party of Lincoln

I learned many years later that the Democrats of my granddad's day were primarily White Southerners. Republicans, the party of Lincoln, had primarily been Northerners.

~ ~ ~

Mom was the only member of her family to graduate from high school. She loved basketball and played on her high school team. Two of her siblings joined the military for full careers, and two found jobs adequate to support families of their own.

She and Dad would be married shortly after her high school graduation and the beginnings of her giving birth to five children, one approximately every three years, commenced. She had become a wife and mother and bent on her role in raising a family.

After the church, the family was central. My parents loved and took great pride in their family. My father worked his entire adult life so that he could support us. His needs or interests were always secondary to the needs of his family. The satisfaction of earning a living came from what it provided his wife and children—a roof over their heads, clothes to wear, and food to eat. And the margins between what the family needed and his income were narrow. Living hand-to-mouth was a commonly heard phrase.

During the school year, the family ate well on Friday night, payday, through Sunday lunch. The meals would steadily decline in both quality and quantity, less meat, and more vegetables, until the cycle could be repeated. The slightest interruption to the pattern was challenging—car trouble, or an unexpected expense of any kind, could be particularly difficult. Summers were different and easier. Teenagers typically had summer jobs to take care of their own interests and often would contribute to larger family needs. Any personal needs or interests of parents requiring the expenditure of money were most likely to be satisfied during the summer, if at all.

My parents loved to play table games, especially those with dominoes. Forty-Two was their favorite. Like the kids she had sent outside to play to enjoy themselves, Mom and Dad would play inside to enjoy themselves. It was inexpensive pleasure, and several other couples shared their approach to entertainment. A great number of Friday and Saturday evenings were passed in this manner. The only occasion that would alter the pattern would be a high school athletic event in which one of their children was participating or some special event occurring at their church.

I didn't appreciate for years how important games were to the structuring and passing of time when our family was together. It was fun, but it also provided a way to minimize conversations. It was a nice way to pass the time. The only discussions that were public, that is, when most of the family was in or close by the same room, were subjects on which there was agreement. Any conversations that might foster differing opinions or discord were avoided or quickly diverted. It was not nice to argue (be different), even among ourselves.

The pattern would continue even as the family expanded. A combination of games, eating favorite dishes following a prayer of gratitude, and an updating of family related information since our last gathering occupied most of our family's together times. Large family gatherings like Thanksgiving were the norm, and we were expected to be there. They would last between 24 and 48 hours. The rituals of our getting together would run their course, and we would return to our separate homes and lives.

In my family's case, the faith of our fathers was primarily interpreted and passed on to us by our mother. She was the one with whom rested the family's final decision-making opinion, what actions taken, or the attitudes to be assumed—how the family would comport itself in the world. Her impact would be profound. She had chewed the fruit, or so it seemed to me at the time, that was passed on for the family's consumption. I could never have known that she was simply passing on the fruit of her family and her larger culture.

Remember my mother was guided by, and provided guidance with a few, powerfully conveyed axioms: "Be nice." "Be a good boy." "Respect your elders." "Don't get too big for your britches." "Give God the credit." "Be grateful for what you do have." Should any of these guides be breached, the offender would hear the exclamation, "You should be ashamed of yourself." And, until early teenage years, transgressions could often be followed by a spanking. Shame and shaming were the most influential tool in my mother's parenting arsenal. All five of her children would bear the marks and scars of its influence.

Communication Primer—Mom's Six Maxims Clarified

"Be nice" primarily focused on interpersonal communication and at its heart was a strong caution against conflict with others. An associated dictum was, "If you don't have something nice to say, don't say anything at all." Differing with others in a public manner was not good or safe and was to be avoided. Having differing ideas, beliefs, opinions produced discomfort, even arguments. Arguments could lead to outcomes ranging from hurt feelings to fights, and no good can come from that. She was known to boast from time to time that she and my dad "never had an argument in front of you children." It was a point of family pride to hear one of the children praised as a "good kid."

The unintended consequences of this attitude were threefold. One was the elevation of niceness over honesty. To maintain an outward appearance of harmony, individual differences, candor, and a degree of personal integrity were sacrificed. The second was that children who had no adult role models for how to productively face and manage the differences in thought, preferences, and actions that are a normal part of life and living were ill prepared to deal with them when they moved away into their own homes. Better (safer) to be nice than honest had its consequences in each child's marriage. The third was the huge toll this approach took on personal development, education, and learning. Raising questions, especially with those in authority, was made to seem wrong and not nice.

"Be a good boy," as indicated earlier, primarily focused on the avoidance of bad things. Smoking, drinking, gambling, stealing, lying, and any form of sexual activity were early childhood biggies. Being disrespectful, failing to mind one's manners, and behaving selfishly followed close behind. The more bad things were avoided, the **gooder** one became. After I became a ministerial candidate, avoiding activities that might lead to bad things took on greater importance. Dancing led to sexual activity, cocktail parties led to drinking, playing cards led to gambling. Being good meant not doing bad. It would also impact relationships. One needed to be careful about hanging out with others who are doing bad things.

"Respect your elders" primarily focused on one's response to anyone older or in a position of authority (parents, uncles, aunts, grandparents, teachers, ministers, police, administrators, bosses, owners). Respect meant being deferential and obedient. "Do as you are told," was operational within and without the family. "Yes sir" and "No sir," "Yes ma'am" and "No ma'am," "Please" and "Thank you," were expected in all interactions. Questioning, talking back, and balking at instructions were unacceptable and indefensible. The family lore held that if you got in trouble at school, church, work, or play for behaving disrespectfully, you would be in worse trouble when you got home. Explanations, reasons, and justifications for breaches of the respect standard were not sought or tolerated.

"Give God the credit" was a focus on the source of all good things (life, love, health, success, weather, victories, beauty). God was the source of all good. We were the beneficiaries of that goodness. If anyone needed help, health, safety, or comfort, praying could bring that help. Prayers of gratitude before all meals, at bedtime, and in moments of celebration, births, weddings, and promotions were a given. Bad or sad outcomes in life were the result of man's limitations or sin, though God would still be there as a comfort. The difficult-to-understand issues of life and living would be made clear in the next life.

"Don't get too big for your britches" was closely allied with the previous one and was a way to ward against the taking of credit. If I achieved, someone else didn't. If I won, someone else lost. If I stuck out, someone else was stuck in. Thinking highly of myself in any form was thinking too highly and was a sure path to shame and failure. Pride was one of the seven deadly sins. Better to be one with or one below others than to risk being above them. "God first, others second, self last," was a popular mantra.

"Be grateful for what you do have" was a summation of all the others. The first five address the world as it was seen to be or was meant to be. What is left is to make peace with the results of that assessment. Accept the world as offered and do your best within that framework. Questioning or challenging any of its aspects is to violate them all. It would be an indication that I hadn't been nice, nor good, nor respectful, nor given proper credit, and I had clearly gotten too big for my britches. Questioning was the ultimate wrong.

In the world of my childhood, binary thinking was routine. In that thinking, there is no in-between; all is black or white, good or bad, nice or ugly. The Bible is either God's Word or it isn't. It is all true or none of it is true. There are either miracles in the world or there aren't. They all happened or none of them happened. I remember the excitement around believing that God could speak things into existence, axe heads could swim, a man could live in the belly of a whale, a chariot of fire could lift a prophet up into heaven, Jesus could feed thousands from one person's sack of food, walk on water, raise the dead, and people could be healed by just touching His clothing. He walked out of His tomb alive three days after he was crucified and pronounced dead. Forty days later He rose into the sky, into Heaven, until He could no longer be seen. He promised that he would return to the earth in the same manner at some point in the future to assemble everyone who believed in Him, living and dead, and have them join Him in Heaven for all eternity. My child-like faith was strong. It got lots of support from my village.

Binary thought is the law of all or nothing, something is perfect or, if not, it should be. My mother's admonishments drew their power from this: Should, ought, must, always were the operative words, and they were intensely personal. In Mom's eye, her son should/ought/must be nice, good, respectful, humble, grateful, and give God credit, and, if not, he should be ashamed. Avoiding the internal feeling of shame remains a challenge for me to this day. It was an enormously powerful tool for her. Interestingly and ironically, though completely outside any awareness on my part in my early years, the six dictums held together as a unit. When one lost its grip, the others would be weakened as well. "Be nice" was the first one to fall for me. It would take years and the change would come through a side door, not the front.

The Helpful Side of a Two-Edged Sword

As a child, I could always find a job—on weekends, holidays, or summers. I was often sought by neighbors for assistance with chores, yard work, or errands and would frequently be paid. At twelve, I had my first salaried job. I sacked groceries on Saturday for the local Brookshire Brothers grocery store. It required getting a Social Security card. I kept that first card proudly for years.

I was always grateful to be hired. I was respectful, trustworthy, and punctual, and worked hard at doing the job well. In the summers of high school and early college, the employers of former years were always glad to have me back. I felt lucky and blessed by God. At a less conscious level, I was the embodiment of all Mom's maxims, and they were clearly being rewarded. What employer would not want a nice, talented, respectful, do-as-he-was-told, and do-it-well employee? It was a powerful reinforcement of the ideas.

Later, even as a counselor, psychologist, management trainer, consultant and executive coach, the drive to want to do my job well to please others served as a powerful motivator. I worked hard at understanding and practicing the skills required in each of my professional roles. After all, had not the patients, clients, and customers hired me? I owed it to them to do a good job.

If what I was doing and the way I was doing it was creating problems for me, or anyone else for that matter, it went completely unnoticed by me for years. Being deferential to others to my own detriment was a slow-to-form understanding. Recall the anecdote mentioned earlier about Harold E. and the two young men who lost their jobs when I was hired. If I was willing to do the work of two for the salary of one, or if I was selling myself short, or in any way undervalued what I might have to bring to any situation, I would not have known it. To even consider such a thought would clearly be exceeding the size of my britches. Lest there be the slightest doubt, I feel extremely fortunate to have developed this mindset toward work and respect. It has served, and continues to serve, me well.

It has proven to be considerably easier to back away from deeply formed behaviors and attitudes than to implant and solidify the new ones that are replacing them. Although I am currently a strong proponent of the capacity for plasticity of the human brain, no newly developed, consciously chosen, patterns of behavior, in my experience, can ever hope to completely overpower the force of the first ones, unconsciously adopted. We are to varying degrees always heavily impacted by our first major influences and influencers.

"Go outside and play" Again

When I reached the ninth grade, I was considered a freshman in our senior high school, and a senior in the junior high school. Each school had parallel sports activities separated by class grade. Eighth and ninth graders made up the junior high teams. Tenth and above constituted the senior high teams. The social lines could become a little blurred at times since all grades, eight through twelve, were housed in one large building and shared the same gym and playing fields.

It was at this point that the link between playing and schooling was firmly joined. School replaced the outside as the place to go play. Choosing up teams, determining who, when, and under what circumstances games would be played was now in the hands of coaches and school administrators. Now the play was organized and formalized. Playing with and against neighbors was replaced with playing against other schools in other towns. Playing school sports was something one did on behalf of, and as a representative of, one's school, one's town. It was both a privilege and a responsibility.

It was magic elixir for me. Being a participant in school sports allowed me to work hard, to exert both my mind and my body. It allowed me to compete and fight and win without violating any of my family's norms for living. After all, none of the athletic activity was for personal aggrandizement. It was for our school. It was for our town. My parents were proud to have a member of their family representing our school and town. The ninth grade completely sealed the deal for me.

As a senior in junior high, ninth grade, I was a member of the first team, a starter in basketball. Within a radius of seventy-five miles or so, we would play all other junior high basketball teams, some representing larger towns and schools, some smaller. The towns that made up our district would all be of similar size. We also managed to play in two or three weekend tournaments. All the games were played within easy driving distance of Jacksonville.

Social changes were occurring as well. I was now playing with teammates from all over town, not just those from my neighborhood; with teammates from every socio-economic, educational, and religious class represented. Collectively, we were all the school/town representatives. We played together—we were the Jacksonville Indians!

In the spring, I was the starting shortstop on the junior high school baseball team. However, a twist occurred, with significant personal consequences. The starting shortstop for the senior high team and his immediate backup were injured early in the season. I was promoted from the junior high team to the senior high team for the remainder of the year's schedule—a ninth grader on the senior high team. It was a very big deal. I earned a varsity letter and was awarded my first letter jacket. I went on to earn at least two varsity letters in each of the three following high school years. School had become the place to "go outside and play." During the years of high school, my body was constantly under development. Developing the mind was another matter altogether.

Studying, learning, questioning, thinking, analyzing, critiquing, debating were of little or no concern. Why should they be? Most of the elements of my life were moving along just fine. Life's basic challenges and answers were addressed and answered each Sunday at church.

The church of my high school days was considered from the outset a mission church. The largest Southern Baptist church in our hometown, Central Baptist, wanted to provide an opportunity for worship for families who lived on the west side of town. Our family, along with four or five other families, volunteered to form the nucleus of the new church. Sunset Avenue Baptist Church had its first meetings in a renovated house. As the congregation grew, it purchased a corner lot and built a church to accommodate the needs of a hundred-plus people. The church, a mission, was in harmony with the self-effacing, serve-others attitude within our family.

Going to school was fun. That's where I played. That's where my teammates and friends were, and in time where my girlfriend would be. I never skipped school. Relatively speaking, I made good grades, Bs and Cs mostly, an occasional A and no Ds or Fs. I was a good boy in class. I was respectful of my teachers, paid attention, and did as I was told. I came to understand much later that my capacity for auditory recall was high, especially so if a person in authority, such as a teacher, was doing the talking. In testing situations, this meant that if the question being asked had been discussed in class, the chance of my remembering the answer was high. If the topic was not covered, or I was expected to have read about it, the odds of recall were significantly reduced. I depended on my teachers to tell me what was important. I never considered that I might study and learn something on my own. That would have been forgetting my place and role in the world and getting "too big" for my own good.

"Go outside and play." Once More

My college experience was not too different from high school. The setting was dramatically different to be sure. East Texas Baptist College in Marshall, Texas, a town of about 25,000 residents, had been founded as the College of Marshall in 1912, following a campaign to create a Southern Baptist college in East Texas. It began as a junior college and academy and became a four-year college in 1944. At the time of my enrollment, the fall of 1953, it had fewer than a thousand students. Most students, faculty, and administrators shared a commonly held set of beliefs. Religious-related activities were dominant, including chapel services five days a week, evening vespers, a school curriculum that, along with traditional liberal arts instruction, also included Bible courses and church history. As a ministerial student, I was deeply involved in all these activities.

Spoiler Alert 5 - Segregated Colleges

Two other denominational colleges were located in Marshall. One was Wiley College, founded in 1873 by the Methodist Episcopal Church's Bishop Isaac Wiley and certified in 1882 by the Freedman's Aid Society. It is notable as one of the oldest historically Black colleges west of the Mississippi River. The other was Bishop College. Bishop was founded in 1881 by the Baptist Home Mission Society to serve students in East Texas, where the majority of the state's Black population lived. Its original administration and faculty were made up of Americans of European heritage. It's first Black president, Joseph Rhoads, was appointed in 1929. The colleges, like the public schools, were completely segregated. In my world, there were no questions raised about this arrangement. It was simply the way it was.

~ ~ ~

The two biggest influences of my high school days—the six maxims that guided all my behaviors and the role and place of athletics—were still my lodestones at East Texas Baptist. I was nice, a good boy who deferred to authorities, depended on teachers to make me aware of what I needed to know and understand, was careful not to think too highly of myself and was in a community where giving God the credit for all good things was standard behavior. I was pleasantly surprised, and a bit embarrassed and self-conscious, to be elected on an occasion as the school's most popular boy. The modesty part came easy; any sense of personal pride over the selection I felt only vaguely.

It was athletics and all that went with it that would profoundly impact my college days, as well as the first few years that followed. The College was essentially a one-sport school—basketball. Football had been eliminated during the years of World War II and baseball would not be introduced until the year after my graduation, 1958. Track was also a sport, but it primarily supported the basketball team. The Big State Conference in which the school participated did not allow spring practices for fall sports. Therefore, the students who were on a basketball scholarship also were required to run track in the spring as a way to maintain fitness throughout the year.

My identity as an athlete felt constant to me, my body changed dramatically as I got older. At the beginning of my senior year in high school, I stood 5'10" and weighed 155 pounds. As an entering freshman in college, I was 6'2" and weighed 195 pounds! While I still felt small, I was seen as something quite different by my teammates and competitors. Little Hoddy Cone was living in a very different body.

I loved the beginnings of my college life; being around lots of people who shared my views of faith, life, and living, being an aspiring ministerial student, picking a schedule of classes, having a roommate in a college dormitory; essentially living on my own for the first time. On weekends, for the first several weeks, I would hitchhike home to be with my girlfriend, who had one remaining year in high school.

Money was becoming a problem. Although I had plenty for beginning fees and costs, despite considerable effort, I was unsuccessful at finding a part-time job to support the additional needs that were coming. Being without a job became the stimulus for a great deal of prayerful appeals to God for help and guidance. Not having a former employer to return to and not realizing that almost all part-time jobs were already spoken for by the older, mostly married upperclassmen who knew their way around town, left me on the outside looking in. Hard decisions were coming.

By early October, I was spending more and more of my free time in the gym playing intramural basketball. Although I had turned down the community college basketball scholarship to pursue the life of a ministerial student, I found playing again to be great fun. The joy was enhanced playing in my larger body! It was something of a palliative in an otherwise difficult financial time. I had also become friends with a fellow freshman, Rodney Beasley, who was attending school on a basketball scholarship. It was this friendship that became the catalyst for the dramatic role that athletics was about to play in my college life.

Story - "Get your ass off the court or ..."

In mid-October, the College basketball team had begun its pre-season practice sessions. When time away from class and job hunting would permit, I would find my way to the gym to watch. The size and layout of the gym allowed for close contact between spectators and players. It was not uncommon for me to be on the side of the court carrying on a running conversation with Rod. Neither was it uncommon for him, during warmup periods, to throw me a ball and say, "Have a shot!" I would readily comply. This bantering and side court behavior continued off and on into November, when the team's official playing season began.

At a Monday practice session following a Saturday game in which the coach had not been especially pleased with his team's performance, I saw a side of the coach I had not seen before. During the team's warmup period, I stood with a ball in my hand on the side of the court. In a very loud and direct voice, the coach shouted at me, "Get your ass off the court or get out here and practice like the rest of us." I had upset a person in authority. I was surprised, embarrassed, ashamed. I immediately left the gym.

That evening Rod came by my room to talk. He thought there might have been some validity in the coach's harsh words. The next afternoon, I went by the coach's office to apologize for any difficulties I may have created the day before. I also made known to him what my friend had said. He acknowledged that there was some truth in the "get out here and practice like the rest of us." He also acknowledged other comments that had come to him from those with whom I had been playing in intramural games. Later that day, I was issued a set of the College's practice uniforms and joined the team. By mid-December, I was offered a scholarship covering all related college expenses except for those being covered by the denomination's contribution for ministerial students. Just like that, my financial anxieties were over, and I was playing again!

I felt fortunate, lucky, and blessed by God, especially blessed. He had more than answered all my prayers. Just as in high school, the six deeply held mantras had worked their magic. I was a good student of the game, respected and learned from the coach, respected and learned from the older and more experienced players, and was proud to be a part of the team—playing on behalf of our school, and I was playing for a Christian school. That year, I was one of only two players on the team who were in the process of becoming ministers. The other, James Morton, was a senior.

By the time I graduated, I was the College's first player to be selected three years in a row to the Big State Conference All-Conference Team, elected the team's co-captain two years, voted the team's most valuable player two years, named to three Holiday All-Tournament Teams, and, for a while at least, the holder of the school's single-game, single-season, and career scoring records. In 1988, 31 years after leaving, I was one of four selected for the inaugural class of the College's newly created Athletic Hall of Fame.

Through it all, I never lost sight of the idea that all these good things were coming from God. I was blessed and fortunate to have had good coaching and good team members with whom to play. His hand was at work through me. God was first, teammates were second, and I was third.

Story - Wearing Little Britches and Giving God the Credit

In the early 1990s, three friends, two of whom had been teammates for two years and one who had played on the junior varsity, and I had agreed to meet in Marshall. Our meeting coincided with Homecoming Week for the College. Ron Wimpy was coming from Florida, Bill Little and I were coming from Missouri, and Jim McBride, who had continued to live in Longview, a town near the College, would all meet. The plan was simple—play golf, attend a Homecoming event, dine, and swap catch-up stories in the evening.

Since I was coming from Kansas City and Bill from St. Louis, we met at Love Field in Dallas and rented a car for the drive to the College. As we were driving toward Marshall, Bill began to talk of his first college game as a freshman playing on the

JV—how excited he had been and how clearly he remembered it. Why? He had personally scored twenty of the team's points, and they had won. We laughed and joked about it. In good fun, I questioned his memory after thirty-plus years as well as his skill level as a player.

At his insistence, we decided to drop by the local newspaper office, the Marshall News Messenger, to go through its microfiche files and prove once and for all the validity of his claim. Three variables made the data search easy. It was the first game of his freshman year, 1954. It was also the first game of the season for the varsity team. One game had preceded the other, and he remembered the name of the school against which he had competed. And there it was, just as he had claimed! His name was in the box score, and he had been credited with scoring twenty points. It was a happy moment.

In the process, I looked at the box score for the varsity as well. I was then a sophomore, and it was my first game as a member of the starting team. To my complete amazement there in the box score, as well as in the body of the newspaper article pertaining to the game, was my own performance. I had scored 32 points! I had absolutely no recall of anything regarding the game—none whatsoever! I did not remember the game, the team against whom we competed, my individual performance, or that we had won. My friend was as stunned as I, if not more so, that I had no memories surrounding the event.

Later that same evening, when the four of us were in Jim's home, we recounted our afternoon experience. Jim's spouse, Jan, immediately left the room and returned with a scrapbook she had kept since her own college days. She and Jim had been college sweethearts. What was my first game as a starter, as a sophomore, was the first game of the year for Jim and Ron as seniors and starters. She quickly turned to a page where the article under discussion was pasted into her scrapbook in 1954. I was amazed.

For the next several minutes, I thumbed through her scrapbook. Every article regarding every game for that year and the year before had been pasted in. What she had maintained in complete detail, I could only locate in partial and hazy memories. I can still remember some of my emotions, in the early 1990s, as I thumbed through the articles reflecting so much of my early college life of the mid-1950s.

~ ~ ~

For the record, the two most lingering and powerful memories of my entire college career as a basketball player occurred one year apart, under similar circumstances, and both were embarrassing. Why is it I can recall those and not remember the achievements? Both memories occurred in a post-conference playoff game with the winner of the Lone Star Conference to determine who would represent our region in the NAIA National Championship Tournament in Kansas City. I failed to make a layup in each case. In one, against Stephen F. Austin, at the very start of the game, the ball I shot rolled slowly and completely around the rim before falling away. We went on to lose the game as well as the two-out-of-three playoff series. It was an embarrassing miss. In the other, against Southwest Texas State, one year later, I intercepted a pass, was dribbling toward a layup, and thinking I would dunk it. At 6'2," dunking was something I had learned to do but had never actually done so in a game. However, in mid-flight, I decided not to slam dunk the ball for fear of being seen as a showoff. While adjusting, I managed to miss the shot altogether. I was mortified. We lost the game as well as the playoff. Keeping my britches the size they should be was, and continues to be, a powerful emotional influence.

As in high school, participating in athletics put me in touch with a large segment of college life, not only among students but among faculty, staff, and alumni as well. Those contacts led to many invitations. Invitations to speak at banquets, youth meetings in churches, guest minister for Sunday services, youth director and assistant pastor of the largest church in a county seat town of about 5,000. The most life-impacting of all, was being selected to participate as a member of Texas Baptists' statewide, summer Youth-Led Revival program. This program made it possible, over three summers, in week-long increments, for me, along with other young ministers, preachers as well as musicians, to have contact with churches of all sizes all over Texas. The Department of Student Work, the denomination's department that coordinated all these activities, was also the hiring agent for my first full-time job, the one discussed earlier, as BSU Director at the University of Houston, and the one for whom I worked when Dr. Patterson suggested that I no longer use the services of Drs. Chafin and Sherman. I had been both literally and figuratively caught up in some of my denomination's most important ministries for their young people. It was an amazing ride. I felt enormously fortunate and blessed— "All things had worked together for good ..."

PART III

Chapter 7

FINAL COLLAPSE OF THE COCOON

In the early spring of 1966, while I was still an assistant minister
of Park Cities Baptist Church in Dallas, I met the president
of William Jewell College, H. Guy Moore. He wanted me to
consider joining his staff as the new Dean of Chapel. In this first
conversation he made two observations that were to have a major
influence on the final decision to accept the college's invitation.
Buried within the second was a challenge that was so personally
fascinating and timely that I accepted his invitation immediately
without much thought. Our contacts, via telephone, mail, and
a visit to the campus, would continue for another four months
before my final decision was made public.

Although, I knew of William Jewell College, my information
existed in the smallest of bits and pieces. The school was
in Liberty, Missouri, a suburb of Kansas City. Within our
denomination, it had a reputation of being liberal and
academically selective in the makeup of its student body. A high
number of the school's grads left the college to further their
graduate and professional education in well-known universities
around the country. I learned that the school was one of the
first private four-year colleges founded west of the Mississippi,
in 1849. It trailed the founding of the country's first four-year
public university west of the Mississippi, the University of

Missouri, by only ten years. I also learned that it was held in high regard by the business and professional community in Kansas City, the state, and the region in which it was located.

Until our first conversation, Dr. Moore was someone with whom I had had no contact directly or indirectly. At the time of our visit, he had served as the school's president for four years. He had been an undergraduate at William Jewell before going on to acquire two additional degrees in theology and philosophy of religion. He returned to the college after a successful career as a minister within the Southern Baptist Convention.

The first of my two profoundly influential observations came about when Dr. Moore explained how he had come by my name as a potential candidate for the newly created Dean of Chapel position. He was contacting me at the suggestion of a former undergraduate schoolmate of his at Jewell who had been a friend of his for four decades. His friend turned out to be my philosophy of religion professor, Dr. John Newport, from the seminary class that had had such an impact on me five years earlier. At Dr. Newport's suggestion, Dr. Moore also had conversations with my former boss during the student minister days, W.F. Howard, as well as the senior minister of Park Cities, Dr. Herbert Howard, where I was now serving. In each case, it was a conversation between individuals who had known of and about each other within the larger organizations of the denomination. They had crossed paths with each other before.

Dr. Moore contacted me as an extension of the visits with his friends and my former and present employers. He wanted us to get acquainted, to meet face to face. We talked in Dallas for most of an afternoon. The topics covered were many and varied, including our family backgrounds and children.

He was interested in me understanding why and how he had become the president of the College and what the experiences of his four years in the position had been like. He also wanted to explain how the Dean of Chapel position had emerged in his mind. After all, he had been serving as the senior minister of a large metropolitan Southern Baptist church in Kansas City when the Board of Trustees initially approached him about the William Jewell presidency. He thought that my decision-making process regarding leaving a church role for a college role might not be too different from his.

Once again, I was being invited to consider a job about which I would have known nothing before the conversations began. And the meeting had come about at the recommendation of a former professor whom I had greatly admired. The discussions were exciting for me. I felt immensely flattered.

I learned in 2014, forty-eight years after this conversation, that a friend whom I had admired since our first meeting in the late 1950s, Dr. Hardy Clemons, had triggered this entire string of events. Hardy had been approached by Dr. Moore initially to fill the new Dean of Chapel position at William Jewell. Hardy did not feel he could leave his current responsibilities at that time, though he could appreciate what the College was attempting to do. It was Hardy who first raised my name with Dr. Moore as someone to consider. Hardy, Dr. Newport, and Dr. Howard were all well acquainted. That Dr. Newport and Dr. Moore had been undergraduate classmates turned out to be fortuitous.

I smile as I recount this conversation with Hardy. Bill Little and I were visiting him at his condo in San Antonio. Hardy's life-long partner and wife, Ardel, had died a few months earlier. Living without someone to whom he had been so devoted for more than fifty years was proving to be a considerable challenge. Bill and I, at his invitation, were to spend three days with him. Our goal was to visit, catch up, and play golf.

Catching up with Hardy was a huge deal for me. I first met him in Fort Worth in 1958. I was a second-year student at Southwestern Seminary; he was a graduate student completing his ThD degree. Our contact there was random, brief, and pleasant. Though I scarcely knew him, I liked and admired him. He struck me as someone who was calm, smart, and kind. And to top it off, we both liked to play golf. Our connection deepened in the early 1960s because of the Student Department of the Texas Baptist Convention. As mentioned earlier, I was the BSU Director of the University of Houston. Hardy, a few years earlier, had been the BSU Director of the University of Texas in Austin and had maintained a close friendship with his former and my current employer, W. F. Howard. I learned more of their friendship when I moved to Dallas. It was not unusual to cross paths at shared meetings and conferences. We had many friends and associates in common.

For all practical reasons, contact with Hardy became limited when I left the Student Department and accepted the job at Park Cities Baptist. After he left the Student Department, he had become a pastor in the Texas cities of Georgetown and Lubbock. Our contact was limited even further when I took the job at William Jewell and moved to Missouri. We would know little or nothing of each other's lives from that point until our visit in 2014.

What Bill, Hardy, and I shared was a common beginning— ministers in the Southern Baptist Convention—a continued interest in graduate education, a curiosity about life and learning, and a high regard for each other. I believe our visit in San Antonio, each in his own way and for his own reasons, was special. For me, strange as it may seem, it provided me a fuller understanding of one of the important stories of my life. I had taken a lot of satisfaction from the idea that Dr. Newport had played an important early role in my being considered for the William Jewell job. To learn that his role was likely complementary at best made more sense. That Hardy had been the college's first choice for the Dean of Chapel job made even more sense. The fuller more accurate story is more satisfying for me to consider than the original ever was or could have been.

The second conversation topic at Dr. Moore's initial visit, the one that played the largest role in my eventual decision to accept the College's job offer, had to do with the structure and function of chapel services within the campus community. I learned the why behind his decision to create a Dean of Chapel position to join the President, Vice-President of Student Affairs, Academic Dean, and Vice-President of Finance as a part of the School's administrative structure.

My alma mater, East Texas Baptist College, held a required attendance chapel service from 10:00 to 10:30 five mornings a week. They were religious in nature—a hymn or two, a prayer, and a brief sermon was the typical format. Occasionally, the gathering would be completely musical, given over to the College Choir, visiting church choirs, pianists, or organists. On rare occasions the president of the College or another person of rank would address the student body.

It little mattered to me that all students were required to attend the services a minimum of eighty percent of the time each semester. To fall below that standard rendered one subject to disciplinary action up to and including dismissal from school. We were, after all, a denominational college committed to honoring God through the development of our spiritual as well as our academic lives. However, I was aware, though not directly touched to any extent, that some felt daily, mandatory chapel was excessive, if not unnecessary. It was also commonplace to tease and chide the fellow students who passed up and down the chapel aisles as the checkers. At the beginning of each service, their job was to verify one's attendance, in the right seat, by the appointed time.

The conversation I was now having regarding the role, place, and value of a chapel service on a denominational college campus was taking place thirteen years after my experiences at East Texas Baptist. In that stretch of time, there had been numerous life situations, including several that have already been cited, that altered, and were continuing to alter, my views of religion in general and my own faith specifically. I had become particularly enamored of the place of an individual's responsibility to think and choose for himself or herself what is worthy of one's life thoughts and energies.

"Do you think that it would be possible to create a concept of a chapel experience that potential students would come to see as another reason for enrolling at William Jewell rather than a liability they discovered after they had enrolled?" was Dr. Moore's question. It was personally fascinating and timely to consider. In its essence it was another "What do you think Harles?" question. And, more exciting to me still, William Jewell, a few years earlier, had already arrived at having only two campus-wide gatherings per week—one on Tuesday (Chapel), devoted to religious considerations, the other on Thursday (Convocation), devoted to topics of general and current interests. An hour for each had been set aside in the school's calendar. I was hooked! I wanted to be a part of such a school and such a program.

The college's position regarding student attendance at these two meetings was stated formally in this manner:

• The administration and faculty have determined that chapel-convocation is an integral part of the learning process at William Jewell College. This conviction underlies the decision to free the hours of 10:00-11:00 each Tuesday and Thursday morning. When appropriate, the guest lecturer will remain the following hour in the Student Union for direct questioning and exploring the ramifications of the presentation.

• Every student is expected to attend Opening Convocation and Achievement Day Convocation.

• Aside from the two mentioned above there are 25 chapel-convocations the first semester, beginning September 19. Of these 25, all students are required to attend 15. Students may select any 15.

• Since this aspect of William Jewell life is intended to be a part of the education process, a student will receive one academic grade point if electing to attend 20 chapel-convocation sessions. The grade point is applicable to all campus groups and honors.

I was especially proud of Southern Baptists for having one of its colleges play such a role. I became aware in the next few years that, in fact, three or four other of the denomination's colleges and universities around the country had similar programs. I simply had not known of their existence. I can now see that this invitation was an incredible fit for my personal and professional life. Only the scope of the fit was beyond my grasp and, in many ways, remains so to this day. The discussions of ideas touching faith and living that had begun with students during my time as a BSU Director and Campus Chaplain and continued with a group of young single adults at Park Cities Church were now going to reach full bloom as the major focus at a small liberal arts college campus. And there was lots of stuff to talk about!

The war in Vietnam was heading toward the 1968 peak of U.S. involvement, including a rapidly increasing draft of college-age young men. Social norms regarding clothing, music, drugs, sexuality, civil rights, voting rights, civil disobedience, and respect for authority were roiling and shifting throughout the country. Sit-ins and protests were beginning to appear on college and university campuses. Churches and people of faith were increasingly being drawn into public conversations. Many were still reeling from the election and assassination of the country's first Roman Catholic president and that of his younger brother.

The assassination of Martin Luther King, Jr. in the spring of 1968 exacerbated the discussions. One would be hard pressed to find a college student of the mid to late 1960s who doesn't have stories to tell about those years. I was proud—and challenged— to have a voice in how some of those discussions could take place in chapel and convocation gatherings on the campus of a college supported by my denomination.

One other item of discussion between Dr. Moore and me warrants acknowledgment, the ramifications of which would be of extreme importance to me as we went forward. In our first extended afternoon visit, I had commented to him about my growing interest in the role and place of personal counseling as a minister and of my strong desire to return to a university setting for further education and training along those lines. He was quick to acknowledge its value. He also pointed out that the Kansas City branch of the University of Missouri, one of the four main campuses of the Missouri University system, was within a 30-minute drive of the College and gave his complete support for my desire to pursue further graduate studies. I learned upon my arrival that several of the college faculty, across a wide range of fields of study, had taken advantage of these opportunities.

My family and I moved from Dallas to Liberty, Missouri, to take on the new job in August 1966. In those first weeks and months the Moores and the Cones became close friends. I quickly got acquainted with the chairman of the school's Department of Religion, Dr. David Moore. Until my coming, he had served as the chairman of what was known as the Chapel Committee, a small group of faculty and upper-class students whose task it was to meet periodically and decide whom to invite as guest speakers and what topics should be considered, for both the chapel and convocation sessions. The committee would remain intact and serve in an advisory capacity. And aside from commitments and arrangements already in place for the first weeks of the semester, the primary responsibility, and accountability, for the speakers chosen and subjects addressed now fell to me. While still struggling with the old anxieties of wanting and needing to please others, particularly the people in authority in my life, as well as not getting "too big for my britches," it was a job I entered with a great deal of excitement and enthusiasm.

The first days and weeks were filled with meeting students, faculty, and new colleagues on the administrative and support staff, as well as active participation in the school's fall events, particularly those having to do with sports and fine arts. The position I was assuming, Dean of Chapel, was high profile and new to the college and to the surrounding community. Considerable curiosity was aroused over exactly what this role meant to campus life and who and what I was like as a new person in their midst. Being addressed as Dean was new and a bit disquieting. I and the position were in a highly public light. In the first days, I made it a point to meet all the local ministers in Liberty.

To better understand the interests and expectations regarding the role and place of chapel in the minds of students, faculty, staff, and influential others in the community, these earliest get-acquainted meetings were very important to me. Since the school's philosophy was to allow students to pick and choose which sessions they would attend, it seemed extremely important to schedule the various topics and presenters as far into the future as possible, thus allowing students to make informed choices. Knowing in advance subjects and speakers also allowed time for promotion of the events both on and off the campus to enhance attendance and participation. In my mind, I felt I was being influenced and guided in my chapel program choices by many of these discussions. Looking back on those times from my current perspective, I am confident that most of what I was hearing was filtered through my own interests and desires. I would be addressing topics that seemed of great importance to me. The thought that there might be several Southern Baptist pastors across the state who held very negative attitudes toward mine never occurred to me.

My family and I (spouse and two daughters) began the process of affiliating with Second Baptist Church in Liberty and becoming acquainted with the families of the men and women with whom I worked at the College. In the spring of 1967, I enrolled on a part-time basis at the University of Missouri at Kansas City (UMKC) master's program of counseling and guidance. The formal pursuit of advanced training and understanding of counseling psychology began.

During the time from the acceptance of the Dean of Chapel role in August of 1966 to a conference I was about to have with Mr. B. G. (Bob) Olson, Interim President of William Jewell in September of 1968, I had devoted most of my energies to trying to create a concept of a chapel experience that potential students would come to see as another reason for enrolling at the College rather than a liability they discovered after they had enrolled. To that end, and with the input and help of numerous students, faculty and staff colleagues, current and former friends, and with the support of the Chapel Committee, I began the process of recruiting a wide range of people to help bring about those experiences.

For the chapel hour, local and distant ministers, seminary professors, theologians, and religious writers provided the bulk of the presentations. I sought a balance between assisting students in the exploration of their religious experiences, providing opportunities for quiet meditation, and times for reflection on the potential ramifications of a believer's role in the larger world. For the most part these clergymen were Protestant and Baptist. Ethnically, there was a generous sprinkling of White and Black presenters. There were also times when it seemed most appropriate that I, as the Dean of Chapel, should lead the worship hour.

Spoiler Alert 6 - Inviting Black People as Guest Speakers

For the convocation hour, the subjects and topics pursued were varied, leaning heavily toward those areas receiving the most national public attention. As alluded to earlier, there was much stuff to talk about on a college campus in the latter half of the 1960s. Politicians, especially those in the public eye, were popular. The fall of 1967 and spring of 1968 was the run-up period to the November presidential election. Senators and representatives from both major parties, a cabinet officer, along with the chairman of the George Wallace for President Committee drew attention not only to the convocation hour but also to the post-presentation question-and-answer period which followed. A representative from the Parliament of India as well as one from Great Britain fell into this political category as well as did a lecturer representing the AFL & CIO Frequent references were made to the Great Society, the war in Vietnam, race relations, the role of women, and the place of college campuses in a democratic country. To this day I treasure correspondence with Martin Luther King Jr. and former president Harry Truman. Unfortunately, neither could accommodate our request.

For the other convocation topics, not quite so overtly political in nature but still very much a part of the country's most-talked-about subjects, there were journalists, writers, college professors, university presidents, semanticists, sociologists, and mental health professionals to lead the presentations and discussions. Their ethnic and gender diversity was a big part of their appeal. Men and women of color were frequent guests. It wasn't unusual for a chapel-convocation event to be the talk of the campus.

From my limited perspective, this was a very engaging, even exciting, two-year period for the college, its students, and faculty. The post-presentation discussions were generally popular and well attended by many from both groups. On occasion, guest speakers would be invited to linger and make classroom visits in the academic disciplines that they now represented as professionals. Spirited discussions were sparked by something said, or an idea that had been presented, either in a speaker's formal presentation, the open discussions that followed, or at a classroom visit. It was also gratifying to hear expressions of appreciation from many of the students and the faculty for the role I may have played in making such experiences available to them.

~ ~ ~

In retrospect, what was lacking on my part was an appreciation for what was happening in those spirited conversations among those who were not happy or enthused by the conclusions or observations advanced by the guest speakers. While I thought of myself as open and desiring feedback regarding the value of the chapel events, I was in fact mostly attuned to the comments of appreciation and gratitude. The comments and reactions of anyone—faculty, staff, or student—who might hold a difference of opinion as to the value and worth of the meetings were lost on me. In the language of those years, I would be clearly identified with those referred to as progressive or liberal. I had considerable difficulty hearing, much less being understanding and supportive of, those referred to as conservatives. The meetings and the topics discussed were of such value to me, how could others not share that same enthusiasm?

Also during this period, there were a number of students who would make their way by my office for a one-on-one private conversation, sometimes as a walk-in, sometimes by making an appointment with my administrative assistant. In my earliest months in the job, the one-on-ones presented a challenge. My assistant and I shared a common space, two desks and not much room for visitors. To have sufficient privacy often meant a quick look up and down the hall for either an empty office or an unoccupied meeting room. Eventually my office would be moved to a space that would accommodate room for a secretary, a reception area, and a connected private office. And unlike my early experiences as a campus chaplain and assistant pastor of a large church, I wasn't surprised when the private conversations with students would shift from lighter topics to issues of deeply personal significance. I was surprised somewhat at the range of concerns as they were presented and the number of students who sought the contact. Like the chapel experience, I was scarcely aware of the few numbers of conservative students who sought my office out for counseling and support. I should have known they were going to the BSU Office directed by a young man I had hired, Fred Hodkins, for those conversations. I was particularly glad, that beginning in the spring semester of 1967, to have begun the formal training in counseling psychology at University of Missouri at Kansas City.

Story - "You're being fired."

On Friday afternoon September 13, 1968—a little more than two years into my job as Dean of Chapel, I was invited to a meeting with the Interim President of William Jewell College, Mr. B. G. (Bob) Olson. The Interim President had been in his new position for about a month. He came to the college in 1967 as the vice-president of development. We were in the first days of the fall semester for the students and four days away from the school's official Opening Convocation, complete with the Academic Procession of the Faculty. The entire college family was expected to attend.

As I was preparing for the conversation with Mr. Olson, the man who hired me as Dean of Chapel in 1966, H. Guy Moore, had been relieved of his job as president of the college a few weeks earlier! The reason stated by the Board of Trustees for his termination was primarily financial in nature. Although Dr. Moore was aware of financial issues and concerns for the College, he felt they were being addressed. After all, he had been a major factor in the recruiting and hiring of the new Vice-President of Development, Mr. Olson, a year earlier for that very purpose. The man whom Dr. Moore had hired to assist him in getting the College back on more sound financial footing was the man I was now on my way to visit.

The termination of Dr. Moore had been surprising, abrupt, and shocking to many. He was handed the decision in the late summer. He and his spouse were asked to vacate their on-campus president's home within a month. To assist in the transition process, they were provided a nice condominium in nearby Kansas City and whatever income would be necessary until another professional opportunity might present itself. Nothing that was provided for their changes altered the sense of devastation the Moores experienced. I will never forget a late August visit with them in the new condo. Hardly any topic could be considered that didn't trigger the expression "those sons of bitches, those sons of bitches!"

According to the statements from the Board, a more financially minded, university-experienced administrative leader was required, and quick action was needed. And while there had been limitations in President Moore's direct administrative experience with academic institutions, he was seen as someone who surrounded himself with the needed experience and sought their input and guidance in his decision making. He and his spouse were viewed as people who genuinely cared for the wellbeing of the students, faculty, staff, and community. They were hurt and embarrassed to have been placed in such a circumstance.

Again, from my perspective, Dr. Moore was popular and well-regarded. His abrupt dismissal was the fuel for countless conversations. That, plus anxieties associated with ramping up for a new semester of schoolwork and the numerous national issues mentioned earlier, made for some high levels of tension and angst in me.

It did not take long for Mr. Olson to get to the reason for asking me to drop by his office. "You're being fired," was its essence. The termination was to take effect at the end of the fall semester that was just now getting underway. We were both aware that the entire chapel-convocation fall program, complete with subjects to be considered as well as the presenters of each, had been completed and published in a widely distributed brochure.

The message was conveyed to me in a respectful, professional, and business-like manner. He made a point of how important it had been to him to advise me as early as possible of his decision so that I could have adequate time to prepare for whatever career changes would be needed.

He also made it clear that he felt the action he was taking, as well as the timing of our conversation, was in the best interests of the college. He pointed out in some detail that there were groups and individuals within the state who had become "troubled" and "concerned" over what they were hearing about chapel-convocation events on the campus. Those cited included some parents who were worried for their children, some ministers who were hearing the concerns of the parents, some minister groups who felt traditional Christian ideas and values were being minimized, ignored, or undermined. Some members of the Executive Committee of the Missouri Baptist State Convention had raised concerns. Some within those groups, he said, thought there was a connection between the declining student enrollment and the religious environment on the campus. As a collective, this group was putting forth the idea that the college had strayed too far from its original roots, and strong measures were needed to get it back on its more proper path. Removing me from the position of responsibility for the chapel-convocation programs was seen as a needed step along that path.

As mentioned earlier, while I had been aware from the beginning of my tenure that some individuals were uncomfortable with the changes going on in the chapel-convocation subjects and presentations, it had never occurred to me that there was anything approaching formally organized and outspoken disagreement with the changes. I was too naïve to have considered that possibility and too caught up in the praise and words of appreciation that I heard routinely. It would be several more years before I could begin to grasp more fully the impact that change can have upon individuals, organizations, and institutions.

It is accurate to say that I had been stunned five years earlier, complete with pounding heart and racing emotions, when Executive Director of the Baptist General Convention of Texas, Dr. Patterson, suggested that I stop the use of two of my favorite ministers as program personnel in conferences for which I was responsible. But on this occasion, stunned is too strong a word. Although there is the similarity of having the value of the decision making associated with my job called into question, the manner of this exchange was altogether different. I was listening to a man with whom I had worked for over a year, a colleague with development officer responsibilities who had become to that of the college's chief executive and now my boss. He was simply conveying to me information that had come to him in his new role, its potential impact on him, me, and the school, and the decision to which he had come as a result. He was a businessman making a serious business decision.

I don't deny that my thoughts and emotions were wide-ranging and strong as we talked. If I had given expression to the strongest of them, they would have been centered in two areas. One would have been why, if there was such a level of concern among parents, minister groups, and denominational leadership regarding what was taking place on the campus, would it not have been called to my attention much earlier? After all, I had been responsible for the chapel events for most of two years, and he and I were having this discussion a full three summer months since the last such gathering had occurred. The timing of the conversation struck me as very strange.

Second, I would have wondered if my being terminated from the Dean of Chapel role in any way related to the recent termination of the college's president, Dr. Moore? I learned over the next days and weeks that indeed it was, and in ways that were perfectly understandable. I would always wonder if Dr. Moore had been confronted with the concerns regarding the chapel programs at Jewell. If he was, he chose to keep them to himself, and I was too naïve to ask him outright.

It was a conscious choice on my part not to raise either of the two thoughts. Strangely to me now, bringing either of them up seemed inappropriate. Mr. Olson and I were not having a give and take conversation. I had been summoned to his office to hear directly from him an important decision to which he had come. I can smile as I write these words so many years after the fact. The smile is coming primarily from my lack of appreciation at the time for the common practice of organizations and institutions to announce potentially upsetting or problematic personnel decisions late on Friday afternoons. But that was it! He had given the matter serious thought and had concluded that it was time for me to go.

Being late in the afternoon, I went immediately home and called Dr. Douglas Harris. Doug had joined the faculty of William Jewell as Visiting Professor of Religion from Carson Newman College in Tennessee at the same time as I had come as Dean of Chapel. The visiting professor had now become a full professor and a permanent part of the faculty. He was thirty years my senior and one who had been very interested and outspokenly supportive of the direction the chapel and convocation programs were going. Doug and his spouse, Zenona, had become close family friends. He was also an outspoken inquirer regarding the dismissal of Dr. Moore. Doug's counsel to me was, "Sit tight until I can talk to Olson." Doug felt strongly that what Olson had done was not in the best interest of the college. He called back the next morning, Saturday, and asked if I would meet with him and some faculty colleagues in Olson's office on the following Monday morning. I said, "Yes."

Since Mr. Olson had joined the staff in 1967, he had made it known that he liked getting to his office early. "5:30," as he often said, "is when I prefer to start my workday." Doug knew this, and being something of an early person himself, had visited with him on occasion when Olson served as the Vice-President of Development. I was asked to be at Olson's office at 5:30 a.m. I was.

When I arrived on Monday, there were seven of Doug's faculty colleagues and a member of the school's operational staff already in the hallway waiting to visit with the newly acting president. There were two from the philosophy department, one from business, one from history, one from sociology, one from education, one from psychology, and the librarian. Two were the heads of their departments, philosophy and business. It had to be something of a significant surprise for Mr. Olson to ascend the stairs of the administration building to the second floor a moment or two past 5:30 a.m. and find ten employees of the college waiting outside the entrance to his office. For nearly three hours, a very interesting discussion took place.

The conversation began on an agitated note, peppered with questions and accusations. There was no spokesperson in charge of the group. "What's going on here?" "Why did you decide to fire Harles?" "Why was Dr. Moore fired?" "Why was the faculty not consulted in either case?" Each question raised also tended to be accompanied by anecdotal examples of how things "used to be," "how much better they are now." Several times a faculty person would cite a highly specific example of how a particular chapel program had spilled over into classroom discussions or to an important one-on-one exchange with a student. This part of the give and take went on for the better part of an hour.

Throughout it all, Mr. Olson responded to the questions and statements with respect and consideration. He also returned to one particular theme. The Board of Trustees, in asking him to serve as the interim president, had made it clear that, from their perspective, William Jewell was "in serious financial trouble" and "was headed in a direction at odds with its original Christian principles and values." He indicated they had tied the drop in student enrollments to the directional shift in religious values. He was expected to provide "new and decisive leadership to get both situations righted."

Mr. Olson was not a Southern Baptist, nor was he very aware of the religious overtones of what was taking place within the state. The leadership of the Missouri Baptist Convention was tilting toward a growing fundamentalism position. His background was in business, publishing, development, and public service.

He said that he had not been privy to any Board discussions that had led up to the termination of Dr. Moore. He had been informed of their decision before it was made public, and that was a part of the Board's appeal to him to accept the interim role. He added one important comment that had the most lingering impact on me. While he did not see a way to rescind the decision to have me step away from the role as Dean of Chapel at the end of the semester, he saw no reason why another role might not be found or created to have me remain a part of the William Jewell family.

I learned later that Mr. Olson aspired to having the interim and acting qualifiers dropped from his title. Two very large hurdles were before him—he was not a Southern Baptist nor was he a former minister, conditions which had been in place for many years in the College's selection of a president. In seeking counsel on how his desire might be given more serious consideration by the Board of Trustees and the leadership of the Missouri Baptist Convention, he was counseled to "get the college back on sound financial footing" and "fire Cone." That was it! The Dean of Chapel role at William Jewell had come to its end. Mr. Olson's career at the College ended a year later. He was replaced as Interim President by Bill Holzapfel, who remained in that interim position until the naming of Dr. Thomas Fields as the official president in 1970.

~ ~ ~

What had begun in the heart of a nine-year-old boy to be saved, born again, and baptized, had bloomed into becoming a minister of the gospel to assist others toward their own being saved experience. In order, my religious life was expressed through the experiences of a youth evangelist, a pastor, a campus chaplain, a denominational staffer, an assistant minister, and a chapel dean. My life as a minister had come to an end! I was leaving the last of the roles I would play for and within the Southern Baptist Convention.

Throughout the fall of 1968, I filled the Dean of Chapel responsibilities as I had done the preceding two years with two major exceptions. I did not make or schedule any chapel-related activities for the spring semester, and by mid-December, I had the new title of Director of Counseling and Testing, a role and position I maintained for another seven years. During that span of time, I completed a Masters in Guidance and Counseling at UMKC and through the cooperation of the departments of education and psychology completed a PhD that qualified me to become a licensed psychologist in the State of Missouri in 1976. The responsibility for planning, scheduling, and recruiting presenters for the chapel-convocation programs was assumed by another college staff member and the position of Dean of Chapel was eliminated. I continued to live in Liberty, supporting the College in a variety of ways until 2009.

Chapter 8

REALIGNMENT

In an earlier section, I made note of the African Proverb, "It takes a village to raise a child." In doing so, I referenced family, church, denomination, friends, public school, college, and seminary as the major components of my "village." I would now like to add to that list religion itself. Together they were a powerful source of encouragement, support, belonging, and happiness for me.

As time passed, however, I became aware of the ripple effect of the impact of changes in the various branches of the village (my Southern Baptist denomination, family, college, seminary, and friends) on me and belief in any religion itself. The experiences opened a unique understanding of the influence of the groups on me as an individual as well as my impact on the groups of which I was a part. As I began to have thoughts and actions of my own, different from those I felt the village had wanted and expected of me, the responses of the village began to shift as well.

I moved from a position of insider in each component of my village to that of an outsider! Strangely, up to and including my termination as Dean of Chapel, I never felt I was leaving anything. After all I was associated with Southern Baptists at each step along the career path. I was keenly aware of shifts in my thinking and values, but I wasn't separating from them. I was the same person with different thoughts and feelings. What those in the larger "village" might be thinking about any changes in my attitudes and actions was of limited awareness or concern to me. My naivete was boundless.

The Denomination

In 1953, at seventeen, I maintained a faith and belief that we Southern Baptists, we true Christians, were all of one mind. My years at East Texas Baptist College, the summers of Youth-Led Revival preaching, my first experiences of being the pastor of two small rural churches, my time at Southwestern Seminary, and the earliest years of working as the BSU Director and student chaplain in Houston had little impact on that starting point.

Niggling exceptions to that general trend occurred in four areas: the shift in attitude regarding my personal role in my lack of learning that started with the contact with Dr. Newport and the philosophy of religion class at Southwestern; the sharp division that occurred among some Southern Baptist ministers concerning the worthiness of a Roman Catholic to serve as the President of the United States; a growing fascination with the importance of one-on-one conversations, as opposed to preaching and teaching groups, as a method of being helpful to others; and after moving to the state office in Dallas, a greater awareness of the range of theological, social, and philosophical differences that existed among my fellow university and college chaplains and BSU Directors.

These experiences, along with the events centered around Dr. Patterson, Park Cities Church, and William Jewell College led to my breaking with the Southern Baptist denomination. In my last position, Dean of Chapel at William Jewell, I was hired by a member of the denomination in August 1966 and twenty-five months later was fired from that same position by another representative of the denomination, but not one of its members.

There were no formal separations, no defrocking of a minister, and no withdrawals from membership in churches. It was more a withering that took place over time. Within five years, however, I would have virtually no contact with anything having to do with the Southern Baptist Convention as an organization. That part of my village ceased to exist.

For me, the first challenge, as it turned out, was Baptist to Baptist—fundamentalists vs. conservatives vs. liberals. Professionally, what began in Dallas with Dr. Patterson's challenge of the use of Sherman and Chafin as program personnel in BSU conferences had ended at William Jewell College with my termination as Dean of Chapel. What had surfaced in 1964 had come to a head in 1968. Now that I was aware of at least three different circles, in which one did I want to live, if any?

Looking back, which can be iffy at best, to me it had become a matter of focus. The more conservative or fundamentalist a church or minister was, the greater the tendency to separate the social problems of current times from worship, missions, and evangelism. With that came major concern for protecting the beliefs and practices of the past and one's personal salvation in the hereafter. Issues like anti-war, civil rights, and social justice were best addressed outside the church. The more moderate or liberal the church or minister, the greater was the opposite belief. If the church has nothing to say to the world's crises, then of what value is it in real life?

The second challenge, and infinitely more personal, was a lot like answering the Park Cities Church question, "What do you think, Harles?" To what conclusions about anything had I come on my own? About anything? It may have started as Baptist to Baptist, but it quickly spread. It soon became religious faith in general and Christianity in particular with a special focus on Jesus, the founder.

The first outward change was my move from a Baptist to a Presbyterian congregation. As mentioned earlier, upon arriving in Liberty in 1966, my spouse and I with our two daughters immediately aligned with Second Baptist Church, the church most closely connected with William Jewell. A son, Elliot, was born in January 1971. The loyalty to church and denomination, despite the dramatic job shift at the college, remained intact until 1973. Then, after fifteen years of marriage, my wife and I separated and then divorced.

First Presbyterian Church, in addition to its worship services and Christian education programs, was also noted for its involvement in societal issues that touched Liberty, Missouri, and the country (Vietnam, voting and civil rights, social justice). I admired the minister, Julian Houston, a great deal. We shared numerous conversations and activities. He and the congregation were supporters of Northland Counseling Center, the center Dr. Lee Minor and I had founded. Julian was the officiating minister at my wedding to Judith White Burson in 1976. During all the years of my association with the church, however, I could never bring myself to become an official member. I no longer wanted to be identified with any specific set of beliefs and doctrines.

Attending a Black Church

The final church shift was to the First Baptist Church of Liberty, a move that took place around 1980. It was a distinctive African American church that had been founded in 1843, making it one of the oldest churches in the area. Several of its members were good friends. Sam Houston and his family and I were particularly close. Sam was a deacon and the grandson of slaves who had lived in the Liberty area. We had gotten to know each other through our shared interests in community service projects. Again, like before, my contact with the congregation was as a visiting participant rather than an official member.

When I consider the portion of my life within the Southern Baptist denomination—twenty-two years—I am flooded with a sense of profound gratitude. Nothing had more far-reaching impact on the direction of my life. In many ways I owe much of the way my life evolved to the Southern Baptist Convention as it existed during the years of my childhood and young adulthood. And when I think of specific individuals along my way— classmates, professors, administrators, pastors, denominational leaders, fellow church members, and colleagues who loved me, believed in me, and supported me—tears of gratitude flow easily. I came to recognize, however, that direct contact with individuals within a group tends to both create and reinforce one's image of the group itself. I saw in those close to me what I was taught to see.

During it all, I proved to be a classic example of an aspect of the yin-yang philosophy. The high price I paid for the propensity to be deferential to authority showed itself repeatedly to the detriment of my own ability to think, reason, and decide.

At each point in my career there were always a few friends with whom I felt closely tied. It was that closeness with a few that generalized itself into the feeling that there must surely be others just like them. As a BSU Director in Houston, as a staff member of the Baptist General Convention of Texas, as an assistant pastor of Park Cities Church, and as the Dean of Chapel at William Jewell College, there were always a few who were closer than others. It was the experiences with those few who had such positive and powerful influence on my life—that helped paint the palette in my mind that we Southern Baptists were all generally of one mind and heart. I did not recognize that as the close ones shifted a bit from assignment to assignment, the new ones reflected more directly the emotional and ideological changes that were occurring within me.

Having that limited mindset made it virtually impossible for me to see the numbers, the passion, and the organization of others within the denomination with views distinctively different from those to which I had come. What was for me freeing, exciting, and challenging was for them a departure from what was true and right and even a betrayal. As far as they were concerned, I needed to be corrected, returned to my starting point, terminated, or ostracized. It was, and continues to be, a very interesting experience.

East Texas Baptist College (University)

My alma mater was another member of the structural village that underwent significant shifting. Some of the shifting occurred while I was still closely connected.

My first spouse and I were married in September 1957, following my June graduation from East Texas Baptist College. She had just completed her sophomore year. Her father was a member of the College's faculty, and their family home was nearby, which meant that we were frequently in contact with both family and school. Following my seminary graduation and during the four years I was with the Department of Student Work, that contact would only be strengthened. I was then able to recommend former classmates as potential candidates for BSU Director positions as well as to be participants in the Youth-Led Revival Teams in the summer, and I did so. Acting in that manner provided me with a great deal of personal satisfaction.

My formal contact with the college happened under the leadership of four of the school's presidents: H.D. Bruce, the president of my student days, Howard Bennett, Robert Craig, and Bob Riley. Each one would be connected, in his own way, with the shifts in my jobs and thinking.

Dr. Bennett, 1960-76, especially during the days of working for the Student Department as well as the early Dean of Chapel days at William Jewell, invited me on several occasions to be the guest speaker at campus chapel services. The presentations followed the pattern of brief services of worship; a hymn, a prayer, an introduction, and devotional thoughts based on verses from the Bible that would be cited. It all took place within a 30-minute period allotted on the school's calendar for its daily period of worship. The relationship between me and the college was essentially that of a former ministerial student returning to talk to current students about issues having to do with our lives and our faith—to minister to students and faculty. This manner and arena of contact underwent rapid and significant change.

Starting with being fired from the Dean of Chapel position in the fall of 1968, the assumption of the role of Director of Counseling and Testing, the completion of a master's degree in counseling and guidance in 1970, the founding of the Northland Counseling Center in 1973, and the launching of a five-year pursuit of a PhD degree emphasizing counseling psychology, made it clear to all that I was no longer living my life as a Southern Baptist minister. Also, my divorce in 1973 further limited the contact with the College community that I had enjoyed through my ex-spouse's father and her family.

Contact with Dr. Craig, 1986-92, as well as Dr. Dawson, 1976-85, was incidental. During their presidencies, my contact with the college was limited to a few occasions when I would return for a visit in association with Homecoming events in the fall. It is worth noting that Dr. Dawson was the first president with a background in professional education rather than in that of a minister. He would also be the administrator when

the official designation of the College was shifted to that of a
university.

During Dr. Craig's tenure, in 1988 the university initiated and
created an Athletic Hall of Fame. I was one of four selected to its
inaugural class. During this period, my relationship was that of a
former student athlete who was proud to be a part of the school's
history.

The tenure of Dr. Bob Riley, 1992-2009, proved to be the
most interesting of all. He was serving as president of Howard
County Community College in Big Spring, Texas, when he was
named president of the university. His time at East Texas brought
about not only my greatest amount of contact with the school but
the most diverse as well.

Dr. Riley knew me as the president of Cone Resource Group,
in which capacity I had been a licensed psychologist and done
a great deal of leadership and management training, as well as
consulting and executive coaching, for many private and public
companies, organizations, and agencies in the U.S. and Canada.
He also learned that many of those services had been provided
for several of his former community college president colleagues
in Galveston, Dallas, and greater Houston. He learned through
a mutual friend that I was a 1957 graduate of East Texas Baptist
College.

During his first ten years as president and under his
leadership, I received the following invitations: to give the
opening convocation address for the University in 1996 and to
lead a strategic planning workshop for the Executive Committee
of the Board of Trustees in 1998. In both instances, I was simply
referred to as Dr. Harles Cone, Cone Resource Group, ETBU
Class of 1957.

In 2002, I was invited to speak at the annual Donor
Appreciation Banquet. I was also selected that year to receive
the J. Wesley Smith Achievement Award, the school's annual

outstanding alumnus award. The Award was presented on October 12 of that year as a part of Homecoming activities at an Alumni Luncheon. In each of these contacts, I was viewed as a former student who was now highly engaged in several business and professional activities. There were no references to my former life as a minister. Earlier in the week, I had been invited to address the faculty and student body at what was known as Homecoming Chapel. I was invited to speak, not so much as a minister, but as the recipient of the Smith Achievement Award. I had long since ceased to be an insider as a desired preacher. The chapel address became the last formal contact I would have with the school family.

A copy of the chapel address is included here as Appendix A. I knew at the time that what I was saying was highly personal and likely to be surprising, if not disappointing, to many. Consequently, for the first time, I read the address rather than speak extemporaneously from notes, as I had always done before. It was, however, an accurate portrayal of how I had come to think and feel over the forty-five years that had transpired since my graduation in 1957.

At the conclusion of the presentation, only one person, a member of the faculty, came to the front of the chapel to offer a comment. To the best of my recollection his words had to do with how different my remarks had been for an ETBU chapel service. I had clearly left the core religious beliefs of my college family. I was no longer a member. My village had splintered further. Aside from occasional financial contributions, I have had no further formal contact with the university. (I was informed in 2018 of a thirty-year celebration of the creation of the Athletic Hall of Fame, and I went to the celebratory luncheon—the only member of the original inductee class to do so.)

One other experience connected to this last formal visit warrants a mention. In addition to the chapel speech, I was asked to participate in a class discussion for upper-level students, juniors and seniors, interested in a major in psychology. The class met on Tuesdays and Thursdays for an hour and a half as opposed to the more typical schedule of three classes a week of one hour each.

After the class was called to order and a brief introduction of who I was and why I was on the campus, the instructor did a very interesting and surprising thing. "First things first," he said to the students, "are there any prayer requests?" After a brief pause a hand went up and a request was made. In a short amount of time, another four or five requests were made. In order, the professor acknowledged the student with raised hand and inquired as to the request. After each request was identified, the professor asked the larger class, "Who would like to voice that prayer on our behalf?" Hands went up and a person to pray was selected for each request. The process lasted for a bit over a half hour. In all my years as a student, as well as all my return visits, I had never seen, or heard for that matter, of a liberal arts class turned over to time for the solicitation for prayer requests. (An opening prayer before a religion or Bible class was not unknown in my college days, but never such a prayer in any arts, history, or science classes and never in any class a time for prayer requests.) As it turned out, there was yet another surprising event to come.

For my part, I spoke briefly of my days at the college as a student who had majored in history and minored in sociology; of how I had come to the interest in counseling and psychology following graduation from Southwestern Seminary and work stints, particularly at the University of Houston and Park Cities Church; and of how I had returned for graduate studies, completing an MA in 1971 and a PhD in 1976, six months before my fortieth birthday and nineteen years after my graduation from East Texas Baptist! I concluded by saying how important and flexible I had found the training in psychology to be. And how

I hoped they would have a similar experience of value, whether they worked as teachers, therapists, ministers, or businesspeople, as well as in their personal lives. I then opened the door for any questions or comments.

Many of the first comments and questions centered on aspects of the return to graduate school as an older student. I didn't lack for anecdotes as to what it was like to be the oldest person in a class or seminar. Neither was there a lack of contrasts to be drawn between my motivation as a student in college and seminary and then in graduate school.

There were also several questions regarding certification and licensure requirements for anyone wanting to work as a counselor or therapist in either a public or a private setting. A dramatic shift in the class occurred when someone asked, "Have you ever prayed with any of your clients or witnessed to them about Jesus?" "No," I said after a brief pause. The ensuing exchanges were mostly about who leads or directs the conversation in a therapy session, the client or the therapist. Eventually one of the students said, "I think a lot of a person's problems would go away if they would just get right with God." The statement generated considerable buzz. Soon after, a bell sounded, and the class ended.

When the class was over, I dropped by the office of the academic dean. Over the period of Dr. Riley's tenure, the dean and I had become friends. He was free, giving us a chance to talk for several minutes. I wanted him to hear of my surprise at the amount of class time devoted to religious actions and themes. I also spoke of the future risk a student might run if he or she applied for graduate studies in psychology. I was especially concerned about any gap that might exist between how this upper-level class was described in the college's catalogue and what training the students might be receiving. The dean seemed genuinely surprised to hear of my experience. Later I learned that the instructor was an adjunct faculty member on a semester contract. His contract was not renewed. I have always wondered if my Homecoming Chapel remarks the next day made it into any class discussion. I have also wondered if I would have received the Smith Award had the chapel speech been presented at some point prior to the award selection process.

An aha!

I have been writing about this journey that began with the certainty of a religious supremacist off and on for eleven years now. I am determined that this will be the last time to review and edit any further than what you are reading now. Why? Because there seems to be no end to the interconnectedness of any single story that I make known with all the other stories that I share.

The "aha" occurred when I took a break from some minor editing dealing with the changes that had gone on with me following my termination as the Dean of Chapel of William Jewell College. The impact of those changes on the various parts of my village that had been important in the earliest days of my faith and religion was a big deal. When I returned to my computer, I took one last look at this ETBU visit and lingered a moment recalling the visit with the psychology students and especially the student who posed the question regarding witnessing to clients/patients about the need for Jesus in their lives and the classroom buzz that followed. A thought popped into my head that seemed to come out of nowhere. What the student asked me might have been something I could have asked a guest speaker when I was a junior or senior at East Texas in 1956! What a profound realization—I had witnessed, believed, prayed for—all of the attributes I was questioning in this young person were parts of the former me—or perhaps the same me.

Were these the same attributes I have now, but redirected to new targets? After all, in those years, 1956-57, I had been deeply involved in all things evangelizing and trying to save lost souls as well as keeping close friends on the straight and narrow path that God had set out for everyone! It was an all-consuming thought.

The mulling since this thought occurred has gone like this: 1) How in the world could I not have had an instant recollection and identification between him and the person I was at his age? Where had the me of those mid 50's days gone? 2) How could the current me, 2022, see so bluntly what the 2002 me hadn't noticed at all? 3) Now, in a similar setting, I would want to acknowledge the student's awareness that a serious conflict could be coming his way if he decided to stay in the world of counseling psychologists. What would he do or say if he knew his patient's background was that of a Muslim, Hindu, Shinto, Hebrew, skeptic, or atheist? 4) What has happened in me to see things so differently today from the 2002 view? 5) The greatest current mystery being mulled by me is how could I have felt so right about each of my former positions when I was in them? 6) And finally, if I live another five to ten years, what will have emerged as me by then? My stories are indeed proving to be mysterious, interconnected, and expanding!!

Family

Regarding my family as part of the village, and particularly my parents, the shifting village was not so much a collapsing as it was a restructuring. After all, I was never not their son nor they, my parents. The restructuring was driven by the changes that had been and were occurring in my life. It rapidly became a process of me making known who I was and what I was becoming as a person—who was in many ways very different from the son they had seen or dealt with in the past.

My gratitude for who and what they were never altered much. What was new for them, and me for that matter, was letting them see and know the person their son had become—and was continuing to become. What they wanted to do with that would be up to them. I no longer wanted to play the cards of my life as I felt they had been dealt. I wanted to play a new and different game. It would be more of a life of my own choosing, and to whatever degree possible, one of my own design. The transition came quickly after the termination as the Dean of Chapel. The journey had numerous twists and turns along the way. Sadly, time with Dad was curtailed by his death in ten years. For Mom and me our shared journey would go on for another thirty years. It demanded a huge amount of unraveling and reknitting the boundaries of how we dealt with each other.

I never doubted my parent's affection nor the warmth and regard that I felt from them. They never failed to give what they could, what they had. When it came to "train up a child in the way that he should go," being saved and teaching me to live by God's laws trumped all other things they held dear. They helped prepare me to live in the world as they knew and understood it. I remain grateful to this day for the foundation which that provided. They could not have known how small and limited the world in which I grew up turned out to be for me—geographically, culturally, ethnically, educationally, socio-economically, politically, and theologically. How could they?

For the most part, particularly if the challenges associated with living in very modest circumstances are ignored, the earliest days of my childhood were happy and safe. I was a member of a family and a clan that included grandparents, uncles, aunts, and cousins. Through the eyes of my earliest childhood, all loved and cared for each other. It was not an accurate view, but it was mine. Many years passed before I grasped the powerful connection between my sense of belonging and being loved and my personal behaviors, within my biological family as well as that of the church.

To the degree that I lived by my mom's guiding maxims and the church's basic tenets I was taught, I was valued, acknowledged, recognized, and even praised. It felt a lot like love. It was when the circumstances of my life put me in positions where the maxims and tenets I had been taught were of questionable, limited, or hurtful value that the upheavals began. My mother would never depart too far from the binary, fundamentalist faith she practiced and taught. Good was good. Bad was bad. Right was right. Wrong was wrong. If she had doubts or questions, I didn't hear about them.

She was a pleasant and unrelenting witness to her faith. For example, on one occasion she and Dad were making a summer visit to our home in Liberty. Mary and I were still married, and son Elliot would not be born for another two years. I was still closely connected with the College but finished with the Dean of Chapel job.

Dad had recently taken up the game of golf. While he wasn't very skilled, he played with enthusiasm and pleasure. There was a nearby golf course owned by the College, Claycrest. We decided to play. It was a warm summer day, and we had a great time. When we were finished, I suggested we go by a local package store, buy some beer, go home, and enjoy a cold one together. He liked the idea but indicated that Mom might not think too highly of our plan. I shrugged it off as no big deal. "What can drinking a can of beer possibly do to hurt anyone?" For a fact, this was the changing me doing the talking, not willing to let Mom's choices be the last spoken, at least not in my house. I loved and respected her. I wanted her to know who her son was becoming.

True to form, Mom was uncomfortable, though she said nothing directly to either of us. It would not have been nice to do so. As she was wont to do, she sighed, suggested our money might have been better spent on something else, and was relieved that my two daughters, five and seven, were outside playing with friends and did not have to see what their father and grandfather were doing at the kitchen table. For the next several months, when we exchanged letters, she would remind me of the importance of my Christian witness in front of others, especially setting the proper example for my children. I have no idea what she might have said to Dad.

The pleasant but steady reminder of my role and place in the world as a Christian witness remained her chief way of dealing with me. "Son, do you still go to church every Sunday? Do you read your Bible often? Do you pray every day?" were standard inquiries. A pleasant "No" would not dissuade her from repeating them at our next visit. If she invited me to pray in her presence, I would defer by suggesting, "If you don't mind, I prefer you say the prayer for both of us." If, at family meals in her home, she would invite me to say grace, I would suggest that we each "voice our individual gratitude to God privately" and immediately bow my head in silence. I made sure my responses to her were always pleasantly and respectfully stated, but firm. I had absolutely no interest in pretending that I felt, or believed, anything different from what might be inferred from my actions.

My being fired in 1968 was scarcely known or noticed in my larger family. Getting divorced in 1973 got a bit more attention, but even that was limited. After all, I was still employed by the college and continued to live in Liberty, five-hundred miles from Texas and the nearest relative. Neither leaving the employment of the College in 1975, marriage in 1976 to Judith, nor beginning a new career in counseling, consulting, and training necessitated any change in my city of residence. In my larger family's eyes, "Hoddy still lives in Missouri."

Dad and Mom met Judith and her two daughters, Angela and Alexis, in the summer of 1975. Judith and her children, along with me and mine, had decided to take a summer vacation together. We chose Galveston, Texas, as the end point so that we could stop by Jacksonville in route for first-time introductions. I called Mom to alert her and explain the situation. True to form, even though she was most likely uncomfortable with me being a divorced dad and traveling with a woman, she said, "Son, any friend of yours is a friend of ours." Mom and Dad liked Judith immediately. After our marriage and the blending of our two families the next spring, we would get to enjoy two extended visits with Mom and Dad. One was a Thanksgiving in Jacksonville; the other was a Christmas in Liberty.

My father died of lung cancer in 1978, the result of a lifetime of smoking that began at the age of thirteen. He was sixty-nine years old. His funeral was the last time our entire family would gather for any event. By the time of Mom's death in 2005, two of my siblings, Bob and Jamie, had died. Although Dad lived throughout my entire ministerial career, he died before I was wise enough or courageous enough to recognize how little he knew or understood about what had gone on in my heart and mind, particularly during my days at Park Cities Church and William Jewell College.

It would not have occurred to him to ask about any of the reasons behind the job shifts that took me from Houston to Dallas, from the denomination's state office to the large, wealthy suburban church, or from the church to the campus of a Baptist college. Neither did it occur to me that we might be able to talk about the shifting plates at the base of my childhood faith. As a family, we didn't talk about troublesome ideas, issues, or people. However, throughout all the professional and personal changes, including the divorce and remarriage, there was never a doubt regarding his affection and regard for me as his son.

Mom would be another matter. I no longer was satisfied with a style of living that prevented any real understanding of how and what each of us thought and felt. I wanted to know more about her. I also wanted her to know me. As is typically the case in such a process, we would both learn more about ourselves. This began a determined effort to relate more openly with her and insist that she be more open with me. We started small.

Following Dad's death, Mom gave little thought to any choice beyond simply continuing to live as she had been living—on Devereux Steet in Jacksonville, with continued activities associated with Sunset Avenue Baptist Church. Though widely separated at the time, each of her children, in their own way, Ray Charles and Evelyn in Denver, Bob and Orie in Austin, Judith and me in Liberty, Jamie and Nelda in Houston, and Nan and Jack in Moore, Oklahoma, would do whatever was necessary to ensure that she could continue living where she was.

In our case, we made it possible for her to fly to Kansas City for extended visits whenever she was up to it. On one special occasion, she joined us for a vacation in Hawaii that followed two days of business for me in Honolulu. On those two days, she and Judith toured Oahu in an open-air Jeep. We stayed another ten days and toured two other islands, Maui and Hawaii.

It had also become a part of my visits to inquire more and more about her thoughts, her life experiences, her joys, as well as her regrets. It took a few years, but we had gotten pretty good at being open and honest with each other.

The early days of more honest exchanges had been extremely difficult. For one, there was the five-hundred-mile gap between our homes. Also, when we were together it was usually in the midst of a larger family gathering and difficult to find time when we could be alone to talk. Finally, my own reticence to ask questions or make comments that might be difficult or upsetting to her often restrained me. After all, I was talking to the author of the "be nice" and "be good" guidelines for interpersonal conversations.

However, I was dogged and persistent in having those conversations. Dad died before I was old enough, curious enough, wise enough to recognize that I knew so little about him—his boyhood, his thoughts, hopes, and dreams. His knowledge of me was equally and profoundly limited. A major sorrow in my life is that gap between us. Now, I was older and wiser. I had been through enough personal and professional struggles to not be fearful of difficult subjects. I was determined that Mom and I would not end with similar gaps of knowledge and understanding.

Early on, I came to a sobering realization. I was as much a part of the current distance between us as was she. I made a conscious decision to pay more attention to what I was doing. I put special focus in two areas: being more open and transparent about what I thought and felt and resisting the urge to help Mom be direct about her own wants and needs.

Our small start consisted mostly of me making comments that would make her squirm. For instance, when she visited us, she was reluctant to make the simplest of decisions. "Would you like something to drink?" "What would you like for breakfast/lunch/dinner?" "Is there anything special you would like to do while you are here?" Those were challenging questions for Mom. At restaurants, she was much more attuned to the price of an entree than to what dish she might enjoy eating. Invariably her responses would be passive and, in her mind, kind, "Whatever you kids are having." "Anything is okay." "Don't go to any trouble for me." "Whatever you have." "I don't care."

When possible, I was pleasantly insistent. I also learned to frame the questions in such a manner that she had to make a choice. "Mom, we're having baked chicken with a green salad for dinner. To drink, we have water, tea, beer, and white wine. What would you like?" The beer and wine were always added recognizing her feelings but wanting her to understand that our choices might be different from hers. Her choice was always 100 percent predictable—"Tea." Getting a 100 percent response from me—"Sweetened or unsweetened?" In the earliest days, there might be an occasional, "Whatever you have or whatever is easiest," reply. I waited until she decided. This little dynamic often got a quizzical glance and a bit of a squirm from her. It might almost get a frown or a cocked head from Judith, whose love for Mom grew with each visit. She did not like me to put pressure on Mom.

Over time, the topics and choice points became subtler and more serious. The Hawaii trip provided fertile ground. A huge surprise for me was the discovery that my mother knew a great deal about the Islands. My surprise was enhanced by the fact that my family only made two out-of-state trips in my entire childhood. One was to Logansport, Louisiana to visit part of her childhood extended family. The other was to Albuquerque to visit my oldest brother. At the time, he was in the Air Force, married, and the father of two young girls. Evidently, interest in Hawaii had been something of a hobby for her. She was somewhat familiar with each island, especially informed about flowers and local customs. In Honolulu, we attended a luau on Waikiki Beach. While going through the food line following the roasted pig ceremony, I said to Mom, "Judith and I are going to join the locals and drink their rum punch. Care to join us?" She said, "Yes." Nothing more was said. She had two cups.

Late afternoon the next day, we flew to Maui. We arrived too late to do anything except locate and check in at our condo. On our first day, following breakfast in the condo, I said to Mom, "Now that you are here, what would like to do or see?" Her reply was not surprising. "Oh Son, I am so grateful to you kids for bringing me here that anything you want to do will suit me fine. I can't thank you enough." I paused a moment, squelched a couple of suggestions, and finally said. "I'm surprised. I thought there would be any number of things you might want to do. Why don't we just wait and see if anything pops into your mind as a preference." The moment was awkward for us all. I remained seated on a couch looking at local brochures. My spouse was noticeably annoyed with me for creating the drama. In what could not have been more than five to ten long minutes, Mom said, "If you kids don't mind, maybe we could drive down to Lahaina and look around." Which we did.

For the remainder of our trip a list of interests that Mom had hoped to see or do was never too far away, and she readily made them available to us. Two other incidents occurred on the Kona side of the Big Island, Hawaii.

On our first afternoon, we went to an ocean-side bar famous for a balcony area with an unhindered view of the setting sun. In the process of ordering something to drink, while looking out over the Pacific, I suggested to Mom that she might enjoy trying a strawberry daiquiri. She agreed. A larger one than was expected was served. I excused myself to go to the men's room. When I returned to the table, she had consumed most of her drink. I exclaimed, "Mom, that isn't Kool Aid!" She just grinned and nothing more was said about it.

The last incident proved to be the biggest shocker of all and occurred between Judith and Mom. Until now, except for a hotel in Honolulu, all our accommodations had been in condos with two bedrooms. The one in Kona had a living area, a small kitchen and one bedroom with two large beds. Soon after lunch on the second day, and back at the condo, she took Judith aside. She said something like, "Why don't I take a walk so you and Harles can have some privacy for a while. I know what it can be like to be married to a Cone man!"

I was not privy to the rest of their exchange. However, Judith assured her that a walk would not be necessary, but her thoughtfulness was appreciated. I could hardly contain the laughter later when Judith told me about the experience. I was immediately reminded that no subject in my childhood had been more studiously avoided than anything having to do with sex. As far as my parents were concerned, the only certainty about sex was that they had the experience at least five times!

When we returned home, several months passed before there would be anything like a serious conversation between us. Whatever contact we had was almost always shared with other members of our larger family. Yet, I was always mindful of the strong desire to relate to her in such a manner that she would not have to guess what her son thought or felt about whatever topics did arise. I was unrelenting.

For her part, she was busy in her church and its activities. She was also heavily engaged with other seniors in the group in her same position—widows and widowers. It was fun to listen to her tell stories about meetings, events, and meals shared with these friends.

One part of her pattern in dealing with me remained constant. She couldn't resist offering suggestions about how she thought I should be relating to others, particularly reminding me of the influence of my behavior on others. As an example, if we were alone, she would invite me to look in on a neighbor while I was in Jacksonville. I would retort that I didn't want to waste any of my limited time chatting with the neighbor. She would say, "It would mean so much to her if you would." I would respond that what I wanted was more important to me than what her neighbor might want. She would frown. I would smile. A similar dynamic played out over time with this as a common theme. What I wanted was being given more attention by me than what some others might want of me. The pattern persisted over the years.

Then, out of the blue, during one of our visits she was able to acknowledge, with considerable discomfort, awkwardness, and embarrassment, that some of her most satisfying moments in her entire life had occurred since Dad's death! That she could acknowledge such a reality to one of her own struck me as one of her most courageous acts. It was in direct violation to the axioms that had guided her and our lives. It was not a nice thing to say. It suggested that her life as a wife, mother, and grandmother might not have been as grand, noble, and universally gratifying as she often made it out to be—that she had other interests and desires that had been hampered and limited by the choices she had made. Dad's death and all her children being out of the house had left her free. Free to choose, to act, to be.

That her son could hear such a comment without any judgment or shock, could see it simply as a very significant sharing, and respond to her in gratitude for this gift of openness was perhaps the greatest surprise of all for her. She had been open about something very personal and nothing bad had happened. Instead, her son wanted to understand and know more. We were off and running on a broader track and neither of us wanted to give it up. Weeks, and even months, might slip by between visits, but we never lost this new track.

Too Soon Old, Too Late Smart.

Toward the end of her life, during one of our routine conversations, I gained a life-altering insight into my mother. The personal force behind her axioms was to become considerably clearer.

The last two years of her life, age ninety-four and ninety-five, were spent in an assisted living facility. She preferred to stay in her home living alone as she had done for the nearly 30 years following Dad's death at sixty-eight and caring for herself. Memory challenges and a couple of falls with no one immediately available to help had been major factors in deciding on the assisted living option. I have some regrets now that we children let concerns for her safety with the attendant risks to completely trump her personal desires. Our interests, her safety, were more to us than hers, spending her days in familiar and personal surroundings. (I never knew if any of my siblings came to feel the level of regret over our choice that I did.)

Being in the assisted living facility brought about some changes in our conversations. Her room was just that, a room. Two visitors could seem a bit crowded. Conversations with one or two others became the norm. There were no longer others around to overhear or participate in the exchanges. Games, but on a much smaller scale, would remain a means for structuring time.

She and I began my visits routinely. She would inquire about my family, and I would inquire about her health and the attentiveness of the facility's support staff. If health and energy allowed, she would always want us to play dominoes. She was competitive and liked winning. She especially enjoyed beating her college-educated son. I loved watching her smile coyly on those occasions when she did.

It had also become a part of my visits to inquire more and more about her thoughts, her life experiences, her joys, as well as her regrets. We had gotten pretty good at being open and honest with each other.

The crucial turning point question of this visit was, "Mom, what did you want to be when you were growing up?" We had earlier in the day been looking at her high school yearbook, the Jacksonville High Class of 1928. Her response was immediate. It was clear and simple. "Son, I always wanted to be a nurse." It came as a complete surprise. I had never heard once of such an early and clear desire on her part. Thinking of my own daughters and how different their lives seemed to be from their grandmother's, I responded, "Why not a doctor?" She said, "Oh Son, women weren't doctors when I was growing up." "Well, why didn't you become a nurse?" I was fully expecting something like "Your Dad and I decided to get married," but instead came the life-altering shocker! "My daddy didn't want me to." "Really," I said, "Why?" in a kind of pleasant disbelief.

Spoiler Alert 7 - "He didn't want me to touch colored people."

I was completely caught off guard, shaken. Black people had been a considerable part of our lives, and I did not have a single memory of my grandfather ever having said or done anything that smacked of meanness or disregard for any member of the race. "Why didn't you become a nurse anyway?" Reflecting again on the mindset of my daughters if someone offered personal objections to their hopes. "Oh Son" she said, "you didn't do what your daddy told you not to." And that was it. The basis of her life choices had been set. When her interests, wants, and wishes conflicted with her father's, they were to be settled by her doing as she was told!

I was never able look at her yearbook in the same manner again. Here was this attractive, athletic, intelligent young woman who had hoped for something out of the ordinary within her family and had it denied. What was she supported in doing— getting married and raising a family, a role and place she would never forget. The trusted authority had spoken. She had obeyed.

~ ~ ~

From that moment on, up to and through Mom's death several
months later, I experienced a wide range of conflicting emotions.
In many ways, cognitive dissonance during this stretch, was my
constant companion. I felt a surprising amount of anger toward
my grandfather, one for whom I had such respect and affection.
How could he have placed such limits on what was clearly
important to his only daughter? How could Mom acquiesce to
something as important as her own sense of self-worth and value?
Was there no one around who could stand up for Mom? Where
was her mom, my grandmother, during these happenings, or did
she even know they were going on? How about her brothers,
my uncles? How did the experiences of my grandfather's
boyhood, and the Southern culture of the late 1800s and early
1900s impact his actions toward his family? The answer seems
obvious now: It would have been unusual for him to have felt any
differently about Black people in Macon, Georgia, in the late
decades of the 1800s.

As things turned out, this conversation was a harbinger
of understandings that would be as jolting on a cultural level
as this one was on a personal, family level. Upon reflection, I
remembered that I never saw a Black person in my grandparents'
home. Those who had occasion to come, and it happened with
some regularity, would approach their home by the back door
and stand politely for someone to respond. Whatever needed
to be understood or acted upon would be handled through the
screen door. Also, in the fields where a great deal of work was
shared, he was always "Mr. Hutto" or "Sir" no matter the age or
gender of the person involved. Everyone knew their place, abided
by it, and peace prevailed—at least that is how it seemed to me.

Be that as it may, Mom passed the same legacy on to her
family. What she would not claim for herself, she would not allow
her children to claim for themselves. "Be nice." "Be a good boy."
"Respect your elders." "Give God the credit." "Don't get too big

for your britches." "Be grateful for what you do have." These all carried the same basic message for me. What I might think, feel, want, or hope for should be delegated to and guided by those in positions of authority over me: parents, teachers, ministers, bosses, and elected officials. Her legacy turned out to be an extremely powerful and double-edged sword. I would experience the impact of the concept of yin-yang long before I could grasp the profundity of it. Coming to understand that there was a racial prejudice element at the center of all her guidelines, even her religious admonishments, was the most shocking! After all, in my grandfather's day, the supremacy of Whites over Blacks was preached from the pulpits of Southern Baptist churches as the Will of God. And how did they know that? The Holy Bible said so!

As a child, I was trained to live in a world dominated by Christians of a fundamentalist Southern Baptist persuasion. My childhood world, late 1930s to early 1950s, played out in two small towns in East Texas—Jacksonville (population twelve thousand), from birth to seven and again from thirteen to seventeen, and Lufkin (population sixteen thousand), from seven to thirteen. Both towns were heavily Southern in their social orientations. My maternal grandfather loved to tell of coming to Cherokee County, Texas, from Macon, Georgia, when he was a boy. The trip was made in a wagon pulled by two mules in the late 1800s.

The universal conundrum for all parents is the question, "In how large a world are you preparing your child to live?" Do you teach the child what to think or how to think? Do you teach them to trust the judgment of others or, when called for, to get all the information they can and form their own conclusions? Do you insist on the rightness of your beliefs or share with them your whys and encourage them to search for their own whys, ones that could lead them to conclusions that might differ from yours? Do you celebrate the child's adherence to your dreams for them or to their finding and following their own dreams—no matter what? These are terribly important questions for parents. The answers provide the superstructure upon which the life of the child begins. It also impacts how children, as they grow and learn, can continue to relate successfully to their parents when their experiences lead them to conclusions and actions that differ from those of the parents. My grandfather gave his only daughter no life choices beyond those that he was taught and had chosen to follow.

My current belief: To indoctrinate a child is one of the most crippling things a parent can inflict. Indoctrination assumes the critical truths of life and living are already understood and need only to be believed and practiced. To do so, robs the child of her most powerful tool, her own mind, her capacity to reason, examine, determine, choose, and solve for herself.

Friends

Discussing the role, place, and impact of friends as a part of the village that raised me requires that I divide them into two distinct categories. There are those I knew in public school days, from second grade through high school graduation, the days before I was called to preach. And there are those who would be a part of my new life as a college and seminary student, youth evangelist, pastor, BSU Director/campus chaplain, assistant pastor, and dean of chapel—the days of my life dominated by roles as a Southern Baptist minister.

Public School Days—I am filled with innumerable happy memories with both boys and girls. As mentioned, playing outside was a huge part of my life. I loved games, sports, Boy Scouts, and church activities. The teenage years of junior high and high school, the addition of girls and social activities, only added to the pleasure of the mix. I think of myself as having a happy childhood. In high school, sports were the hub around which most of my activities revolved.

During the period, I think it fair to say that I would have been considered popular by classmates. I was voted as such on two occasions. I mention this because, with four exceptions, I had limited to no contact with any junior high or high school friends once I left for college and engaged in the ministerial pursuits. My class, Class of '53, would have three reunions that I attended. The first came after twenty-five years. The other two, with a declining number of participants each time, came after fifty years and our last after fifty-five. I attended all three with great pleasure. It was a matter of renewing old acquaintances and recalling those years we had spent together. It was fun and satisfying on many levels.

I had many friendships; none but four proved to have enough depth or substance to be lasting. The four exceptions included my high school girlfriend and three guys with whom I had a great deal of contact during our days as teammates on the school's various athletic teams—Harold Davis, John Clark, and Charlie Brazil.

Harold, 'Burr' as he would be known all his life, two years younger, was the friend of longest standing. We were across-the-street neighbors when I was five. His siblings, especially his younger brother, a sister my age, and two of his older brothers all lined up well in age with my own siblings—a younger brother and sister and two older brothers. Add to that, our mothers were friends and, for a period of nearly fifty years, the mothers would attend the same church. During visits and calls with my mother during her last years, she would routinely ask, "Have you been to see Mrs. Davis yet?" The Davises were close to being a part of our extended family.

It was this family relatedness as much as anything else that kept our friendship together. Burr and I would be in town at the same time, typically around holidays, and we would always get together and catch up. And while our conversations might seem shallow and lacking in much personal depth, our tie to each other was strong. I knew of his successes as a college football player, a stint of professional football in Canada, a high school coach, and the owner of a small business. He knew, in the broadest of terms, about the changes and shifts in my life. I enjoyed those visits and miss them now. He died in 2020.

My girlfriend, who was one class grade behind me, was a different story. The shift in our relationship came in stages. In high school talk, we went steady for two years. As a couple, we participated in all school events, academic, social, and athletic. We went to movies together on weekends and attended the parties of friends. When time and circumstances would allow following all events, we would find a private place to park to enjoy and express the physical side of our affection. With the exceptions of hugging, kissing, and hand holding, I experienced all sexual firsts with her. We were serious about each other. Like other adolescents, we looked forward to our lives together— married with children.

Being called to preach in the summer following my senior year would alter all that. I was now very serious about my faith, my religion. My life's direction was now clear. I was going to be a preacher. From mid-summer on, I was completely caught up in my summer job, church activities, and getting ready to go to college. We continued to go steady. We loved each other.

Since all the religious and career decisions I was making were of my own choosing and not the product of discussions we might have shared, my girlfriend, by default, was caught up in the huge shifts occurring in my life. At the time, I was incapable of anything approximating an objective discussion of what I might have been thinking and feeling. I was doing and following God's Will for my life. I was trusting and obeying. I was swept away.

During the first weeks of college, without the part-time job I had expected to have, I would hitchhike the seventy-two miles home every Friday afternoon for us to be together. I could always manage to get a week's dirty laundry in my suitcase for my mother to include in her Saturday morning trip to the laundromat. A typical weekend included attending a Friday night football game (watching my friend Burr Davis play), doing a variety of things on Saturday, attending Sunday School and Church on Sunday morning, and hitchhiking back to Marshall, clean laundry in the suitcase, on late Sunday afternoons. Throughout this entire time, we continued to find a time and place to be alone. I had little or no appreciation for how difficult her senior year may have been, particularly with an out-of-town boyfriend—and a preacher at that.

These early college days included classroom studies, attending daily chapel and vesper services devoted to prayer, Bible study, and worship, trying to find a part-time job, and hanging out at the gym. To the best of my memory, the only change in my relationship with her growing out of my new life had to do with dancing. I would no longer participate. It was sinful to do so, and good Christians refrained, especially preachers.

Receiving the basketball scholarship in late fall pushed our times together farther apart. It was a rare weekend, except for holidays, from November through February that did not include a Saturday afternoon or evening game, at home or away. I do not have any clear memories of this period except that I was very caught up in my life as a college athlete and that we continued to go steady.

The end of basketball season and the spring semester, however, would introduce a completely new stage. In April, I was asked to become the pastor of the Ironton Baptist Church.

Ironton is a small rural community fifteen miles west of Jacksonville. The community consisted of a combination grocery store-service station and one church, Ironton Baptist. Being asked to serve as pastor meant being willing to deliver two sermons each Sunday—one for morning worship and another for evening. There could be as many as thirty to forty members for morning worship and half might be expected back in the evening. Here I was at eighteen years of age, a freshman in college, serving as the pastor of a church. My religious beliefs and role within the denomination were serious business.

I followed the pattern of hitchhiking home on Friday and returning to college on Sunday on a 10:00 p.m. bus from Jacksonville to Marshall. In late May, with my first year of college behind me, I once again worked for Heidelberg Construction Company and continued as the pastor of Ironton Baptist. My role at the Church now included leading the Wednesday night prayer service and being in the community on Saturdays for home visits with families of the church. I wanted to be a good pastor.

Time with the girlfriend was now limited to Friday nights, occasionally for events during the week, and some Saturday afternoons. On many Sunday mornings, she went with me to the Sunday morning services. She was now a high school graduate and was making plans to enter Lon Morris College, the junior college in our hometown, in the fall. One of my strongest memories of this period was that of being constantly busy. In our minds though, we were still going steady, and behaved accordingly.

Back at East Texas in the fall, basketball season was approaching, with its heavy demands of games played on Saturday night. It was clear that I would no longer be able to remain at Ironton. I resigned as pastor. Strangely, at this point, I have hardly any memories of times with this young woman

in my life. When at home on the early fall weekends, I picked
her up and dropped her off at her college dormitory. I was not
part of any of her activities at Lon Morris. There were no more
high school sports events to share nor was she a part of my last
Sundays as Ironton's pastor. It was as if we both understood that
whatever had existed between us, no matter how intensely close it
had seemed, was ending. We never discussed it, and there did not
seem to be any hurt or disappointed feelings. My last memory
was saying goodnight at her dormitory door on a Friday night. I
have had no direct contact with her since.

The relationship with John Clark, 'Johnny' to me, and
Charlie Brazil continues to this day. I had not realized until this
writing that to be a close friend of one of them was to be friends
with them both. They were classmates, neighbors, teammates,
and inseparable friends since their earliest days at East Side
Elementary School. They were a grade ahead of me and the only
two who proved to be a part of my college athletics as well as my
life as a Southern Baptist preacher.

As mentioned, my first-grade schooling was completed at
the one-room schoolhouse in the community of Cove Springs,
outside Jacksonville, and second grade was at Joe Wright
Elementary, also known as Northside. When I was in second
grade at Northside, Charlie and Johnny were third graders at
East Side. My family moved to Lufkin, Texas, toward the end of
my second grade, and we remained there through the completion
of my eighth grade at Lufkin Junior High. Then we moved back
to Jacksonville.

The friendship with Charlie and Johnny began in the spring
of my ninth grade and was centered in athletics. My promotion
from the junior high to the high school baseball team meant
playing as the shortstop next to Johnny who played third base.
Simultaneously, Johnny and Charlie played doubles partners on
the high school tennis team. For the next two years, all three of

us played on the basketball team, Johnny and I on the baseball team, and I was a fan of their tennis skills. We shared a common religious faith, and we were all active in our churches. Johnny and Charlie were members of Central Baptist, the original sponsoring church of our mission church, Sunset Avenue Baptist.

I mention the churches because the pastor of their church, Dr. James T. Draper, was the father of the young evangelist Jimmy Draper, who had such impact on me the summer following my high school graduation. They were all students at East Side and members of the same church. In 1951, the Drapers moved to Houston at the end of Jimmy's tenth grade. Although I have no clear memories of it, if Johnny and Charlie were in Jacksonville following their first year in college, I am confident they would have been a part of the Youth Revival that Jimmy had been in town to lead.

Upon graduation, Johnny enrolled and played basketball for our local junior college, Lon Morris. He later moved to Baylor, and upon graduation, spent a very successful career as a high school football coach and athletic director in Texas. Many years later, we discovered that we were distant cousins. Charlie enrolled in and graduated from Stephen F. Austin State Teachers College, later Stephen F. Austin University. He went on to a career in public education and education administration in greater Houston.

Like no one else, I always felt supported by both for what was happening to me as a preacher and an athlete. During the period I served as the pastor in Ironton, it was not unusual to look out and see them among the Sunday morning congregation. The two of them remain active in their local Baptist churches to this day. Charlie, as far as I know, is still the discussion leader of the Sunday Morning Men's Bible Class in Houston.

In March of 1957, my senior year at East Texas, our basketball team won the Big State Conference Championship.

Stephen F. Austin was the champion of the Lone Star Conference. In those days, both schools were members of the National Association of Intercollegiate Athletics (NAIA). The NAIA format called for a best of three-game playoff between the conference champions to determine which school would represent the Texas region in the national tournament in Kansas City. SFA sent ETBC home after the first two games. Both Charlie and Johnny were in attendance for game two, and we had a brief chance to visit following the game.

The high school sports, the Ironton church activities, and the 1957 basketball playoff games are mentioned for one basic reason. To this day, if we are thrown together for any reason, it is one hundred percent predictable that our shared anecdotes will center on them. It is a reconnecting ritual that we each enjoy and treasure.

Our closeness has been severely limited in recent years. At least it is for me. Both are aware that I have gone through major shifts in terms of my religious faith and professional career. In those arenas, I am a radically different person in my thoughts, beliefs, and behaviors from the young man they knew who trusted without question the fundamentalist teachings of my childhood and young adulthood. By unspoken mutual consent, we step around discussions having to do with those shifts. I think they sensed I would answer any question posed as honestly as possible but that the answers would draw sharp distinctions between their lives and mine. When they speak of the faith-based ideas that govern their lives, I am respectful and considerate. I am happy for the satisfaction it seems to bring. Bottom line, there are no friends from my public-school days who know very much about my current life.

College—Friends in college also fell into two distinct categories: teammates in athletics and those who shared the ultimate desire of preparing to enter full-time church work. Regarding the latter, there were many with whom I happily shared religious activities. In addition to Sunday events in a local church, the college had much to offer. There were morning chapel services, Noonspiration, and evening vespers five days a week. The noon and early evening gatherings were not too different from chapel, only a bit briefer and more causal. There was prayer, singing, and a devotional thought from some Bible passage. In order to demonstrate how serious we were about our faith in Jesus and our desire to serve and be a witness for Him, there was a small group of us who attended as many of these as possible. We felt close to each other.

In my freshman year, the weekend visits home to be with my girlfriend, and the sexual nature of our contact, had little to no impact on my religious life in college. Somehow, I convinced myself, God understood. We loved each other and would one day be married. I just never talked about it with anyone. Neither did it interfere with any discussions I might have had about the importance of pure thoughts and chaste living for sincere Christians. Hypocritical might have described me in the minds of others if they had known. It was never a self-descriptor. Uncomfortable and awkward on occasion, but not a hypocrite! When the relationship ended in the fall of my sophomore year, so, too, would end this stark contrast between word and deed. Following the pastorate in Ironton, other preaching opportunities came. There was not another serious girlfriend until first spouse, Mary. That relationship began in friendship during the second semester of my junior year, early 1956. It culminated in marriage in September 1957, following my spring graduation and a summer of Youth-Led Revivals.

Like most of my high school friends, with two exceptions, the friends associated with college religious activities faded away with time. The two who lingered a bit longer were ones I recommended for the role of BSU Director for the State Convention. One was the best man at my wedding. After his own stint as a BSU Director in Texas, he returned to Marshall and distinguished himself as a pastor. The other became active in administration of a Baptist university.

Friendships associated with college athletics was another matter. The period from the spring of my sophomore year through my senior year was pivotal. I was completely focused on both my religion and sports. In many ways, it was the best of times for both. There was a worst of times lurking to which I was completely oblivious. The collision occurred because of my belief in the absolute rightness or wrongness of certain behaviors and my strong belief that the Bible was God's Word on all matters. As it turned out, and only realized after many years, the way I practiced my religion severely tarnished two critical relationships. One was with the most authentic friendship I had had to that point in my life. The other was with my younger brother, Jamie.

Rod Beasley and Bill Little proved to be significant friends. No fellow student had more impact on my life than Rod. We were buddies. Recall it was he in my earliest days of unemployed studentship who encouraged me to come to the gym and hang out. He also thought I should talk with Coach Dorsett after he yelled for me to "get my ass off the court." That one event changed the immediate direction of my life like none other. Our basketball years mirrored each other. We were on the starting team as sophomores and remained so for three years. We began under the direction of Coach Ray Dorsett as freshmen followed by Coach Lenny Fant for the final three years.

We spent a lot of time in each other's company. We, with four others, ate most of our meals together in the college dining hall. On those days when an evening home game was scheduled, his dorm room was the afternoon gathering place to rest up for the game. He had a combination record player and radio. It was fun to lie around, listen, and talk. Often, I would leave those occasions early enough to attend vespers and still get to the gym at our team's expected arrival time. On away games, when an overnight stay was required, we were often paired as roommates at the hotel. In the spring, we trained hard and participated as members of the track team. We also, for the first time, took up the game of golf.

The largest part of the summer following my sophomore year I spent working with Rod at the Lone Star Steel Company in Daingerfield, Texas. It was a town twenty-five miles away from his family home in Kildare. Rod's dad was the safety engineer for the company. He was known as Safety Sam. His direct influence made it possible for me to be hired, along with Rod, as a summer utility laborer. It was the highest paying job I had or would have until graduation from Southwestern Seminary seven years later.

Lone Star Steel had three shifts, day (8 a.m.-4 p.m.), swing (4 p.m.-midnight), and graveyard (midnight-8 a.m.). There was only one utility laborer scheduled per shift in the open-hearth area, where we were both assigned to work. We served as a replacement for a worker on a week vacation. Whatever the job of the vacationer, assuming we had the necessary skills, became our job. Whatever the pay scale for the vacationer would become our pay scale. Each week we were expected to rotate shifts. Swing followed day, graveyard followed swing, and back to day. It wasn't unusual for one of us to be going to work when the other was returning. Work on the weekend was rare for a utility person. All hours over forty meant a pay scale of fifty percent more—time and a half. As a rule, the extra time was happily

accepted by regular full-time employees. Mr. Beasley, a member
of management, only worked days.

To help me save as much money as possible, I was invited to
live in the Beasley home, as a guest the entire time. In addition
to Rod and parents, there was a younger brother, John, and
a younger sister, Ruth. An older sister, Sammye, was living in
Marshall. It was an amazing summer. The family were active
members in the local Baptist church. Safety Sam was a deacon.

Because of the work schedules, Rod and I didn't spend much
time together. During a typical work week, if evenings were
free, I often drove to Marshall to play fast-pitch softball with the
LeCuno Oilers. Younger brother John, on occasion, would make
the trip with me. On a typical weekend, to help lighten the load
on Mrs. Beasley, I would go home to be with my own family and
be a part of my home church. On the few occasions when a work
week ended at Friday midnight and the next began on Monday
morning, I would stay in Kildare and attend church with the
Beasleys. A great many summer hours were spent in a back
bedroom, with shades drawn if it was daylight, sleeping.

In my mind, the most telling event of the summer for Rod
and me occurred at its end. Since the fall semester of college was
to begin near September 1, we opted to resign our jobs at Lone
Star in late August. We had a plan. I was going to move out and
go home. A few days later Rod was to come by Jacksonville and
pick me up. We were going to drive to Galveston, find a motel
convenient to the beach, and spend a few days on a vacation. We
were resting up for the coming basketball season.

I am both amazed and fascinated at how few details I
remember about the trip. One experience overwhelms all else.
We chose a motel that was directly across the highway from the
beach. We walked across in bathing suits and were in and out of
the water the three days we were there. We both suffered from

sunburns. That is the extent of my recall except for our last night. That night is crystal clear.

We had both heard tales of Post Office Street in Galveston, a street dominated by "whorehouses," as they were called. We decided that it would be fun to see if we could find the street and drive down it. It was easy to locate and not far off the beach. One stretch was exactly as we had heard. While driving slowly with our car windows down there were many invitations extended from women standing in groups of two or three on the curbs. It was a bit much. It was titillating.

Two blocks farther, there was scarcely anyone standing on the corners. We passed a two-story building with a small balcony on the second floor. As we passed a young woman on the balcony announced loudly to us, "Three ways for five! Three ways for five!"

Sex was a subject Rod and I had never seriously discussed. I scarcely knew anything about the girls he dated in college, only that he had never gone steady with anyone. Unless the girl was connected to one of the activities of serious Christians, our paths were not likely to cross.

He knew of my high school girlfriend and had met her once when we were freshmen. How serious we were about each other, he might have observed; however, it was something I never talked about. At some important level, I was incapable of a conversation that could lead to the inherent contradiction and hypocrisy which existed between my oft-stated beliefs as a fundamentalist Christian, a preacher, and my actual behaviors regarding sex.

Following the young woman's invitation, we turned the car around and parked in front of the house with the balcony. The invitation was extended again with a finger pointing toward the entrance that would lead us upstairs. There was a quick look at each other, a "Why not?" and we headed for the door. We could both afford the $5.

The apartment, as it turned out, was one large room that doubled as the main living area as well as a kitchen in the corner. There was also a bathroom and a bedroom toward the back. In one corner of the living area, in a large, padded chair, sat a much older woman who said nothing. She simply observed. We gave our money to the young woman, and she gave it to the older woman. It was all business—pleasant, but business.

"Who wants to go first?" was how it began. My response was immediate and nice. "Go ahead, I'll wait." It was a long, silent twenty-five-to-thirty-five-minute wait interrupted only by the sound of bodies shifting positions on a bed. When they were done, Rod appeared at the door dressed, except for the shoes and socks in hand. I then repeated the process.

Two things will forever be lodged in my memory. One was how mechanical, robotic, and affectless I felt. I felt overwhelmed and disconnected. It would be forty years before I would have any understanding, much less appreciation, for the term cognitive dissonance. I was not real enough to face words like guilt or sin or contradiction or hypocrisy.

The other curiously baffling item in my memory bank was how little Rod and I then, or ever, talked about the evening. For that matter, until now, it was an experience that I never revealed to anyone.

When I emerged from the bedroom, Rod had already left the apartment and was standing by the car when I came out. The drive back to the motel was dominated by small talk. We agreed the rumored reputation of Post Office Street was deserved. How weird it had been to have sex with a young woman while having the much older woman in an adjacent room. We agreed she seemed more like a grandmother than a madam.

When we got back to the motel, we immediately took hot showers, Rod first. I remember nothing after that, save it was late. We went to bed with a plan to rise early and hit the road to return home. The ride home was consumed with talk of our coming junior year in college and what lay ahead for our basketball team since two of our most important players from the previous year had graduated. Registration for the new semester was three days away.

There was one more, and final, contact that Rod and I had with prostitutes. It occurred a few months following the Galveston experience. We, and two other teammates, were going to "cruise the neighborhood." I knew enough about the expression to know that it essentially meant leaving the dorm early on a Friday evening and driving around all night. The details included driving northeast from Marshall to Texarkana, south from Texarkana to Shreveport, Louisiana, and west back to Marshall. The cruise ended at Ward's, a local 24-hour café, for breakfast. Saturdays were typically spent sleeping it off.

I remember very little about the experience. What is important to me now is the acknowledgement that I was a participant in it. The prostitutes were housed in a large frame house in Texarkana. For $15—$10 more than the Galveston fee—the deal was completed. Also, as in Galveston, the experience was never discussed. It is not clear if I felt any cognitive dissonance at that time, either. I think not.

Beginning in the spring of our junior year, the time Rod and I spent together became more limited, but we remained buddies. We still ate most of our meals together, talked basketball, ran on the track team, and played golf. All the while, I was becoming more engaged in matters having to do with being a young ministerial student. There were more invitations to be a guest preacher on Sundays at churches in the general area of Marshall. There were also opportunities to speak to youth groups, especially Sweetheart Banquets and weekend retreats. In the fall of my senior year, I was invited to become the assistant pastor, or youth pastor, of the First Baptist Church of Mt. Vernon, Texas. It was a church within an easy weekend drive from the College. And, as explained earlier, I was invited by the Student Department of the State Baptist Convention of Texas to again be a member of their Youth-Led Revival movement for the coming summer. I was the only student preacher at East Texas to receive such an invitation. I felt proud, honored, excited, and blessed.

No activity would have more impact on the direction of my life at the time than this work for the State Convention. In the first summer following my junior year, I became acquainted with Bruce McIver, Associate Director of the Baptist Student Department. He oversaw the Youth-Led Revivals. The association with Bruce led to meeting W. F. Howard, Bruce's boss and the Department Director. In the spring of 1960, W. F. Howard was the one who hired me to be the BSU Director of the University of Houston. In 1962, he hired me as an Assistant Director in his state office. I joined the line as a follow-on to Bruce McIver to help give direction to the Youth-Led Revival program in the summer.

Just as high school athletic experiences led to playing with students from all over Jacksonville, my Youth-Led Revival experiences led to meeting and working with Baptist college students from all over Texas (Baylor, Hardin Simmons, Howard Payne, Wayland, Corpus Christi, and Southwestern Seminary). It also led to working often in the largest Baptist church in small towns as well as large suburban churches in big cities. I still felt lucky, fortunate, blessed. I gave God the full credit for my good fortune.

I need to say a word about my sermons. As a preacher, in conversations with individuals and small groups, I could talk easily. Bible study and prayer became a large part of my life.

When making a statement about what was right or true, I could almost always quote the Bible—book, chapter, and verse—to support any comment. It wasn't what I thought, it was what God said that mattered. I was simply quoting God.

Standing up behind a pulpit and speaking to crowds was different. Not too unlike my experience playing basketball before crowds, I was always careful not to get too full of myself, to show off. Who was I to decide what to tell others about God, life and living, death and dying in sermons? As a pastor, how was I to know what subjects to address, and in what order, to essentially to a repeat audience?

The maxims that had guided the largest parts of my life were guiding the smaller parts as well. Others knew far more than I, especially those older and in positions of authority. I just needed to learn who they were and what they were saying. I did this by studying published books of their sermons.

Beginning as the pastor at Ironton, through my time as the youth pastor in Mount Vernon, the pastor at Purley, the youth evangelist in Texas, the supply preacher in Houston, the assistant pastor at Park Cities in Dallas, and the Dean of Chapel at William Jewell, when it came to sermons, I followed a predictable pattern. The basic structure of my sermon originated with someone else, with personal examples taken from my own life experiences or additional thoughts woven in. And like the books I read for Dr. Whaley and the speakers I invited to Jewell's chapel program, the selected sermons were what I would have wanted to say if I but could.

As my own thinking changed, so did the sources for my sermons. One of the earliest sources, in 1954, was Herschel Ford, pastor of the First Baptist Church, Longview, Texas. Two of the last sources, in 1966-67, were Harry Emerson Fosdick, pastor of Riverside Church in New York, and John Claypool, pastor of Crescent Hill Baptist Church in Louisville. There would be any number of others in between. The shift I underwent from the certainty of fundamentalism to the skepticism of liberalism could be traced through the authors I had chosen to read. And the last, the chapel address at East Texas Baptist in 2008, was solely from my own experience!

Back to the college friends. Bill Little came from Gideon, Missouri, to East Texas in the fall of 1954, one year behind Rod and me. Like me, he was a young minister who loved athletics, particularly basketball. Unlike me, he was married with a young daughter. He has remained an interested and interesting friend. Also, he featured prominently in events in the spring of my senior year that I recall now as the worst of times.

As the 1954-55 season was getting underway, Lenny Fant had replaced Ray Dorsett as the basketball coach at East Texas Baptist. Bill approached Coach Fant regarding the possibility of playing. After the conversation and a trial period, Bill was offered a scholarship and joined the team. His time was short-lived. A few weeks later, H.D. Bruce, the President of East Texas, learned of the scholarship for Bill and suggested to Coach Fant that it be revoked. Dr. Bruce didn't think it appropriate that a married minister with a child should be wasting his time playing basketball. Bill's scholarship was withdrawn. Without it, Bill was unable to continue playing. His time was taken up with part-time jobs and pastoring small churches in the area to support his family.

Bill's scholarship status remained the same for the remainder of my time at East Texas. However, in my junior and senior years, his contact with the team was rekindled. Somehow, he managed to find a way to support his family and play at the same time without the scholarship. He was a part of all practice sessions and all home games. He also became a part of the track team.

Although most of our time together was severely limited to the gym and the track, Rod, Bill and I became good friends. We all liked talking ball, competing against each other in practice, running track, and playing golf. On occasion the three of us devoted evening time to study together in Bill's apartment on preacher row.

As fellow preachers, Bill invited me on two occasions to be the guest evangelist for a revival in churches where he was serving as pastor. The first, in Bassett, Texas, occurred during basketball season of my senior, his junior, year. We had to be absent one night of the revival due to a conflict with a home game for the college. The other, in Geneva, Texas, was during Bill's senior year and my first year as a (married) seminary student. To this day, when we visit, it is rare for one of us not to make some reference to those two revival weeks.

I mentioned the worst of times, which came toward the end of my college senior year in 1957. We had a successful year in basketball. I had served as the assistant pastor in Mount Vernon and was preparing for my second summer as a Youth-Led Revival evangelist. I was at that time engaged and planning to be married at the end of the summer revivals before we moved to Fort Worth to begin my seminary education.

Collision 1—Rod. I was sure he needed my help. He was important to me. He, and his family for that matter, had been very helpful. We had been and were close friends!

While the details surrounding the event are long lost, the central idea is clear. A verse from God's Word says, "He who causes a sinner to be converted from the error of his ways, shall save his soul from death and shall cover a multitude of sins." (James 5:20). Recall that I, the minister, was now comfortable interacting with individuals and small groups. If the subject had anything to do with good-bad or right-wrong, all I needed was a

Bible verse to guide me. Rod, I thought, was headed for trouble if he wasn't there already. I wanted to help protect him from the error of his ways. The sin? He had begun dating a Marshall girl, Martha Muse, and they were talking about marriage. She had been married once before and was now divorced. Divorce was wrong, and I knew it. According to Matthew 5:32 Jesus said, "But I tell you that anyone who divorces his wife, except for sexual immorality, makes her the victim of adultery, and anyone who marries a divorced woman commits adultery." In Matthew 10:11-12 Jesus said that "Anyone who divorces his wife and marries another woman commits adultery against her. And if she divorces her husband and marries another man, she commits adultery." I knew nothing about Martha, her life, or her circumstances. At that point, nothing was more important than what the Bible taught, and I wanted my friend to know about it. It was my duty both to God and to Rod to make the truth known. It was the right thing to do. Once again, I was doing God's Will for my life. The irony of me doing this at that time, after our sexual pursuits together, is so glaring, that even I ought to have acknowledged it—at least to myself. I did not. Right had blinded me to the good and kind!

How did our friendship evolve from there? All I can remember is he essentially said nothing about my counsel and nothing about the shared sex-related experiences with his preacher friend. He was invited to attend my wedding. I was not invited to his. I went off to seminary to continue my journey as a preacher, and I would know nothing about his life for the next six years.

I next saw Rod in 1963. I was in Dallas working for the Texas Baptist Convention, Department of Student Work. Somehow, I had learned he was in the army and stationed at Fort Rucker, Alabama. I called and as luck would have it, I was passed through to Captain Beasley. He had finished training as a helicopter pilot and was in the process of being transferred to Fort Huachuca, Arizona, for advanced training in aviation communication. He was glad to learn I was in Dallas and promised to drop by so we could see each other. "It will have to be brief," he said. Dallas was going to be on his driving route to Huachuca. We had a great visit, though severely limited by time.

On the day of his visit, he gave me a late morning, one-hour-away heads up call. Since my office in Dallas was only three blocks off his route, and easy to reach, we had a bit longer for a visit than I had hoped. With curbside parking available, I was standing there when he drove up. I was struck by the sight of my 6'5" friend, in military fatigues, unfold from a VW Karmann Ghia sports car. We both laughed.

Over lunch, I learned that he had been drafted into the army as an officer candidate, chose the army air force, specifically helicopters. With some pestering from me, I learned that during his training, he passed very quickly through the 2nd and 1st Lieutenant ranks, as well the qualifications to pilot a helicopter. And finally, I learned that Fort Huachuca was his last stop before being sent to Vietnam.

What we did talk about at length was our days of playing ball at ETBC There were dozens of anecdotes to share over the four years we had spent together. I inquired about his parents and his younger brother, John. He wanted to know about my parents and younger brother, Jamie. Nothing was mentioned about Galveston or Texarkana. Neither was anything said about our wives and families or my job. Our time was up, and he was gone. I did not see him again for 12 years.

In the fall of 1975, we met again. I still lived in Liberty, had recently resigned from William Jewell, and had been divorced for two years. I was within a few months of completing the PhD. degree and actively engaged in both counseling and management training. Rod was in transit to a new assignment, the U.S. Army War College in Carlisle, Pennsylvania.

I don't recall exactly how the meeting came about, but Bill Little joined us. Bill was serving as the pastor of Christ Memorial Baptist Church in St. Louis. It was the first time the three of us had been together since graduation and the second face-to-face visit for Rod and me. We met at my apartment in Liberty, and our time together was very much like the Dallas visit. The three of us talked non-stop from late afternoon through dinner at a Kansas City steakhouse and into late evening back in my apartment. A couch that made into a bed was where the two of them would get whatever sleep there was to be had. Two things remain stuck in my mind: the first was that though Rod was dressed in civilian clothes, his bearing was very militaristic; the other was the narrow range of our conversation.

Because of some work I had been invited to do through the Chaplain's Office of the Staff and Command College at Fort Leavenworth, Kansas (thirty miles from Liberty), I knew that a captain would never be invited to Carlisle. The War College was reserved for officers that someone of rank felt to be worthy of general officer consideration. When I made that comment early, Bill and I learned that our friend was now Colonel Beasley. From then on, for the greater part of the visit, neither Bill nor I could resist referring to him except by his new title. We were impressed.

We drove to dinner in Rod's car. It was nothing like the Karmann Ghia I remembered from Dallas. It was four door and full sized. After leaving Interstate 35 into Kansas City and approaching an intersection Rod did a noticeable thing. We were already aware that he drove the fifteen miles into the city well within the speed limit. A comment made about the speed simply got a "What's the rush?" response.

At the intersection, and although we had the right-of-way, he came close to a complete stop, looked carefully both directions, and drove slowly through before speeding up again. Bill turned to look back at me, and we both looked at our driver. By this time, we were approaching the next intersection. Without taking his eyes off the street, Rod simply said, "When approaching an intersection, my first responsibility is to make sure it's secure!" Then after a quick glance at us, he continued, "Then my job is to see that we get across safely." We laughed. He smiled and repeated the process for the three intersections to the restaurant.

The restaurant was popular, and even with a reservation, we had to wait a few minutes before being seated. Once settled in, we jumped immediately back into telling the stories of our earlier times together. Our stories slowed down the process of placing an order. Our young waiter would have preferred greater speed from us and did his best to let us know that at several points in the process. I tried to assure him that we understood the value of turning tables and that I would "make it up to him when we were done." Rod simply stared at him.

"No," was our reply to the waiter's question "Would you care for any dessert?" We did tell him we would like another round of beers (this was the first alcohol Rod ever saw me drink). This was too much for the impatient waiter. It was obvious we were in no rush to leave. When the beer was served, so was our check. It seemed clear that our service from him was over.

By the time we were ready to go and the credit card process was over, none of us was in any mood to leave a tip of any size. My be nice manner was missing. I didn't appreciate the waiter's treatment of my best friends from college days. I had a plan. I took two pennies from my pocket and inserted them into the folder with the signed check. I thought the two cents message would be stronger than no tip. Rod didn't think he would get the message. He did. As we were crossing the street both front doors of the restaurant swung open loudly. The young waiter threw the pennies at us and shouted, "You sons of bitches," and went back inside. We laughed. He had gotten our message. "Be nice" had lost its hold on me.

Back at my place, we continued talking about a narrow range of topics, just as we had done in Dallas. By far most of our time was spent recalling our time at East Texas. Twenty years later, the stories were still fun to hear and to tell. We also tried some "I wonder whatever happened to" explorations, especially regarding former teammates, but none of us had much to contribute. It was quickly clear that talking about Vietnam was not going to happen. Very little information was shared beyond cursory comments like, "I spent a little time there," and "It's over and there's really not much to say about it."

It remains of great interest to me that so little was asked or offered about our personal lives, especially our families. We were in bed around 1:30 a.m. Both had to leave soon after we got up the next morning.

Highest Price Paid for Religious Certainty

The Liberty visit was our last. Rod died of a heart attack less than a year later on May 7, 1976, while living in Pennsylvania. He was buried in Arlington National Cemetery, and Bill and I attended the ceremony. Bill was asked by the family to be the minister providing the non-military portion of the eulogy and burial service. We learned from a summary of his career that he not only had served in Vietnam—he had served three different tours as a helicopter pilot and officer. He received numerous citations for courage and valor, up to and including the Silver Star Medal. We were awed and proud. Over time, the single most powerful and lingering memory of his funeral was seeing his spouse, Martha, his two sons, and his daughter—his family that I knew nothing about! Doing God's Will with Rod had cost me any knowledge of or relationship with his family!

My sense of personal loss was palpable. **It remains the single most disappointing and shameful memory of my entire life as a Southern Baptist minister!** My religious certainty had cost me the most important friendship of my college career and perhaps the most unique of a lifetime!

Collision 2—Bill. An experience with Bill, also in the spring of 1957, was not too dissimilar from that with Rod. I felt Bill was putting his marriage, and maybe even his ministry, at risk. I believed the interest he was showing to some single female students, one in particular, was putting his marriage vows in jeopardy, if it had not already done so. Unlike Rod, Bill was a brother preacher. He would or should have more knowledge and appreciation for keeping our lives in line with God's teaching.

During this period with Bill, The '57 Martian, the college's annual yearbook, was released. When asked to sign it, I took it upon myself to offer in addition to my signature, a reference from the Bible for his encouragement. As with Rod, I felt it my duty to him and God, to speak the truth in love. The chosen verse was Ephesians 6:16. It was one of several verses used to encourage believers to stay true to their faith. "Above all, take the shield of faith, with which you will be able to quench all the fiery darts of Satan." Exactly why I chose to put the verse in a place where anyone else looking at his yearbook might see it is open to question. I can only suppose I felt it was my duty. Quick to blame circumstances outside myself for personal thoughts and behaviors was a very strong pattern in me.

Unlike Rod, Bill and I never lost contact with each other for any long stretch of time. He is the only college friend who would never be too far away from all the major changes in my life, and I, his. In several ways, our lives would mirror each other's, including being divorced and remarried.

After his graduation from East Texas Baptist, Bill returned to live in Saint Louis and remains there. From Saint Louis, he commuted to Midwestern Baptist Theological Seminary and completed his degree. Midwestern was located in Kansas City and was no more than ten miles from Liberty, the home of William Jewell College. Later he completed a PhD at Washington University in Saint Louis. Following the Washington University degree, Bill became a licensed psychologist in Missouri, the host of a late-night talk show for a local radio station, a sports psychologist for the Saint Louis Cardinals and the Kansas City Royals, as well as pastor of a church. During this entire time and for years later, he was the singular pastor of the Christ Memorial Baptist Church. I was one of the church's guest speakers at a fifty-year anniversary celebration of his ministry.

Bill and I shared many things in common that kept us in frequent contact to both play and talk seriously. Proximity was a big one. For a period of thirty-plus years, I was often in St. Louis as he was in Kansas City. The similar starting point was another—Southern Baptist ministerial students at East Texas Baptist and sports teammates. And even though our religious paths would become different, the differences never altered the friendship appreciably. As far as theology was concerned, Bill would be known as a liberal, in the extreme. Shared interests in things psychological was a third commonality, especially counseling, management training, leadership development, and sports psychology.

Regarding what I called the tarnishing events with my two friends, there was an all-important difference for Bill and me that I missed with Rod. Bill and I had enough continuing time and contacts for him to know how foolish I came to feel about the words I had spoken and written in the spring of 1957. And to this day, he draws considerable pleasure out of reminding me of those earlier times, most especially the "fiery darts" comment.

Religion Itself

Many of the books cited on the 1965 and 1966 Reading Lists (see Appendix B) touched on aspects of Christianity. None however, to the best of my recollection, dealt with the history and phenomenon of faith and religion itself. Starting around 1970 and running actively for the next twenty or so years, that all changed. As time and energy allowed, I became absorbed with the historical beginnings of religion in general, holy men, shamans, rabbis, priests, Jesus, churches, denominations, the Bible, fundamentalism, and faith. I came to feel some kindship with Albert Schweitzer, who titled his account of his searching, *Quest for the Historical Jesus*, except my looking went considerably beyond Jesus's personal being. My growing realization that there was no actual evidence for any of my most deeply held beliefs was both devastating and exciting. What I had done was to simply accept, and agree with unquestioningly, the beliefs of those I loved and who loved me, those who taught me.

Once I had a taste of the excitement and joy of searching for information to form an opinion of my own, there was no turning back. To quote one author, I had tasted "new wine" and I liked it! For sure, there were times when what I was reading was jolting, anxiety provoking, even frightening. Especially was that true in those areas in direct contradiction to beliefs taught by the authorities in my life and to which I had fully, though blindly and trustingly, committed myself.

I can see now that I wasn't looking to discount my own religion directly. That would have been a sin of the highest order. I merely wanted to know about others, authors who had wrestled with the ideas that had and were troubling me. For whatever reason, the voice to hang in there and keep looking when ideas were personally upsetting always won out over the voice of this is wrong, you ought to be ashamed of yourself for doubting.

The desire to find verifications and justifications for claims made was replacing the drive to "trust and obey." I moved from one who felt he knew the basic verities of all the great questions of life (Who are we? What is the purpose of life? How did we get here? Where is it all going?) to one who was more comfortable with ideas like, we really don't know much. We are surrounded by incredible mysteries, open to curiosity, to discussions and attempts to understand. I eventually got to a place where the mysteries associated with life and living were more satisfying to consider than the unquestioned certainties I had claimed for so long. In recent years, I find great peace, excitement, and joy thinking that living is an unending mystery to be experienced, not a problem to be solved nor a dogma to be believed.

Early in the searching period, I found the work of a group known as the Jesus Seminar to be significant. The writings of Dominic Crossan, Martin Borg, and Robert Funk were especially interesting. Others that I found helpful were John S. Spong, Leslie Weatherhead, Matthew Fox, Karen Armstrong, Gregory Riley, and Bruce Chilton. For stronger medicine, I read Richard Dawkins, Matthew Alper, and Edward Wilson. There were many others.

To say that I had become a skeptic at first struck me as too harsh a title, but the first definition of skeptic is a person inclined to question or doubt accepted opinions. So, I suppose I can live with it. I do have an enormous interest in understanding the basis for anyone's claim of rightness or accuracy on virtually any subject. My skepticism began primarily in doubting those who claimed an understanding of an all-knowing, all-powerful, and eternal being and who in that being's name did harmful things to people around the world. It soon expanded to include any group or person who claimed to know an absolute truth, especially those who couldn't or wouldn't explain the basis for their claims. I came to think of such persons as religious supremacists and made peace with the idea that I had been one of them. I, too, had believed my ideas about an eternal God who could, in His infallible, literal book of rules-to-live-by (the Bible), justify the subjugation of women and condone slavery. I believed my understandings to be the only right ones. Competing understandings, through all ages, were wrong.

The thought that there have always been individuals who claimed to know, with certainty, the mind and will of a being who is responsible for the creation and operation of our universe is hard to get my mind around. Even harder is understanding that there have always been individuals, like me, who willingly accepted their pronouncements and found comfort, safety, and life-direction in trusting and following their stated views.

As the philosopher Camus observed, "We humans spend our lives trying to convince ourselves that our existence is not absurd." And on top of that, I learned how emotionally comforting it can be to gather with a large company of fellow believers who think exactly as I do—on any topic.

Yet, my certainties were gradually replaced by a sense of wonder and awe regarding the many mysteries associated with being a human in such a complex world. For instance, instead of believing specific items about Jesus, I became fascinated with how distinctive he must have seemed in his time and place to have attracted such attention, fascination, and interpretation from any who knew him and from many of those who came after him. One thing was certain, I could never again be a part of any group that felt it had an exclusionary claim on what or who was right. The world for me ceased to be black and white, or even gray for that matter. It had become both excitingly and frighteningly kaleidoscopic!

The Bible, the inerrant Word of God, King James Version, was the centerpiece of the living room of the homes of my childhood. Here is a brief, simplified historical overview of the Bible in general and the King James Version in particular, none of which I knew during the years I served as a youth evangelist or as a young pastor. What I did know was that what the Bible said was central to all truth.

• Job is likely the first book ever written, circa 2000-1500 BC.

• All 39 books of the Old Testament (KJV) were completed by 300 BC.

• The Septuagint Bible (Hebrew translated into Greek) added 14 additional books. The Apocrypha, a set of texts included in the Septuagint, were added to the original 39, circa 200 BC.

• All 27 New Testament books were completed by AD 45-100.

• Athenasius of Alexandria declared the 27 books the "Official New Testament."

• Many other important writings were circulating at that time, but not recognized as official, including a Gospel of Thomas, a Gospel of James, a "Q" and the Didache. There was also a III Corinthians, an Epistle of Barnabas, and an Apocrypha of Peter, circa AD 323.

• Jerome translated the Greek Septuagint into the Latin Vulgate. The Roman Catholic Church declared Latin the only language of Christianity, circa AD 600. This idea stood for nearly 1000 years.

• John Wycliffe translated the Latin Bible to English in 1382. He was found guilty of heresy. Forty-four years after his death, his bones were dug up, burned, and strewn across a river.

• The invention and creation of the Gutenberg Printing Press, circa 1455, made the scriptures accessible to more people. Until this event, all writings, copies, and translations had been accomplished by hand.

• Martin Luther translated the Vulgate into German. He nailed to the Wittenberg church door his 95 Theses, which stated his challenges to the existing norms of the Catholic church. The Protestant Reformation was born, in 1517.

• The King James Version, published in England in 1611, became the most printed book in the world from then to present day.

• Once out of the exclusive hands of Roman Catholic Church clergy and into the hands of the general public, "modern" denominations arose, each with a strong sense of the rightness of their view in contrast to the first Catholic one: Lutherans, Presbyterians, Methodists, Baptists, Christians, Church of Christ, Unitarians, and Mormons.

Summary Observation about the Bible. The Christian Bible, as I knew it, came together over a period of more than two thousand years. The first images of God—all powerful (omnipotent), all knowing (omniscient) and everywhere present (omnipresent)—took hold in primitive times. The idea that God is love began taking hold in the first and second centuries AD The Bible's stories were first told and then written, by dozens of authors in multiple languages. As the ability to read and

write grew among humankind, so did interest in getting the
religious writings into a common collection and into a common
language. Latin won the language race and dominated for nearly
a thousand years. Sixty-six different writings were roughly
agreed upon and became known as the books of The Bible.
Beginning in the late fourteenth century and running through the
Age of Enlightenment—thanks to Gutenberg's Press—printed
and bound copies of the Holy Bible in English became readily
available to anyone who wanted one. Elizabethan English would
always be the language of God for me.

Chapter 9
LIFE LESSONS

Lesson 1

With limited experience and information, I was capable of believing anything, no matter how absurd it might turn out to be. In my first born again state, I believed that the universe in which I lived was spoken into existence by God (an Omnipotent, Omniscient, Omnipresent being). Let there be light. The process was completed in six twenty-four-hour days, and the earth is the center of this vast universe, with Heaven above and Hell below. (I did not believe the earth was flat, however. Civilized people had advanced too far for that.)

The profundity of the simple thought "people had advanced too far for that" never once caused me to raise an eyebrow regarding other areas where people might have already advanced! Even as I came to understand aspects of the evolution of life, I insisted that God remained the author of all creation. So what if a day of creation turned out to be hundreds or even thousands of years, it was still all God's doing. There was nothing to doubt about that.

I believed when Christians died, they went immediately to heaven to be with Jesus. I also believed at the end of time there would be a great judgment day when every human being who had ever lived would stand before God to receive a final sentence regarding eternity in heaven or hell. That the two beliefs were contradictory never occurred to me!

As noted, I believed the God I worshipped was in fact omnipotent, omniscient, and omnipresent. At seventeen, the first time I heard George Beverly Shea sing the solo "How Great Thou Art" at a Billy Graham-led revival, I was thrilled beyond words.

How Great Thou Art

O Lord my God, When I in awesome wonder,
Consider all the worlds Thy Hands have made;
I see the stars, I hear the rolling thunder,
Thy power throughout the universe displayed.

Refrain
Then sings my soul, My Saviour God, to Thee,
How great Thou art, How great Thou art.
Then sings my soul, My Saviour God, to Thee,
How great Thou art, How great Thou art!

When through the woods, and forest glades I wander,
And hear the birds sing sweetly in the trees.
When I look down, from lofty mountain grandeur
And see the brook and feel the gentle breeze.
Refrain

And when I think, that God, His Son not sparing;
Sent Him to die, I scarce can take it in;
That on the Cross, my burden gladly bearing,
He bled and died to take away my sin.
Refrain

When Christ shall come, with shout of acclamation,
And take me home, what joy shall fill my heart.
Then I shall bow, in humble adoration,
And then proclaim: "My God, how great Thou art!"
Refrain

In many ways this mindset toward God proved to be the biggest conundrum of my religious experience. How could I feel so passionate about an idea on one hand and behave as if the opposite were true on the other? If there really is a God, and if He really is omnipotent, omniscient, and omnipresent could He not speak anything He desired into existence just as He had done with the Earth, Moon, Stars and the first human couple? It seemed to be obviously true from the first verse in the book of Genesis to the last verse in the book of Malachi, the entirety of the Old Testament. Years later, with a broader appreciation for the historic Age of Reason, the seventeenth and eighteenth centuries, I came to understand that the ideas about God in the Old Testament were shaped by individuals who had lived 1000 to 1500 years earlier.

The fourth characteristic of God—Love—would be powerfully added to the original three in the days of the New Testament. Two verses stood out for me above all others. John 3:16 states that "For God so loved the world that He gave his only begotten son ..." and 1 John 4:8 states that "He that loveth not, knoweth not God, for God is love." That's what the Bible is all about. That's why I found the George Beverly Shea song, "How Great Thou Art" so thrilling. If so, what could God possibly want or need from me or any other human being, except to be worshipped?

Not being able to see the forest for the trees is an apt description of my earliest beliefs and actions as a fundamentalist Christian. In my case, the inherent contradiction between the

forest of my actions and the trees of my belief that described the
essential nature of God—all powerful, all knowing, everywhere
present, and loving—was never confronted.

For example, two political events in the earliest days of being
a Southern Baptist preacher set the pattern for years of my social
behavior as a born-again believer living in the United States.
First, in 1954 President Eisenhower signed into law a bill passed
by Congress adding the words "Under God" to our national
pledge of allegiance. I was nineteen years old. The pledge was
originally created in 1892 and formally adopted by Congress
in 1942, when I was six years old. That means I said the pledge
hundreds, if not thousands of times at schools, churches, World
War II related moments, and sporting events without any direct
reference to God. My Boy Scout oath was different and more
specific. "On my honor, I will do my best to do my duty to God
and my country ..." I gave both the pledge and the oath with a
proud mind and loyal heart every time. Surely God knew I meant
it.

How is it then that I could feel so excited about this two-word
addition? Wasn't I already giving God the credit for everything?
It seemed to reinforce my zeal for God, Boy Scouts, and country
for the entirety of my public-school days. What would have
happened to us as a country if we had not given God his due?
Is God less present, less knowing, less powerful, less loving if we
don't say that he is? Huge questions!

The second political event occurred two years later, in 1956.
I was a junior in college and one year away from Southwestern
Seminary. On this occasion, President Eisenhower signed into
law another bill passed by Congress dealing with God and
language. This bill declared the phrase "In God we Trust" the
new motto of the U.S.A., replacing "E Pluribus Unum." The
latter, translated from Latin, "Out of Many, One" had been
in use since 1776. Once again, the omnipotent, omniscient,

omnipresent, loving God of the universe was being elevated in the public eye. The motto soon appeared on all U.S. currency, coins and paper bills, tying God to democratic capitalism. What had served our country since its initial founding was no longer enough. I was happy for my God and for America. He was getting the national recognition that He should have been getting all along! At the time of the bill's signing, President Eisenhower stated: "In this way we are reaffirming the transcendence of religious faith in America's heritage and future; in this way we shall constantly strengthen those spiritual weapons which forever will be our country's most powerful resource in peace and war."

I knew nothing of this statement at the time. Had I, it would only have enhanced my joy over my God getting His due recognition. My first presidential vote was for Ike. I liked him! I didn't have the slightest idea that clever politicians were using my religious zeal for God and country to enhance the likelihood of my voting for their party. Not to vote for them was the perilous road toward godless communism or socialism, or both. (As noted earlier, my second presidential vote was guided by a desire to protect protestant Christianity against encroaching Catholicism.)

How could that be? How could an all-knowing, all-powerful, everywhere present being in the universe be in any danger of anything? Therein lay the conundrum.

In sum, I unknowingly surrendered my own thinking, my mind, to the minds of others who had done the same thing with theirs. A question was born in me: From whose mind did the first fundamentalist thoughts come into my world, the world of a Southern Baptist? "Communism is a religion that is inspired, directed and motivated by the Devil himself who has declared war against Almighty God," stated Billy Graham.

Public issues dealing with contraception, abortion, homosexuality, transgender, same-sex marriage, poverty, education, housing, political party and immigration remain highly charged if followers can be led to believe that God's Will for the country is on trial.

Lesson 2

With limited experience and information, an individual's beliefs, by their nature, can be enhanced and strengthened when they are surrounded by others who believe the same things. I was proud of my child-like faith in the truth of all Biblical claims and miracles. The simplicity of it provided some status within the group. The more preposterous the belief—Noah building an ark that saved all living creatures amidst a flooding of the entire globe—the better to demonstrate the degree of my loyalty and commitment to my group. Being in the presence of like-minded people provided me an enormous sense of comfort and support.

Also, thoughts can become tied to deeply experienced emotional reactions, and a deeply felt idea can be equated with, and experienced as, the factual truth. The question "How do you know for sure that you are right?" can be satisfyingly answered with, "I don't know, I just DO!" An often-sung favorite hymn in Southern Baptist churches, "He Lives," has a final chorus line that states "You ask me how I know He lives? He lives within my heart!"

Lesson 3

With limited experience and information, judgments can be made regarding the actions and beliefs of others that have profound consequences. At an Inquisition Trial in 1633, Galileo was found "vehemently suspect of heresy" for supporting the idea that the earth was round and rotated around the sun. Such an idea was heretical because it contradicts the sense of Holy Scripture. He was forced to recant or suffer excommunication. He recanted and lived under house arrest for the last eight years of his life. Three hundred and sixty years later another pope would exonerate Galileo from the original charges.

I was taught and believed that the millions of people who lived on Earth before the time of Jesus's birth, life, death, and resurrection were doomed, following their death, to an eternity of some form of conscious existence in a lake of everlasting fire called Hell. John 14:6 was key: "I am the way, the truth and the life. No man cometh to the Father but by me." It doesn't get any clearer than that. Buddhists, Muslims, Jews, Hindus, Sikhs, Taoists, Mormons—past, present and future—were damned to a similar fate. Why? They did not know of, understand, or accept the idea that Jesus was the sole source of eternal salvation. Other historic figures like Buddha, Confucius, Krishna, Abraham, Muhammed, and Joseph Smith held no sway. I was also strongly attached to the opening phrase of John 3:16, "God so loved the world ..."

Lesson 4

A particular religion can be a creator and defender of a culture's status quo or a challenger to it. During the Civil War, there were those who believed that slavery was evil, the work of Satan, and fought vigorously against "the peculiar institution." There were others who vehemently believed slavery was the divine Will of God for both races, White and Black. Two Southern Baptists, Richard Furman and Basil Manly Sr., played prominent roles in founding the Southern Baptist Convention itself at Augusta, Georgia, in 1845. Manly Sr., while serving as Pastor of First Baptist, Charleston, second President of the University of Alabama, and Pastor of First Baptist, Montgomery was a major religious supporter for the secession of southern states creating the Confederacy. He was elected Chaplain of the Confederate States of America and offered the invocation prayer at Jefferson Davis's inauguration at Montgomery in 1861. He was a powerful advocate for White supremacy over African slaves as the divine Will of God and the owner of a plantation in Alabama populated with slaves.

Today I wonder, if Basil Manly Sr., instead of J.M. Bradford, had been the pastor of my childhood family church, would I have become an unquestioning religious and racial supremacist? The answer seems obvious!

Lesson 5

Being indoctrinated into a particular religion is confused with learning about God and faith. "Give me a child until he is seven, and I will give you the man," is a famous quote attributed to Saint Ignatius Loyola, founder of the Jesuits. Once I was in, studying the Bible was little more than searching it for those stories and verses that underscored and confirmed the specific ideas that I already believed to be the truth. I read the Bible for confirmation, not information.

Lesson 6

A person can become so personally connected and identified with the ideas (thoughts) in his or her head that questioning them, or having them challenged by others, can feel like a life-threatening event. Questions and challenges to my first thoughts I experienced as an attack on my sense of me! Believing that my religious ideas originated with the one true God of the universe and obeying them meant following His Will intensified their power over me.

Lesson 7

Standing up for God and His Will is powerful medicine and a strong motivator of public and private action for all whose worship includes a here and a hereafter, a heaven and a hell. It can lead a person to live and act against his or her own

best interests as well as the interests of all others. The positive
emotional force of believing that following God's Will while
on Earth—the here—when doing so pleases God and leads
to an eternity of heavenly joys and peace—the hereafter—is
infinite. Likewise, the fear associated with displeasing God by
not doing His Will here because it leads to an eternal hereafter
of hellish fire and torment is equally infinite. The history of the
fundamentalists' religion is the struggle over what to do about
unbelievers, immorality, and justice.

Knowing the true Will of God for the public was tricky
business for we Southern Baptist, especially those of us in the
fundamentalist wing. Unlike Muslims with their Ayatollahs or the
Roman Catholics with their Pope, we had no elected hierarchy
to speak on behalf of God. Our best hope for leadership
was found in the Bible and those leaders who knew it to be
inherently true. Those leadership voices tended to come from
those most broadly known, more times than not the pastors of
the largest Baptist churches in our convention. Billy Graham,
the hero of my young adulthood, though not a pastor, was a
great example. His popularity in the world was "a sure sign that
the hand of God was upon him" and that God was using him
to help save thousands of souls from an eternity of Hell's fire.
When Billy Graham spoke, people listened. This popularity
as an evangelist put him in contact with every U.S. president
beginning with Harry Truman and ending with Donald Trump.
Having Graham as a friend meant huge political support
whether you were a Democrat or Republican. Issues touching
war in Vietnam, poverty, race, communism, and Muslims
became religious in nature, and it became a challenge to know
whether he was supporting a president or being used by him for
political gain. The 1947 role played by the newspaper publisher,
William Randolph Hearst, who instructed his reporters to "puff
Graham," shocked me. The action of repeatedly putting Graham

in a favorable light on the front page of popular newspapers, per Hearst's instruction, was likely the single most significant factor in Graham's national and international popularity.

Chapter 10

TRUSTING SELF

Life After the Death of Being Born Again

Coming to my own conclusions rather than trusting and obeying the conclusions arrived at by others is a profound shift. I was a slow learner, but when the student is ready, the teacher will come.

What follows is my attempt to understand and share the forces at work during the first twenty-five years of my life and how I either worked through them or came to understand and accept them. As I write this, I am acutely aware of the limitations of such an undertaking, and most especially my capacity for self-deception. That, plus my advanced age and my limited ability to untangle the thoughts and emotions of the present from those remembered across the years, add to the challenge. My intention is to share how it all seemed to me in the hope that my experiences may have some value as others seek to understand themselves and their key relationships more fully.

Orthogonal Learning

In physics, as I understand it, there is a concept that says particles, even the subatomic, can learn only from their own experience or the experience of their immediate particle neighbors, particularly those that exist at right angles. Learning from one's experience is direct; learning from a neighbor is indirect or orthogonal. The term orthogonal learning can also be called side-door or back-door learning. If trying to learn directly through the front door, and it is blocked, and there is no alternative avenue, such as a side or back door for getting information, the particle or the organism is at risk of limitation, damage, or death. Borrowing on that concept to understand human learning has been of great value to me in attempting to understand my most challenging life issues.

My mother's guideposts tended to block the front door of learning for me in some essential aspects of living. They were all interconnected.

The following were not to be pursued:

• Seek to learn, understand, or expand any area of study that was at odds with the world as it had been presented to me.

• Question or challenge the veracity and value of any information, instructions, or directions given to me by those in authority over me.

• Question or doubt the virtue, morality, or intentions of those in leadership.

• Trust and make known to others through comments or actions any thought that was different from existing norms.

• Seek to gain more comprehensive knowledge regarding almost any topic.

• Form my own conclusions regarding the knowledge gained and publicly behave in the direction that the conclusions led me.

How does one learn or develop such skills in a world where, for the most part, their exact opposite was honored and rewarded? Where are the potential side doors when the front door is closed?

Major Side-Door 1—Athletics

As cited earlier, athletics in junior high school, senior high, and college were important, if not central, in most aspects of my young life. In my non-athletic life, standing up for myself, speaking my mind, arguing, fighting, wanting to come out on top, behaving selfishly, being different, or standing out would have received frowning at best and punishment or shaming of some sort at worst. In athletics, a form of each of these forbidden behaviors would be required, even encouraged. Because all the behaviors were a part of the collective, the team, and the team was attempting to win on behalf of the school or town, they became positive characteristics. The entire school and town were supportive. To be sure the coach was still the unquestioned authority, but even he was open to questions, suggestions, and observations in a way that was designed to enhance the team's chances of winning.

It was amazing. I could do and be for the sake of the team, school, or town what I could not or would not do or be for myself. I was learning, through a side door for sure, and outside any conscious awareness as well, that team achievement brought personal advantages to me. To be clear, I never thought of the skills or accomplishments in any personal terms. They were simply the by-products of trying to be the best teammate possible. Learning and being on behalf of others as an orthogonal way of helping myself was a style of life for many years to come. And all the while, my deepest longings and needs were being impacted and changed. My future life was unfolding.

Important Life Lessons from Athletics:

• Good health and fitness: One can only perform at the level of the body's fitness.

• Competence and discipline: Every position on a successful sports team requires a certain set of competencies and the discipline to learn, maintain, and enhance them.

• Endurance/stamina: The game isn't over until the final whistle blows.

• Competiveness/fighting spirit/willingness to excel and outdo others: Within the framework of a team, its best performers are needed at each position.

• Teamwork/cooperation: Individual success or failure is less important than the team winning.

• Giving and taking physical punishment: Football, basketball, and baseball all have an element of physical contact. Giving as much or more than you are getting is a part of winning the game—preferably within the rules.

• Another game is coming: Celebrating wins and bemoaning losses are best if controlled and short lived. The next game requires its own preparation and performance.

• Leadership within the team: The best leaders do so by example and word. The second best do so by example. There is little or no value in leading by word only.

• Coaches: Effective coaches over time tend to be those who know the sport, can communicate their understanding and expectations clearly, and treat their players justly. They are also willing and able to learn from their players.

• Teams: Most teams are made up of players with diverse backgrounds, attitudes, and skills: Learning to play well with personal differences requires respect, understanding, and appreciation of those differences.

• Competitors: Whether fellow students competing to play the same position or opponents trying to win the game, they are just fellow competitors. They are not lesser beings or an enemy!

As I write this section, I am sharply aware of both the short-term and long-term values I learned through participation in athletics. The greatest short-term value, by far, was that I could develop these skills and understandings without violating any of my mom's guideposts. I could learn and practice them and still remain, "nice," "good," "respectful," "humble" (small britches), "praise God," and "grateful" for all the opportunities. The long-term value would show itself when the adult games being played were between players with different ideas and values who were contesting over which ideas and values would win. These new games were played out in offices, boardrooms, conference centers, factory floors, laboratories, school rooms, neighborhoods, political elections, wars and yes, even churches.

Major Side-Door 2—Training in
Counseling and Psychology

One of the first post-master's courses I took at UMKC was a
graduate seminar in social psychology—a study of the way one's
personality, attitudes, motivations, and behaviors are influenced
by social groups and, reciprocally, the influence of individuals
upon groups. The seminar was led by Dr. Neil Willis. The
basic format was significant for me. There were eleven other
participants. We met once a week for three hours, seated at a
large round table in a side room of a Pizza Hut adjacent to the
university campus. Topics to be discussed were announced in
advance accompanied by extensive reading lists and reference
materials. We were expected to be familiar with the assignment
and come to the seminar prepared to discuss our personal
thoughts, reactions, and conclusions. In other words, everyone
was encouraged to "speak your mind." In an important sense,
each participant was demonstrating the thoughts and feelings
that reflected the influences of their social interaction to this
point in their lives. The conversations tended to be pointed and
direct. There was no acceptable place to run and hide from the
discussions. Dr. Willis made it clear that our exchanges around
the table were as important to success in the class as the materials
to be read and understood.

One assignment stands out above all others—read research
studies that indicated that a preponderance of the men and
women who entered the professional world of psychology,
psychotherapy, and psychiatry had done so primarily driven
by a desire to understand themselves! It was certainly not true
of me! My pathway, in my mind, was clear. At the University
of Houston, I had a sharp sense that many of my interactions
were with individuals in search of understanding, support,
and counseling. True, I knew Bible verses to cite and quote for

direction and guidance. I also knew how to pray and ask God for leadership and comfort. I was well-trained in the truth and how to proclaim it. I had been a preacher, a speaker, a talker, a declarer. What I wasn't was a listener, an understander, or a respectful inquirer to expand understanding. I had a strong sense of wanting to become one who could do those things. But why? To be able to understand and help others more adequately, of course! What else could possibly be going on?

At Park Cities Baptist Church in Dallas, I was in a position to promote the reading of periodicals and books that raised life questions regarding religious faith and living that warranted thoughtful consideration. Concerns and questions could be discussed openly and with respect for one another. In my mind, I was choosing topics and subjects that I thought would be of benefit to attendees. I wanted to do whatever I could to help them more fully understand themselves and the world in which they lived. The one-on-one conversations were not too different from those I experienced in Houston. I was aware of how little I understood about the impact of families and cultures on the development of personalities, attitudes, emotions, habits, and behaviors. I wanted to understand more, and for the same basic reason—to be of greater help to and for them.

Incidentally, when I think back to the reading commitment I made to Dr. Whaley during this Park Cities period, the one that resulted in my exposure to more than one hundred books (Appendix B), I am fascinated with one insight. In my mind, I had accepted the challenge primarily to "be a good boy" and "respect my elders" in order to have him think well of me, which he did. That I may have been reading them to satisfy a deep hunger for more personal understanding and knowledge would have meant that I was forgetting my place, putting myself ahead of others, and expanding the size of my britches. All of which would have been emotionally unacceptable behaviors.

My experiences at William Jewell College continued in a similar vein, but here I was adding social, political, and philosophical subjects in the convocation programs to the moral and religious topics that were encompassed in the chapel programs. As strange and fascinating as my personal blindness at the time strikes me now, during those years, I was not conscious that I was pursuing topics, inviting speakers, reading books, and having conversations that were in fact meeting my own most profound personal needs and interests! To have been aware, I would have had to confront the six maxims that had so powerfully ordered my life, especially putting my personal needs and interests above those of others. Thinking, questioning, and acting on the personal judgments that would come as a result was too much. There would be more, and perhaps even more essential side doors coming as I moved into the world of counseling psychology, management training, consulting, and coaching.

With one or two exceptions, no one in the social psychology class, including Dr. Willis, felt I was being honest with myself regarding my motivation for wanting to pursue studies in this field. What seemed so pure to me (my main desire was to be helpful to others) seemed ridiculous to them, bordering on self-deception and delusion. And they told me so. It was a long three hours. I am smiling as I write this. How accurate my classmates were regarding my profound passion for self-understanding. And how strong the desire remains forty plus years later. They could see beyond the side door of my limited awareness to the more direct, personal hunger for understanding and self-acceptance.

I was completely unaware that a similar, if not identical phenomenon was going on in the way I approached my new counseling psychology world. I wanted to learn all I could about how the brain worked, how people related, and what made us tick. Without acknowledging it, I was as hungry for

the verifications and justifications behind the claims of the
authorities, such as Freud, Jung, Pavlov, Skinner, and Maslow,
in the field of psychology as I had come to be in the world of
theology. I was completely taken aback when I realized that I had
come to similar conclusions regarding their claims. I could not
bring myself to take sides, to join any one group, to be identified
as a true believer. There was respect, even awe over their insight
and work, but never enough to want to quit looking on my own.
I became known as an eclectic. I drew from each what seemed
to be valuable, of worth to me, and held at bay or discarded
the rest. To me—what an incredible concept. I was becoming
my own authority. I didn't think of myself as someone who had
found the right answers. The conclusions to which I had come
and was coming suited me. I felt no need to deny them. I confess;
however, I may have suffered a bit from an urge to defend them.
I came to have an increasing appreciation of a passage in *Crime
and Punishment* by Dostoyevsky: "To go wrong in one's own way
is better than to go right in someone else's."

The orthogonal (side-door) learning was not limited to
the lecture and seminar rooms. I sought the help of other
professionals as well. And still, in my mind, the goal was to be of
more value and worth to those with whom I was working.

A friend introduced me to a psychiatrist in Kansas City, Dr.
Clyde Martin. While pursuing the PhD, I was still developing the
Office of Counseling and Testing for William Jewell. Dr. Martin
agreed to visit with me once or twice a month to review whatever
cases I might choose to discuss with him. They tended to be
the ones that seemed the most complex for me to understand
and manage. Without disclosing any identifying information, I
reviewed conversations I had had with the persons in question,
along with what I had said or done. He invariably listened
carefully and made his own observations and comments. I found
them to be very helpful. He was always careful to simply share

his thoughts about the issues and people. He never put himself in the position of an authority telling me what to do or think. The next actions were always left in my hands. These conversations went on for about six months.

At the end of our time of working together, Dr. Martin suggested that I might want to participate in what he referred to as a sensitivity workshop or T-group. The goal of the workshop was straightforward—to assist participants in broadening their understanding of how their words and actions trigger emotional reactions in others and, conversely, how the words and actions of others trigger emotional reactions within themselves. In the broadest sense, the goal was increased self-understanding and self-awareness. Specific attention would be paid to the challenges of having successful interpersonal communications with the important people in a participant's life when strong emotions are engaged, especially those of fear, hurt, anger, and envy. One was scheduled to take place in a few weeks. I felt it would be a helpful experience to have and happily signed up.

He explained the format. There would be eight to ten young to middle-aged participants, mostly present or former patients of his, and a counselor with the Midwest Christian Counseling Center in Kansas City. The gathering would be held in a large house and begin on a Friday evening and conclude near noon on Sunday. The group conversations would take place in the living room with participants sitting around in a variety of chairs or on the floor. Participants were to bring a sleeping bag and wear comfortable clothes. Sleeping and eating were to be minimized. The interactions on Friday and Saturday usually would last until the early morning hours of the next day, ending anywhere from 1:00 to 2:00 a.m. Saturday and Sunday mornings would begin promptly at 8:00. Sleeping would take place anywhere one chose, all on the floor somewhere in the bags brought. A variety of food would be made available in the kitchen to serve oneself.

He said that becoming physically and emotionally fatigued was a part of the self-understanding process. It was believed that the more exhausted the group members became, the rawer the comments and interactions and disclosures would become.

For our group, that dynamic held true. Under his facilitation, we participants were encouraged to share the range of our emotional reactions to the actions and comments made by our fellow group members as the weekend progressed. The emphasis was on the simple acknowledgment of the reactions as opposed to judgments and conclusions. A variety of group interaction techniques and exercises were used throughout.

The most popular one was speaking to an empty chair. In turn, each participant was asked to have an imaginary conversation with someone in his or her life who had played, or was playing, an important role, typically with unsatisfactory, hurtful, or painful consequences. An empty chair was placed a few feet in front of the participant. Most commonly, the person placed in the chair would be an intimate friend or lover, mother, father, sibling, spouse, or partner. Questions like "What would you like for (insert name) to understand about you that she/he doesn't seem to get?" or "What would you like to say to (insert name) that so far you have been too reluctant or fearful to express?" or "What would you like for (insert name) to stop doing that is currently going on or to start doing?" was usually enough to get the experience started. As the process unfolded, individuals within the group entered the discussions by identifying their own reactions to the conversation with the imaginary person in the chair. Sometimes the comments were directed toward the empty chair, "Why can't you understand? Get off her back. Leave him alone." Sometimes toward the participant, "You don't sound like you mean it. You're holding back. Is that really what you mean to say?" The exchanges became highly charged at times, usually expressed in tears or shouting.

When my turn came, the person I most wanted to talk with was my mother. Who else could it have been? My comments literally tumbled out. They went on for several minutes without any comments or interruptions. It was obvious that she was a topic I had spent considerable time and energy thinking about. When it seemed that I was done, Dr. Martin asked, "Is there anything you want to say to your father?" I was surprised. I paused, thought about it, and said something like, "Not that I know of; he and I got along great." Dr. Martin simply nodded, and we moved on to the next participant. This occurred early on Friday.

Later that same evening, though by now it was early Saturday morning, and we were getting ready to call an end to the session, Dr. Martin turned to me again and said, "How about your father, still nothing to say to him?" Though I was even more surprised by him asking this a second time, after pausing and trying to think about it, I said something like, "Nothing, honestly, we got along really well, we still do." Dr. Martin simply nodded, but a seed had been planted.

Saturday passed much like Friday. New exercises and techniques were introduced. The group remained energized and focused; a kind of friendship and respectful bond seemed to be developing. As the day wore on, fatigue began to show itself, primarily in our postures. We were sitting back more deeply in our chairs or stretched out more completely on the floor.

On Saturday evening, Dr. Martin began something like a review, going back over ground covered on Friday and earlier in the day. To my surprise, in two or three cases, there was a noticeable edginess in voices. Some conflicts between and among participants emerged. The group's collective energy was rekindled, only this time there seemed to be less bonding and more defending one's views and beliefs. Tension was noticeable.

During this stretch, Dr. Martin turned to me a third time to inquire after my dad. I was surprised again, and this time I was aware of my own tension. I felt annoyed. Hadn't I been open and clear earlier? I voiced the annoyance by saying something like, "What's with you and my dad? You are barking up the wrong tree here!" He simply nodded and moved on. The tension within me only increased.

The entire episode came to a head just before we came to the close of the day's session. It was early on Sunday. For a fourth time, I heard the father question. And with this one, Dr. Martin added, "Are you SURE there's NOTHING there?" I felt the emphasis of his voice with *sure* and *nothing*. I remember lowering my head ready to make one more dismissal. While staring at the floor, and seemingly from out of nowhere, and as far as I could tell not aimed at anyone, I quietly said the words, "I wish he had stood up for himself!" They were said so softly Dr. Martin asked, "What was that?" I repeated the words. I felt mocked, even embarrassed, when with a bit of what seemed like ridicule, he said loudly, "I still can't hear you." In an instant, with tears gushing out, I shouted, "Just once, I wish he had stood up for himself!" My tears flowed, and I just sat there staring at the floor for the next several moments. Hardly anything else was said. I just sat there. As we were breaking up, a few made a point of touching me on the arm and shoulder as they passed.

I have no memory of the final few hours on Sunday. I know I was struck by the force of the unexpected emotions I experienced, embarrassed somewhat, but at the same time I felt okay, even relieved. It was a lot like standing on completely new ground and in a state of bewilderment as to how I had gotten there.

Years went by before I would relate the retreat experience to anyone. Within days, I became so caught up in activities around my new role at the College, the demands of a graduate

education, and circumstances within my family that it fell out
of my awareness. This dissonance was gone. Dr. Martin and the
workshop had been the teacher. The student, while there, had not
been fully available—yet.

I am comfortable now with the thought that Dr. Martin had
seen or sensed something about me and my father from our
earliest times together that warranted serious attention by me.
I think, too, that he was wise enough, kind enough, to include
me in his weekend retreat as the methodology he chose to see
if I was capable of such an understanding. I think he must have
realized that there was not much access to me through a direct
front-door confrontation. Instead, he made available a side-door
opening. I will always be grateful for his caring friendship and
patient mentoring.

My changed role at William Jewell, graduate school demands
at UMKC, and family circumstances distracted me from delving
deeper into this new experience. Each one of these three items,
in its own way, would immediately be making heavy demands on
my physical, mental, and emotional energies.

Heavy Demand in the New Role—I was considered by many
of my friends, colleagues, and students a good counselor, a good
therapist, helpful, interested, and concerned. There were enough
who felt this to create a growing stream of new referrals, or
clients as I learned to think of them. I couldn't bring myself to
think of them as patients. That would have made me a doctor—
heaven forbid. I was increasingly busy.

In my own view, though, the praise and support were pleasant
to receive, it would often create some anxiety around the "big
britches" issue. I did genuinely care, experienced empathy for
each one, and worked hard at trying to understand and be as
helpful as possible. I didn't want to seem helpful, nor did I want
to think of myself that way. It was important to me to hear from

them that what we were doing was noticeably and practically helpful! And, even then, and remaining to this day, I have a strong sense of embarrassment when I hear expressions of gratitude.

A Client Who Enlarged My Spirit—As observed earlier, the minister of First Presbyterian Church, Julian Houston, was a strong supporter of me and the work of Northland Counseling Center. No referral of his, however, would have greater impact on me than that of a man in his mid-forties who said at our first meeting, "Julian thought it might be helpful if you and I talked."

Our first contacts were frequent, usually early evening, in my office. He was articulate, intelligent, compassionate, and a practicing physician. In time I became well-acquainted with his spouse and on one occasion at his home met his two teenage daughters. His nearly twenty-year marriage was under severe pressure. Likewise, a major shift in his professional life was impending.

The triggering event was this. In a Kansas City park known to be popular among gay men and women, he and a friend, for whom he had great affection, had been caught alone, and to a limited degree knowledge of the liaison had become public. The essence of his life struggle was simple. How does a gay male child find his way to adult life and living when he is raised in the world of a heterosexual family in the grip of religious fundamentalism? His personal efforts toward conformity to their norms had been monumental. He had done his best to live successfully in a manner in opposition to his basic nature.

There was no therapy involved in our sessions. In fact, I did very little. I listened to his childhood and early adulthood stories. On one side were feelings of being weird, different, alone, ashamed, and afraid. His religious stories added feelings of sin, guilt, weakness, lost or saved. Hearing the slang labeling of his adolescence as "homo, queer, and fag" was especially difficult. From my own memories, I understood how we fundamentalists knew how right we were regarding the truth of the Bible, God's Word. That the words in Leviticus prohibiting homosexuality were laid down about five-hundred to three-hundred years before even the birth of Jesus was unknown and inconsequential to us.

He decided early in his college career to devote all his energies to living his life as normal as others seemed to be living theirs! He was arguably successful. He completed college and medical school and joined a group of other doctors providing a full range of medical care. He met and married a remarkable young woman and parented two daughters.

Remarkably, at this point in his life, his family, spouse, and children were able to collectively get to a place where all agreed that husband and dad had suffered enough living against his given biological nature. It was time for him to live in peace and openness with his sexual orientation. His medical practice was another story. The group of which he was a part felt it would be best if they went separate ways. His medical skills and experience found new expression in the international group Doctors without Borders in the African country of Chad. The remainder of our contact was limited to occasional emails and special holiday greetings. My contact with his spouse was regular and casual. I learned of his death in Portland, Oregon, following a brief illness in 2012. I will always have a sense of great indebtedness for what I learned about life from this fellow human being who was deeply impacted by others who believed their Bible was the literal Word of God.

Heavy Demand of Graduate Studies—As the demand grew for the counseling services, so did my curiosity and craving for a greater understanding of the entire field of psychology. As a student, my appetite for learning was high. I no longer waited for a teacher to teach; the new student looked for any opportunity to learn from reading, conferences, and conversations. It was perfectly clear that I could only be as helpful to clients as my knowledge and skill could allow. I had moved a long way from the young evangelist who felt he knew the answers to all, or most all, of life's serious questions. Schooling took up huge chunks of time, inside and outside the classroom. That I was learning orthogonally about issues of lifelong importance to me personally continued to escape me.

A Changed Student—By the time I had reached my last semester of classroom instruction, and before a final internship assignment, I was scheduled to take an advanced course in theories of personality. At the close of the first class, the professor, Dr. Bernie Kleinman, chairman of the psychology department, asked me to remain a moment to talk. He already knew me well enough to understand my interest in the subject and that I had already taught an undergraduate course on the same topic as a faculty member at William Jewell College. He suggested I might be better served if I picked three or four theories or theorists that I would like to understand more fully. With his approval of the list, we agreed that I would pursue my interests in each one independent of the class. I was on my own. When I felt I had enough understanding of a theory or theorist, we would have a private, extended conversation in his office. What an experience that proved to be! There were no written reports or exams; just three conversations with him. I am confident that I invested more time in research and study in preparing for those sessions than I would have ever invested in a routine class setting, even at this graduate level. The student was as alive as he was ever going to be, and a teacher was readily at hand. I had traveled a long way in the few years since Dr. Newport's philosophy of religion class at Southwestern Seminary.

Heavy Demand of My Personal Life—Along with my changing professional role and my new commitment to graduate studies, the third area of my life demanding energy and time, pushing even farther back in my mind any real understanding of the retreat experience with Dr. Martin, was altogether personal, my marriage. My first wife and I were raised to believe that "marriages are made in heaven" and marriage is "until death do us part." Divorces in our extended families were few. We had been married for fifteen years and had three remarkable children.

We had invested considerable time and energy over the previous five years trying to gain a fuller understanding of any hurtful gaps and differences that existed between us and how they might be moderated or relieved. The period included seeking professional help as well as conversations with close, trusted colleagues and friends. No one, to my knowledge, among our larger families, parents or siblings, had any awareness of our struggles. We divorced in 1973. From then to now we both have lived our lives in such a way as to limit, as much as possible, any hurtful impact on our children from the dissolution of our marriage.

It was not until writing this document that I would make the connection, connect the dots as it were, that I was as much impacted by my father's style of living as I was by my mother's spoken maxims! I came to understand that Dad's quietude was at least as potent a force, if not more, in the emergence of my sense of self as anything spoken by Mom. Dr. Martin and the workshop had been the teacher; the student, while there, had not been fully available—yet.

What I came to understand was that Mom's dominance in our family was in great part traceable to Dad's reluctance to challenge, publicly at least, her or her ideas, or assert his own. Dad was physically strong. His arms and back were muscular. As teenagers, Mom could always get our understanding and cooperation with the threat, "If you don't [whatever she wanted us to do or stop doing], I am going to tell your dad when he comes home." It unfailingly got her what she wanted.

Important Life Lessons from Training in Counseling and Psychology

In general understanding—Four main areas of study ranged from looking at 1) the realm of the unconscious; 2) the behavioral stimulus-response-reward theory; 3) the pure conscious rationale of human beings; and 4) the new Gestaltists and Existentialists.

During this eight-year period, I:

• was exposed to the theories of psychoanalysis of Freud, Reich, Adler, Jung, and disciples; the behaviorism theories of Pavlov, Skinner, and disciples; the humanism theories of Maslow, Rogers, Ellis, May, and disciples; the work of Gestaltists, particularly Fritz Perls; and clever blendings of some earlier ideas like the Transactional Analysis work of Berne and Harris; and the studies in neurolinguistics put forth by Bandler and Grinder.

• participated in workshops and conferences led by Carl Rogers, Albert Ellis, Rollo May, and Virginia Satir.

• became aware that the purists of each theory were not too unlike the spokespeople of the various religious perspectives I had experienced and witnessed. Freudians, Adlerians, Jungians, Rogerians, behaviorists, et al., had core beliefs and basic practices they believed to be right or best.

• realized that the extent of my education and understanding lay primarily in my own hands, driven more by my own level of curiosity than in the hands of my teachers and instructors. I became the opposite of my first impressions of life and learning. When the student is ready (curious and wants to understand) the teacher(s) does, in fact, come.

• learned how to listen to others for the sole purpose of understanding, including listening to the voice(s) in my own head. This includes the words that come through my ears when others are speaking and those that come through my eyes when I am reading. At all levels of my life, this skill, this understanding, this insight, has proven itself to have the most far-reaching consequences. No aspect of living has been left untouched by it. Its impact on me is as potent today as it was from its outset. It has been, and continues to be, like riding an emotional roller coaster of ups and downs, highs and lows, wins and losses, and joys and sorrows. So much so, I now treasure a quote attributed to Mark Twain. "It ain't what you don't know that gets you into trouble. It's what you know that just ain't so." In a binary world, there are only two positions—right or wrong/good or bad. In such a world, as a product of my culture, my family, my church, my school, my college, and my seminary; I came to believe that I knew (Twain) the right and good. In that state of mind, I accrued considerable attention and appreciation from those who helped train me as well as from the churches that engaged me as a spokesperson. I was seen as someone who was doing an outstanding job. While I may not have always put the right thoughts and behaviors into practice, I was certain I knew what they were. As a consequence, I fell into a communication/relationship hellhole with no awareness that I had done so.

On the whole, I routinely confused my keeping quiet while another was talking with listening; my asking, "What do you think about …?" with wanting to understand what another's thoughts might be; my asking manipulative questions as if they were honest inquiries: "Have you ever considered? Are you sure you've thought this through? Is that what you really think?" Let me resurrect two earlier anecdotes and add a third.

First, beginning at the 1957 Youth-Led Revival in Houston and the young girl from Atlanta who responded to a comment by her friend, with "You don't really believe all that stuff do you?" I still recall being stunned and the uncomfortable emotions I experienced from simply overhearing the comment. She, as far as I could discern, was not attacking or ridiculing anything or anyone, particularly me. She simply seemed genuinely incredulous that anyone could believe such ideas as those expressed in my sermon. At that time, however, I was completely incapable of considering ideas other than my own—or more accurately, those I had been taught and incorporated as my own. All I had at that moment was a deep sense of disquietude!

In many ways, in terms of my own understanding of myself, this story carries great weight, when paired with the "What do YOU think Harles?" story from my days at Park Cities Baptist in Dallas. What did I think—really?

Second, recall the palpable sense of loss I experienced at the funeral of my friend Rod Beasley, in 1976. The sense of loss was driven primarily by the realization that our friendship needn't have taken the turn it did, with each of us knowing virtually nothing about the other's life as husband, father, soldier, or -preacher.

For all practical purposes our friendship hit its ceiling in the spring of 1957, the same year the young woman from Atlanta found some of my pulpit comments incredulous. In Rod's case, there had been no reason for me to listen to him when talking about Martha. I had heard enough to "know for sure" that what he was doing was wrong. I wanted him to know what I knew. So I told him! The damage was done. I think Rod, at some level, may have understood that I was incapable of considering, much less understanding and supporting, some areas of his life. From that point on, he simply kept those to himself. One of those was the growth and development of his family. I will always be the poorer for that loss.

To introduce the third anecdote, I need to bring the first two forward to 2005 and more thoughtful days. I was present for the graveside burial service of my younger brother, Jamie. He died of liver cancer on March 4 in Houston at the age of sixty-seven. His body was laid to rest in Corrine Cemetery, a country cemetery outside our hometown of Jacksonville. He joined five generations of family members who were already buried there. The church was filled with family and friends from across many years. Two ministers officiated. In their remarks, they chose contradictory passages of scripture, and I am confident that few in the audience, if any, noticed. Each scripture choice enjoys popular usage at funerals.

One is a reference to the scene surrounding the story of Jesus's crucifixion when a fellow victim was reassured by Jesus with the words, "Today shalt thou be with me in paradise!" (Luke 23:43). The idea that believers, at death, are immediately taken to heaven to be with God/Jesus and other loved ones is a strong one.

The other minister's remarks were centered on the hope for a safe future that believers enjoy at death, as opposed to those who die with no hope. In doing so, he cited the passage from 1 Thessalonians 4:16f where the writer declares, "For the Lord himself shall descend from heaven with a shout, with the voice of the archangel, and with the trump of God: and the dead in Christ shall rise first: Then we which are alive and remain shall be caught up together with them in the clouds, to meet the Lord in the air; and so shall we ever be with the Lord. Wherefore comfort one another with these words." The idea that Jesus rose from the dead three days following his crucifixion, that he comforted his followers for forty days, that he bodily ascended into heaven, and that he would return again to the earth in the same fashion at a future point to claim all believers living and dead is also a strong one.

As I listened to the ministers, I could not help but notice that the writer of 1 Thessalonians 4:14-16, even though his work was written nearly two thousand years ago, seemed to feel that he would be among the living at the time of Jesus's return. I was also reminded of a third strongly held idea among believers regarding end times, particularly a singular judgment day when all living beings, past and present will stand before God before a final decision regarding where he or she would spend all eternity. Though there are numerous references to a final judgment day throughout the Bible; passages from the Gospel of Matthew and the book of Revelation are enough to illustrate.

Matthew 25:31f states:
When the Son of man shall come in his glory, and all the holy angels with him, then shall he sit upon the throne of his glory; and before him shall be gathered all nations; and he shall separate them one from another, as a shepherd divideth his sheep from the goats; and he shall set the sheep on his right hand, but the goats on the left. Then shall the King say unto them on his right hand, Come, ye blessed of my Father, inherit the kingdom prepared for you from the foundation of the world; Then shall he say also unto them on the left hand, Depart from me, ye cursed, into everlasting fire, prepared for the devil and his angels; And these shall go away into everlasting punishment; but the righteous into life eternal.

Revelations 21:12f states:

And I saw the dead, small and great, stand before God; and the books were opened; and another book was opened, which is the book of life; and the dead were judged out of those things which were written in the books, according to their works. And the sea gave up the dead which were in it; and death and hell delivered up the dead which were in them; and they were judged every man according to their works. And death and hell were cast into the lake of fire. This is the second death. And whosoever was not found written in the book of life was cast into the lake of fire.

I tie the happenings of Jamie's burial service to the experiences in Houston with the young woman from Atlanta and Rod's funeral for one reason. In 1957, I was completely convinced that anything and everything in the Bible was absolutely true. At one point, I too, had believed everything each minister was claiming. Each idea had to be true because the Bible was God's Holy Word! There was no questioning that conclusion. I was living my life based on that faith. Like the two ministers at the burial, I feel completely confident that I could easily have made any number of statements and claims in my sermons that were exaggerated, illogical, and even contradictory without the slightest sense that I was doing so. In that context, the comment, "You don't really believe all that stuff, do you?" seems somewhat kind. And Rod's keeping of so much personal information from me was a wise thing for him to do. In 1957, what I knew for sure was too strong for me to hear any other ideas for consideration.

In this same vein, another incident with brother Jamie further underscores the communication/relationship hellhole into which I had fallen. The incident has remained a painful reminder of the price I paid for believing that I knew for sure right from wrong and good from bad.

Jamie's athletic experiences especially in basketball, greatly exceeded mine. In 1955, his senior year in high school, he and his teammates won the Texas State High School Basketball Championship for Division II-A. At season's end, he was selected as one of the top five players in his division to the All-State First Team. Second and Third Team selections were announced at the same time. Our family was proud, his teammates were proud, our town was proud! It was Jacksonville's first ever state championship in any team sport. Banners still hang from the ceiling in the current high school gymnasium honoring the team, the coach, and Jamie.

That spring any number of calls from colleges and universities offering full scholarships to come play basketball for them came his way. I was particularly impressed with two—the University of Houston and the University of Kentucky. Both were led by men who were on the path to becoming legendary coaches—Guy Lewis at Houston and Adolph Rupp at Kentucky.

For reasons that were not clear to me, surprisingly, he opted to remain in Jacksonville and play for our local junior college, Lon Morris College, a two-year Methodist liberal arts school. I remember teasing him when together at family gatherings as a "Momma's boy who didn't want to venture too far from home." He seemed to enjoy his Lon Morris choice and had an experience very similar to that of high school. In his second year, Lon Morris won the Junior College National Basketball Championship and Jamie was named as a First Team All-American player. Once again, the family was proud, the team was proud, and our hometown was proud.

For the second time in his post-high school career, Jamie was flooded with scholarship offers from four-year schools to finish out his career. The offers included repeats from Houston and Kentucky. And as before, he opted for a less heralded school, Texas Wesleyan College (TWC) in Fort Worth. TWC was in the NAIA and a member of the Big State Conference, the same as my alma mater, East Texas Baptist College. Though I do not recall any distinctions associated with basketball in his time in Fort Worth, once again he seemed to enjoy himself. He graduated in 1959 with a bachelor's degree and a teaching certificate in secondary education for the State of Texas.

Following college, he married a classmate, Nelda Herring. The two of them, until retirement, lived out their years as professionals in the world of Texas Public Schools teaching and coaching. Jamie also became an active member of the Southwest Basketball Officials Association. They gave birth, and lovingly cared for, two sons victimized by cystic fibrosis. The youngest died at 16. The oldest survived a lung transplant and lived until age 32.

For the four decades from the sixties to the nineties, Jamie and I were together on scores of occasions that bring family members together—vacations, holidays, birthdays, reunions, marriages, and funerals. No contact across all those years, however, would have the lingering impact of one that occurred in the last months of his life.

Toward the end of 2004, the severity of the liver cancer, from which he would eventually die, was known. Early in 2005 it became very important for me to spend time with him. By then my business was such that my work schedule was completely within my control. He, spouse Nelda, and I found a few-day stretch in which I was welcomed for a visit in their home in Pasadena, the suburb of Houston where they had lived the bulk of their married lives. It was our last time together.

Jamie's stamina was limited. An early bedtime and at least one extended nap was required each day. Even so, the three of us stayed busy. We ate our meals together, usually at home. We participated in a daily small group session with others who were exploring alternative methods for dealing with cancer. Two old Jacksonville friends, mentioned earlier, Burr Davis and Charlie Brazil, managed to drop by for a quick front yard visit.

Mostly what Jamie and I did was talk. Nelda was often included, but she had other things to do, and I suspect she just wanted to leave us be. And talk we did. After all we had sixty-plus years of shared stories of childhood, parents, grandparents, relatives, siblings, homes, schools, friends, athletics, kids, life, and death from which to draw. One story stood out above all others.

It started out with Jamie saying, "You never did know why I decided to stay at Lon Morris to play ball did you?" My laughing response was something like it had always been, "You mean beyond hanging onto Mom's apron strings?" We both laughed. Then he said, "That's okay, not many people do." And he began to tell me—and what a story it was!

The essence of it was simple. Some local businessmen, fans of Lon Morris, made him an offer he couldn't refuse. The offer included a monthly stipend for personal spending. It was good for as long as he stayed at the college. It also included access to a car on the weekends if one was needed for being with friends or dating. The car simply had to be requested, picked up at the lot, and returned when the weekend was over. I was amazed! Citizens of our little hometown doing what they could to encourage one of its gifted athletes to stay close by. Those were different times from today's more tightly regulated collegiate sports.

In the midst of my total surprise, Jamie quickly added a comment regarding the basketball coach of Lon Morris, a name I knew well. Moments after the announcement was made public, the coach indicated how happy he was to have Jamie on his team. He also made it clear that, "Under no circumstances do I ever want to know the reasons why you chose us." Jamie never told him. And while I am sure many shared my own astonishment at the 1955 choice, I don't recall Jamie ever offering any explanation beyond, "It's what I wanted to do." As far as I could tell, the entire episode remained between my brother and the businessmen. I am confident that our parents were also among those that didn't know. How Jamie managed the money in an unnoticed manner remains a mystery. With modern eyes, this would clearly be against the rules, but it was a more common practice at that time.

The story did not end there. "What about TWC? Why there?" I asked. Jamie's response was something like, "You knew I never really cared much for school, right?" "Right," I said. "What I enjoyed big time was playing ball and hanging out with my friends." He went on to explain how easy some of the courses he took at Lon Morris had been, how helpful fellow students were, and how forgiving many of his teachers had been when class expectations conflicted with the demands of traveling and playing on behalf of the school.

Texas Wesleyan, like Lon Morris, was a liberal arts college owned and operated by Methodists. In a manner not altogether clear to me, the college's basketball coach became knowledgeable of Jamie's love for the game and his apprehensions around the need to perform as a student. The coach promised the college's full support to assist in the process. Support included academic guidance, personal tutoring, and a scholarship that included summer school participation. It was a process, and it led to the bachelor's degree in education and a Texas teaching certificate.

I loved the story. I experienced it as human and real and, apart from his spouse and sons, it had touched upon one of the most important dimensions of his life. In many ways, it had been his secret. To be let in on it, I felt honored, flattered in a weird sort of way. He seemed glad to now have his brother as a part of the story. Interestingly, this exchange occurred toward the front end of my visit, and it was never mentioned again. We had other stories to tell, other subjects to cover.

A question I am left with is a simple one. Why did Jamie want to tell me about this experience? Or better yet, why was he willing to tell me at this time and not at any other point across the fifty years since it all started out? It wasn't as if he was confessing something. We were more like brothers getting caught up to date with each other after a period of separation. And after he had told me, that element of the catch up was complete.

The answer I give myself to the why now question is equally simple. At that moment in 2005, all I cared about was knowing him, being with him, being known by him. Whatever he wanted to share with me was great by me. I think at some important level Jamie understood that and felt similarly. We did a lot of sharing.

I think Jamie knew me well enough in 1955, like Rod in 1957, to know that I was incapable of respectfully listening to his experiences with sympathetic affection and understanding. It would never have occurred to me that Jamie would have had thoughts, feelings, and preferences of his own that were guiding his decisions. He didn't need, or want, anyone else to tell him how he should live his life, especially someone as self-righteously blind as I.

In my born-again life, I had finished college and seminary. Within the church, I served as an evangelist, a pastor, a student chaplain, a denominational executive, an assistant pastor, and chapel dean. I had been married and fathered two children. Jamie knew me well.

In my life after the end of being born again, I had fathered a third child, become divorced after fifteen years, and married a second time. A marriage that has lasted for forty-nine years. I had worked as a counselor, a college professor, a psychologist, a management trainer, a consultant, and an executive coach. And, throughout all the experiences and lessons learned in those years, one conclusion stands out above all others. To live, work, or coexist with other human beings successfully, success by any definition, requires at its base a respectful understanding of their feelings, thoughts, and actions. I would also argue that the more important a person is to your sense of wellbeing, be it spouse, partner, child, parent, sibling, relative, boss, or colleague, the more respectful understanding becomes. And how does one get to that place? By learning to listen to him or her for the sole purpose of more clearly understanding!

Important Lessons from Interpersonal Skills

(At the end of this PART III discussion, there is a list of books and authors I found to be the most insightful.)

• How to face/attack/discuss the problems and issues of our lives without attacking the persons with whom we are having the issues and problems. And the reverse—how to get beyond what is intended as a personal attack from others to understand the issues and problems that have provoked the discussion.

• Once a person thinks he/she knows something, it is the end of curiosity and learning in that area. Once a person feels he/she knows him/herself, it is the end of personal growth and development. In my own mind, I was Exhibit A. I had felt so certain of my original beliefs about life and living that the curiosity and questioning of ideas for learning and growing were profoundly squelched.

• Personal growth/learning/development/change/insight (this phenomenon goes under innumerable descriptors) almost always includes a process of unlearning and relearning. "Once I was blind, but now I can see," says the Bible. And, as far as I can determine at this time, the process is unending.

• Life can only be lived in the present moment; the past is gone, and future is not yet.

• Assertiveness is an attitude, a state of mind, and it is called into being at the intersection between egoism (concern for oneself) and altruism (concern for others), and a clear choice is required. The assertive person, depending on the circumstances at hand, may choose either to act in his/her own interest or defer and act in the interest of another—being accountable for, and accepting the consequences of whatever choice is made is another equally important consideration.

Connecting the Most Important Dots of a Lifetime

As my life unfolded, it was the combination of the development of the first two techniques (listening for the sole purpose of understanding and learning how to separate the issues involved in a conflict from the persons with whom we are experiencing the conflict), along with the shift in attitudes and beliefs to support their validity, that would provide the couplings that brought the disparate parts of my life to something approximating a coherent whole. Beginning first with the self-deception that seemed so apparent to classmates in Neil Willis's class in social psychology at the beginning of my graduate school training in psychology. Next in line was the powerful drive to want to be genuinely helpful to my counseling clients from the very beginning. There was also a coming to understand and appreciate the profound significance of the dad experience at Dr. Martin's retreat, and finally, coming fully to appreciate the advantages of orthogonal or side-door learning until I could find the front door of my own interests and desires.

Regarding the self-deception: It seems to me now that I was wanting things for myself that might have been considered a breach of several of my mom's maxims ("be good, be nice, don't get too big for your britches"). It seems frighteningly strange to me now that I could have tied an interest in wanting to learn and understand more about life and living to something wrong or sinful. But, I did.

How did I manage to get around the cautions and restrictions? Unknowingly at the time, by the same side-door or orthogonal way I learned to compete, train, and win over opponents as an athlete in high school and college. I was doing it all for someone(s) other than me. In athletics, it had been for the good of the team, the town, the college. As a counselor, therapist, trainer, and coach, I was doing it for the sake of clients, their families, customers, and for the corporations and organizations that hired me. I genuinely did want to be helpful to them. I also wanted to be considered thoughtful and effective as a professional. I just couldn't see at the time that those areas in which I was viewed as being the most helpful were the very ones in which I was the most needful.

How did the retreat experience regarding my dad and my tearfully expressed thought that "Just once, I wish he had stood up for himself!" fit in? The fullness of my understanding took years. It proved to be the most intricate and convoluted of all my childhood and cultural influences. It was not unlike the old expression: "It's a lot like peeling an onion: it comes apart one layer at a time and sometimes you cry!"

I mentioned earlier that my father was physically strong. His hands were coarse and rough. I also mentioned how my mother could instantly bring order to her children, if they were being too rowdy by simply saying, "If you children don't stop, I am going to tell your father when he comes home." The risk of punishment from Dad was not worth continuing any activity.

"How could that be?" is a fair question. It is especially pertinent if one adds to this mix that Dad was considered both inside and outside our family a kind, generous, and even gentle man. I offer two insights and an anecdote from one of his later years—an event that occurred after we children were all grown and gone.

I have only one memory of my father physically punishing me. I remember the setting and the house with crystal clarity. Knowing the house, 122 Alton Street, Lufkin, Texas, means I was in junior high school in either the seventh or eighth grade, twelve or thirteen years old. The family moved back to Jacksonville in time for my ninth grade.

It was suppertime. The three daily meals of my childhood were breakfast, dinner, and supper. Our family was gathered at a round table in the dining room. I had been teasing Jamie before being called to supper and was continuing to do so after we were seated. I am confident that I was told to stop and "behave yourself." I didn't completely and immediately stop. My father, in an instant, rose from his chair enough to reach across the table, and hit me with the back of his hand across the side of my head. He struck me with enough force to send me and the chair in which I was sitting over backwards to the floor.

I think the shock of the experience was greater than any pain I may have experienced. It became an indelible memory. My father meant what he said, and he was not inclined to repeat himself! And, although the incident may seem harsh, even brutal to some, I never felt it as such. I am absolutely comfortable with the thought that his own life circumstances were so pressurized that in this brief moment he simply lost his temper and was for a brief moment, out of control. As I am writing about this incident, I am aware that the story's hold on me, or my hold on it, is dramatically reduced from what it was for years.

The story still begs the question of my father's profound influence on my own thoughts and behaviors that were brought to the surface at Dr. Martin's retreat. To understand that required more looking. Part of the answer lies with a non-verbal pattern of how my father dealt with us children when our behavior around him was moving toward an unacceptable place, and we were in a position where we could both see and hear him. Just like my mother, Dad had his own non-verbal, but clear signals of annoyance.

If we were out of his sight, in another part of house, Mom could bring correction by simply coming to the door and saying something like, "If you kids don't stop, your father is going to come in here." Dad was also known to come by the door, tap on it, and say something like, "Don't make me have to come in there!" That would be sufficient to correct anything that was going on. Arguing or talking back was not accepted. In Dad's case, it had to do with respecting authority. Mom could pile on and make it even more unacceptable because it was neither "nice" nor "good" to do such a thing.

His non-verbal communication pattern, when he needed to correct us, was twofold. One was a facial expression. There was a look about him, a tilt of his head, a sideways glance at you that conveyed what I would describe as a look of annoyance. The other was a sound that he made with his teeth and tongue, a clicking sound. It is a sound that I can imitate to this day but find it hard to describe in writing. The expression "Tsk! TSK!!" comes close to capturing the sense and intent of the sound. The sound he made had two quick parts, similar in nature, with a slightly sharper emphasis on the second part. Bottom line, if one saw the look or heard the clicking, you stopped immediately whatever was going on, and the tension would quickly dissipate. And commonly, after several minutes had passed, the whole sense of warning and discomfort had passed, too.

These two ways Dad had of dealing with frustration and anger could show themselves if we were traveling by car as a family. We children in the back seat needed only to keep an eye out for a quick turn of his head to look back at us or watch the rearview mirror carefully. There was frequently too much noise associated with auto travel to hear any clicking sounds. Obviously in my dinner table story, I clearly did not see the look, nor did I hear any clicking!

During a family gathering around either Thanksgiving or Christmas, my spouse and children were with me for a visit with my parents. The family visits were almost always tied to a holiday period. Dad's brother-in-law had come over to our house. He and Dad's sister lived in West Texas, making frequent times together with them difficult. So when they dropped by, it seemed pretty special.

Through the years, he and Dad had often spent some visiting time together. Mostly their visits would center on outings for hunting or fishing. As they grew older, the visits often involved the remembering and retelling of some of those early outings. This was one of those occasions. I have no recollection how this story came to light. It was one I had never heard either from Dad or Uncle T. L., or T-Bone, as he was known among Dad's siblings. I remember that it was told as something funny— weird, but funny. They were both laughing as they remembered it. I wish I could recall at what point in Dad's life the event had occurred. I was only aware that I was now older, more thoughtful, and was hearing about a revelatory event, a window to a deeper understanding of my dad.

It was a deer hunting story. The two of them, along with six other men, had made their way to a hunting lodge deep in East Texas. The lodge had a program designed to accommodate a maximum of eight hunters per session. The number of hunters was set by the fact that there were eight different deer stands spread over several hundred acres of heavily wooded land. A stand was a small elevated and camouflaged tree house. There was an opening on each of its four sides to allow the hunter who occupied it to see and shoot in all directions. The elevation allowed for an extended range of vision. The day began, as T. L.

told the story, with the two of them arriving at the lodge around sunup. Breakfast had been prepared by the owner, and while eating, the guest hunters heard the ground rules by which they were expected to abide. On a large map, the eight stands were located. Each one was separated from the others by several acres of land. Ponds, creeks, and springs—the sources of water on the acreage—were pointed out. As a safety feature, the hunters were instructed to stay either in the tree house or in its immediate area only. Everyone was warmly dressed, and each was provided a large thermos of hot coffee and a sack lunch. Three or four jeeps were waiting outside to take them to the stands. T.L. said, "We were told they would be back at sundown to pick us up and would help if we had killed anything." At the end of the day, the pick-up occurred. Three of the hunters had been successful in shooting a deer.

The drama of the story began when T.L. returned to the lodge and did not see Dad. He went to the owner and asked, "Where's Ray?" As T.L. said, "Then all hell broke loose." Somehow Dad's stand was overlooked in the pick-up process. By the time the owner could send someone back to get him, it was nearly two hours after sundown. Dad had long since run out of coffee, food, and patience. T. L. said, "I was really relieved to see him finally come through that front door!" The comment was meant to be the end of the story. We, of course, all wanted to know what happened between sundown and when they finally came to get him. "Not much," was about all Dad had to say about it. "I just sat there trying to stay warm. They just kept apologizing over and over when they finally came to get me."

Later that night, and long after T. L. had returned to his own family, Dad and I were alone in the kitchen. I commented on what an amazing story I thought it was and that I couldn't begin to understand what it must have been like to sit in that cold blind for so long. I added, "I can't believe you didn't have some

strong words to say to the owner when you finally got back."
Dad paused long enough for me to sense that the story may have
stirred some old feelings. Then he said, "Hoddy, I was afraid if I
said anything at all I might have killed him!"

There was something about the way he said it that touched me
deeply. He was giving me some very important information about
himself. It was as if he was trapped within two options, keep
silent or risk physical violence. While I don't believe he would
intentionally kill the man, I do believe that he was fearful of what
might happen if he lost his temper and struck the man. Simply
telling the owner of his annoyance and anger at being forgotten
did not exist as an option. Neither did asking for an explanation,
waiting to hear, before deciding what action to take next. I could
eventually understand that what might have happened on the
deer hunt was not too different in basic dynamics from what did
happen all those years ago when he slapped me away from our
supper table.

His studied comment in answer to my question ended up being
one of the most helpful insights I would ever have regarding
the range of behaviors open to us human beings under the
pressure of stress and conflict. I was interested in how one,
including me, might think, feel, and act when frustrated, hurt,
and angry because of such an experience. I became particularly
interested in learning about the attitudes and skills required to
attack the issues without attacking the person(s), physically or
verbally, with whom we are engaged. When communicating with
others, I came to understand the difference between making
an observation and expressing an opinion, between describing
an experience and judging it, between speaking of facts and
speaking of feelings. The more I genuinely wanted to help others
with the development of these skills, the more those skills showed
themselves in my own relationships.

To summarize, here is how I finally came to understand the dynamic of conflict management within our family. My mother's approach was to be nice, remain as pleasant as possible, and hope any existing tensions would subside or go away. Within the family, she would remind us to be nice and if we failed to do so, she would say, "You should be ashamed of yourself" for the failure. My dad's basic approach was to stay silent, to be quiet. He tended to not say anything. Within the family, his glance—and teeth and tongue clicking—was enough to take charge. I have almost no information regarding how he managed the frustrations and conflicts that arose between him and other people. The deer hunting story seemed to provide a bit of a window to understanding, however.

As an aside, I was aware from childhood days that Dad suffered from stomach ulcers. Milk of Magnesia was always in the bathroom medicine cabinet. Peptic ulcers had been the medical diagnosis that made him an unacceptable candidate for military service during World War II. In my early graduate school days, when discussions would occur connecting mind to body and body to mind, I would often think of Dad. I found myself wondering if his reluctance to speak out about anything that might be eating on him meant the difficulties remained in to do their eating. I would also wonder if there were incidents of fighting in his youth that had led to violence.

My parents' styles of dealing with differences, taken together, made it easier to understand how my mom's proud boast, "Your dad and I never had an argument in front of you children," could actually have a lot of substance. If she was ever upset with Dad over thoughts and actions that differed from hers, what could she possibly have done or said in front of us? And conversely, if Dad was ever upset with her over similar differences, what was he going to do beyond being quiet?

When I left home in 1953 to go to college, I was armed with two extremely powerful behavior traits for dealing with any difficulties that might come my way. I knew how to be nice. I also knew how to keep my thoughts to myself, to be quiet. Any additional alternatives I would have to discover on my own. It proved to be a challenging and bumpy process.

Finally, as a counselor and therapist I was considered the most helpful by those clients who were trying to cope with any forces— people or circumstances— that threatened their own sense of happiness and wellbeing. I was especially alert to those who felt that nothing they could say or do seemed to make any difference at all; those who felt they were alone in facing their problems; and those who wanted suggestions and or support for efforts to make things better. In other words, I had a great eye for those who were having life experiences very similar to my own. My later time as a management trainer, an organizational consultant in leadership and teamwork, and an executive coach was but an extension of the same phenomenon. What seems remarkable to me now is how passionately I wanted to be of help to others, how devoted I was to searching for ideas and methods to do and be so for them, with scarcely any awareness that all the while I was seeking understanding and healing for myself.

There were numerous and wonderful teachers available for ideas, insights, and methods to assist me in helping others. Here are but a few that come quickly to mind. Books included:

How to be an Assertive (Not Aggressive) Woman by Jean Baer; the work of Thomas Gordon, particularly *PET & LET (Parent Effectiveness Training and Leader Effectiveness Training); The Intimate Enemy: How to Fight Fair in Love and Marriage* by George Bach; *People Skills* by Robert Bolton; *Working With Emotional Intelligence* by Daniel Goleman; *The Leadership Challenge* by Kouzes & Postner; *Leadership and the New Science* by Margaret Wheatley; *Mistakes Were Made (But Not By Me)* by Carol Tavris; *Brain and Culture* by Bruce Wexler; *The Developing Mind* by Daniel Siegle; *The Last Word on Power* by Tracy Goss; *Getting to Yes by Fisher & Ury; Thinking, Fast & Slow* by Daniel Kahneman; *Your Brain at Work* by David Brock; and *The Righteous Mind: Why People Are Divided by Religion and Politics* by Jonathan Haidt.

There were also numerous journal articles, conferences, seminars, and symposia to read or attend devoted solely to personal understanding and skill development for managing conflicts in one's personal and professional life.

Two other comments regarding the impact of studies in counseling and psychology seem worth noting: For one, the earlier referenced specific skills, techniques, and observations became the foundation for a thirty-year career in leadership development, management training, consulting, and executive coaching. They simply lived under a slightly different umbrella— one that embraced such subjects as effective communication, conflict management, team building, decision making, and strategic planning. The orthogonal, side-door learning had become a front-door way of living and working.

The other, my general interest in this field has currently morphed into a highly specific area of focus, the biology of the brain. Interest in the various theories of personality (i.e., analysts, behaviorists, humanists, and existentialists, and their impact on human understanding) has shifted to all things neurological—neurobiology, neurochemistry, neurophysics, and neuropsychology. The student is as curious as ever and teachers are ubiquitous!

PART IV

Chapter 11

MY SOUTHERN CULTURE

My resignation from the staff of William Jewell College in the mid-1970s took two attempts to complete. In the spring of 1974, I indicated to my boss, the vice president of student affairs, that I intended to resign as the director of counseling and testing at semester's end. He knew I was interested in expanding a marriage and family counseling practice, Northland Counseling Center, which a college colleague and I had begun three years earlier and which mostly was restricted to evenings and weekends. He also knew that I had, on a few occasions, provided training seminars for business, professional, and government groups. This was another area of work that I enjoyed and was being encouraged to expand.

During our conversation, I was taken completely by surprise when he inquired, "Are there any conditions under which you might be willing to stay?" I was so flattered I eventually responded with, "I don't know. Let me think about it." The experience wasn't too different from the one ten years earlier at Park Cities Church. This was also an early glimpse into the possibility that an employer might consider me of higher value to the organization than I would have.

Since my future plans imagined my continuing to live in Liberty and each of my new interests was in its infancy, a different transition plan did have the attraction of letting me proceed. My contract with the College, like those of all administrative staff, had been on an annual basis. We agreed first that I would proceed with a nine-month contract (more typical of the contracts of the teaching faculty). However, rather than three months off in the summer, I could use up to three days a month off throughout the year for the emerging consulting and training business. The Northland Counseling Center would continue to have a late afternoon, evening, and weekend focus. This approach to managing my time would govern my last year as an employee of William Jewell College. The ten years there were filled with many engaging and challenging experiences. Not only do the memories remain strong, but many friendships and associations, with both students and faculty, that began there survive to this day.

I know now that what I was on the cusp of experiencing, in many ways, was a lot like another birth. Separating that change into something so dramatic for these writings felt at first like I was taking a step too far. It seemed more of an outgrowth of the first two (my birth and "rebirth" when I was "born again"). However, with time, it has proven to be an awakening with the broadest impact on how I perceive and live my life. The student was very much alive. Teachers remained everywhere. And it all started under the most ordinary of circumstances.

One aspect of the new business role of management training provided the groundwork for a triggering agent in my personal evolution. Fred Pryor Seminars, a management training company specializing in day-long training seminars, open to the public, was founded in 1970, and located in Kansas City. It quickly grew in value and size to become national in scope. Within a few short years, the company was providing business-related training seminars in dozens of the major cities in the U.S., including Alaska and Hawaii.

For those of us who were engaged from the early days, the biggest change centered on the travel demands required to meet the company's increased popularity. It was not uncommon to lead two to four seminars in a week and in as many cities, two to four weeks per month. It was both exciting and fatiguing. The time, physical, and emotional demands were such that I gradually removed myself from Northland Counseling.

I was not one who could sleep comfortably on plane rides from city to city. Reading became my number one way to relax and manage the travel time between assignments. I became enamored with one topic in particular, the U.S. Civil War. Over the next thirty years, that interest would morph specifically into a focus as much, or even more, on the historian as the history itself.

It all began with Michael Shaara's book *The Killer Angels*. I particularly enjoyed the character development and the personal and human side of key players on both sides of the Battle of Gettysburg, the focus of Shaara's work. The names of Lee, Longstreet, Stuart, Pickett, Armisted, Pettigrew, Buford, Reynolds, Hancock, Chamberlain, and Meade along with numerous others had my attention. In varying degrees, many of the names on the Southern side of the battle were familiar. Of those on the North, aside from brief references to Lincoln, I knew little. That quickly changed.

In the weeks, months, and years that followed, I discovered that no part of the entire American historical experience had received more attention than the Civil War. The work of popular historians like Catton, Foote, Pfanz, Trudeau, and McPherson became commonplace in my readings, along with dozens of others not so well known. My list of interesting characters grew quickly as well: Davis, Jackson, Hood, Forest, Beauregard, Johnston, Burnside, Grant, Sherman, Sheridan, Pemberton, Halleck, McClellan, and Rosecrans to mention a few. My critical focus eventually centered on Lincoln. Reflections on his life and times often led me back to my own experience in small town in East Texas.

My first serious exposure to anything directly regarding Lincoln came as a gift from the brother of a close friend in Liberty—*Lincoln: A Historical Novel*, by Gore Vidal. A few years later, and during a period in my work life when interest in all matters dealing with leadership was extremely high, I read Doris Kearns Goodwin's *A Team of Rivals*. Her discussions around the relationships among Secretary of the Treasury Salmon Chase, Attorney General Edward Bates, Secretary of State William Seward, and President Lincoln were riveting and proved to be of great value to me personally and professionally.

The apex of the Lincoln interest began in the fall of 2009 and lasted through all of 2010. It was centered in the ten-volume *Abraham Lincoln: A History*, by John G. Nicolay and John M. Hay. Nicolay was the personal secretary for Lincoln throughout his public career and Hay was Nicolay's personal assistant. Their work was published over a span of years from 1890 to 1894. By the time of their writing, they had access to not only all of the materials that had touched Lincoln directly, but also to the historical records of the Union and Confederacy, especially the Official War Records of 1861 that had been gathered and kept by the Library of Congress. The sheer volume of their work was dictated by thousands of reproduced documents (i.e., messages, notes, letters, proclamations, speeches, directives, and editorials). Most had been published somewhere. Some had been preserved but never published until they brought them to light.

The Davis Library of the University of North Carolina made available their original copies of all ten volumes for my reading in the building's upstairs study carrels. Turning the pages of books printed a hundred and twenty years earlier was exciting. It was also my first experience with a history and historians driven primarily by the presentations of the documents under consideration rather than a writer's interpretation of documents. Once again, the phenomenon of orthogonal or side-door learning would make its presence known.

I cite the following two examples. Each, in its own way, had significant impact on my broader born-again experience. This time, however, my shift in thinking was more associated with the culture in which my fundamentalist religion existed than with the religion itself.

Louis Wigfall (1816-1874)—First, the name of Louis Wigfall caught my eye. He was a U.S. Senator from Texas during the run-up to the Civil War. He was known as one of the southern Fire Eaters, a group of outspoken secessionists who strongly advocated for expansion and preservation of the Planter Society, an aristocratic social structure dependent on slave labor. Wigfall was born in South Carolina in 1816 and was buried in Galveston, Texas, in 1874.

His adult time in Texas was spent in the towns of Nacogdoches and Marshall. Nacogdoches, in East Texas, was only twenty miles from Lufkin, my hometown for much of my early years and was considered our archrival. Marshall, also in East Texas, was the home of East Texas Baptist College, the school where I spent my first four years preparing for the life of a Southern Baptist minister. My curiosity over his connection to two important towns of my youth was high. I began to search for more information about Wigfall. I felt again like a graduate student trying to do research that would be acceptable to a professor. Except in this case, I was both student and professor. I was deeply driven to discover whatever I could.

Following secession, and after the outbreak of the Civil War, Wigfall served briefly as a Brigadier General of the Texas Brigade. He moved on to the Senate of the Confederacy and eventually to the staff of Jefferson Davis. His early association with the Texas Brigade, one of the more noted brigades in the entire Confederate military, only added fuel to my curiosity fire. And like many earlier experiences, my curiosity in one area led to broader understandings in others. The front door of one idea led to the side door of another. I wasn't at all prepared for it.

Not only was I able to locate numerous historical discussions of Wigfall's actions before and during the Civil War and the Confederacy, but I also found connections to others even more directly involved in the history of Texas in this period. Specifically, there was his relationship to Sam Houston. As far as I could determine, Wigfall was best known in Texas for his pro-slavery attitude and for his vocal and written opposition to Houston.

Sam Houston (1793-1863)—The historical profile of the Sam Houston of my childhood and early student days was simple and direct—he was the Father of THE Republic of Texas. He was the hero of all things Texan. He defeated Santa Anna and his army at the Battle of San Jacinto, securing the independence of Texas from Mexico in April of 1836. He was immediately elected president of the new Republic and again in 1841. He led the Republic of Texas into becoming a state in the United States. I had seen the San Jacinto battlefield area and the monument to his memory. The largest city in the state had been named in his honor. It was the museum honoring him to which I had taken the bus of international students from the University of Houston. That, in a nutshell, was where my understanding and appreciation for Sam Houston started and ended. I had zero information regarding any connection he may have had to the Civil War and the Confederacy. "A coward and a traitor to Texas and the South" was what Wigfall had to say about Houston. I was shocked and startled when I first read those words. How could that possibly be?

As a U.S. Senator after Texas became a state in 1845 and as the governor in 1859, and in spite of his acceptance of slavery in general, Houston believed in preserving the Union. He opposed secession, and he refused to join the Confederacy. He was removed from office in 1861 after Texas voted to secede. He died in 1863 before he could know the war's eventual outcome. How could I have missed such noteworthy information about arguably the State's most important historical figure?

Spoiler Alert 8 - Racial Bias and Political Leadership

My education from first grade through seminary was crafted to enforce a specific view of Southern history, including omitting the role of the Southern Baptists in the Civil War.

~ ~ ~

Although from this distance I cannot be positive, my confidence is high that this information about Sam Houston was not included in public school Texas history books in my day. It may be available now, but it was not then. How could that have been? Why would that part of his life be omitted from the history of the state into which I had been born and which I loved? Was the history of Texas as I was taught it designed to help me understand my home state more fully? Or was it an interpretation of events, a story if you will, about events designed to express an already existing conclusion? My answers to these questions left me confused, disappointed, cheated, and bewildered. This was not the way things were supposed to be! This was not the way things could be.

Frederick Douglass (1818-1895)—The second shift in my thinking that was connected to readings dealing with the Civil War period had to do with African Americans in general and Frederick Douglass in particular. This one had a strong note of personal embarrassment, if not shame. And like the other broadening of understandings, it began by going through one door and coming out another.

Soon after arriving in North Carolina in 2009, and while deeply engaged in reading the Lincoln work of Nicolay and Hay, a person who became an extremely close friend, changed everything. Knowing of my interest in the Civil War, David Perry thought I might also want to know more about the role and place of my new resident state during that period and gifted me several books on the topic. David retired as editor-in-chief of UNC Press in 2013 where he had specialized in history and southern studies, with a special focus on the Civil War and military history. Combined, the books proved to be both broad and narrow in scope. Broad in the sense of looking at the State of North Carolina as a whole and narrow by looking at the Town of Chapel Hill specifically and the University of North Carolina in Chapel Hill. I quickly became familiar with the names of Clark, Manley, Vance, Holden, Pettigrew, Swain, Graham, Bragg, Pender, Hill, Polk, and Johnston; with the towns of Wilmington, New Bern, Bentonville, Goldsboro, Raleigh, and Durham; and with the historical sites of Roanoke Island, Fort Fisher, and Bennett Place.

Three books, in the order mentioned here, had the greatest personal impact, *Fire of Freedom*, by David Cecelski, *A Fool's Errand*, by Albion Tourgee, and *Pickett's Charge in History and Memory*, by Carol Reardon. Cecelski's book covered the life and times of Abraham Galloway, a slave born of an African mother and a White planter in 1837 in Brunswick County, North Carolina. During his life he lived and worked in Wilmington as a bricklayer; escaped to freedom on a boat bound for New Bern, North Carolina; served as a spy, a guide, and a recruiter for Union forces in the area; became known as an orator and activist for abolition as well as women's suffrage; had an audience with President Lincoln; and was elected the first Black senator in the state in 1868. He died unexpectedly in 1870 at the age of thirty-three. As far as can be determined, he could neither read nor write. I was literally amazed by his life, as I was by his times.

Fascination with Galloway quickly shifted to other African Americans, most specifically Frederick Douglass. Douglass, like Galloway, was born a slave. Also, like Galloway, he escaped his home in Baltimore to freedom in Philadelphia, Massachusetts, and New York. Unlike Galloway, he taught himself to read and write and would be noted for the oft-repeated statement, "Education is the pathway to freedom."

Douglass lived nearly three times as long as Galloway. During his lifetime, he became the most famous Black man in the Western world—a writer, a newspaper man, an orator of note, an abolitionist, a social reformer, a statesman, and a world traveler. He became the greatest counter example to slaveholder arguments that slaves lacked the intellectual capacity to function as independent American citizens. His first book, an autobiography, *Narrative of the Life of Frederick Douglass: An American Slave*, was particularly eye opening for me.

In most of his roles, he was often in contact with Abraham Lincoln, sometimes directly, sometimes as a friend and protagonist, sometimes as an antagonist. The two of them were the absolute embodiment of self-made men. They shared by pragmatic and personal experience that reason can only go so far and that power would concede nothing without a fight. So overlapping were their lives, times, and styles, John Stauffer wrote a biography entitled, *Giants: The Parallel Lives of Frederick Douglass and Abraham Lincoln.*

My sense of embarrassment, and even shame, regarding Douglass related to my childhood in East Texas. My hometown of Jacksonville was, of course, completely segregated. The N-word was a part of the everyday fabric. Both Whites and Blacks knew their place: where to eat, where to stand, where to sit in movies, where to drink water, where to attend school, and lived within those parameters. I attended Joe Wright Elementary School and Jacksonville High. Black students attended the segregated high school, Fred Douglass High.

The embarrassment? I was well into reading about the life and times of Douglass before I made the connection to the name on the Black high school. To my best recollection, I do not have a single childhood memory of either hearing or seeing the name *Frederick* associated with the school. From my current age and perspective, that a person of such profound significance and importance to the history of this country could have his name simplified and trivialized to such an extent in my hometown serves as tribute to the power of the historical stories a culture shares and tells to support its existence. I have often wondered what name was used by the parents, students, and teachers at the school when references to it were made. Were the Black kids taught any of the history of their school's namesake? Did they read any of his many writings?

The second of the three books that broadened and extended an understanding of the impact of the Civil War on my life was that of Albion Tourgee's, *A Fool's Errand by One of the Fools,* published in 1879. While the book was written as a fictional story, it mirrored the early adult years of the author. Born in Ohio in 1838, Tourgee grew up in Ohio and New York. He was attending the University of Rochester when the Civil War broke out in April 1861. In the war years, he served in the Union army and was wounded on two occasions. He was captured and spent from January to May 1863 in a Confederate prison in Richmond before being exchanged back to the Union. He was released from the Army in December 1863 because of health considerations resulting from his wounds, and he returned to Ohio. While there, he completed his law training and was granted his bar license. In 1866, for health, a warmer climate, and personal reasons, he moved to Greensboro, North Carolina, where he bought a nursery and began to practice law. Greensboro was his home for the next fifteen years—the years of Reconstruction that followed the Civil War.

During this period, he was extremely active in Republican politics, served as editor of the Union Register, represented Guilford County at the State's first Constitutional Convention following the war, served as a judge for the state's Seventh District Supreme Court from 1868 to 1874, was a champion of Black suffrage, advocated for equal civil and political rights for all people, and helped found Bennett College for young African American girls. In 1881, he returned to live in New York. It was a move primarily driven by an increasing fear for his life and that of his family's.

The impact on me of these two books, Cecelski's and Tourgee's, was the final unmasking of ideas of my religion and my East Texas Southern culture regarding the history of the Black race in the U.S. The probing that followed introduced me to a world about which I knew absolutely nothing. I would, however, over time, become somewhat familiar with Civil War cruelties to Blacks, specifically at Fort Pillow and the Crater, and more generally regarding their pay as soldiers, their risks as soldiers of the Union when captured, and a pervasive view, in both the North and the South, that their character, intelligence, and capabilities were suspect.

I also learned, beginning primarily with the era of Reconstruction and for decades to follow, of White on Black confrontations like massacres in Wilmington, North Carolina;

Colfax, Louisiana; Opelousas, Louisiana; Atlanta, Georgia; East Saint Louis, Illinois; Tulsa, Oklahoma; Rosewood, Florida; and Slocum, Texas. I read of the origins of the White supremacy movement and the Ku Klux Klan and an assortment of atrocities put upon any and all of the Black race, as well as anyone else who dared to speak in support of them. Of note was the discovery that my home state, and especially the section of the state in which I lived, ranked third in the nation for lynchings! It was exceeded only by Georgia and Mississippi. In Texas, between 1885 and 1942, there were 468 known lynchings—339 Blacks, 77 Whites, 53 Hispanics, and 1 Native American. There is no way of knowing how many there might have actually been.

All this taken together helped me understand the core attitudes and behaviors that drove my grandfather's response to my mother's desire to be a nurse. He forbade her to pursue a career that involved physical contact with a Black person.

Important Life Lessons from Readings Dealing with the U.S. Civil War
(The lessons learned from my life of religion
are essentially the same.)

The less one knows or understands, the easier it is to construct or believe a coherent story with limited facts. When I consider what I believed to be true about the Civil War as a child and young adult who had grown up in the South, especially when comparing those first ideas with what I discovered by extensive reading and study of the subject as an older adult, I struggle to find an adequate adjective to describe my emotions. Bewildered, shocked, embarrassed, and disappointed are never very far away in my thoughts.

With virtually no factual historical data, I believed our side, meaning we Southerners, had fought for a Noble Cause, had fought against Northern Aggressors who were out to destroy our way of life and living, and had fought for states' rights. In my mind, being a Texan only enhanced those distinctions. After all, we were champions of freedom from tyrants, were we not? Hadn't we proved our willingness to die for independence at the Alamo and San Jacinto?

And as for slavery, while a bit awkward in my mind, it still seemed to be in harmony with what was prescribed by God. It was a mystery that would be understood later in Heaven. After all, it was a part of God's overall plan. It was God who chose one of Noah's sons, as well as all his decendants, to be the slaves of the other two sons (Genesis, Chapter 9). Even the Apostle Paul commanded, "Slaves, obey your earthly masters with respect and fear, and with sincerity of heart, just as you would obey Christ. Obey them not only to win their favor when their eye is on you, but as slaves of Christ, doing the will of God from your heart" (Ephesians 6:5-6). Hearing ideas like these expressed in churches made it an easy step to believe that Black people had been better off in slavery than they would have been otherwise. They were not capable of better, and for the most part their masters were kind and respectful of them and their families. And even after emancipation, they preferred to live in their own neighborhoods and attend their own churches and schools.

As incredible as it seems now, these and many other similar ones were the normative stories of my childhood regarding the U.S. Civil War. Walt Disney's Song of the South epitomized the story line. What facts did I have for such stories? None. Did it ever occur to me that there might be more to the story, a great deal more? No, embarrassedly, it didn't.

The search for adjectives to describe the contrast between my earliest attitudes toward the Civil War and what I had come to understand after years of serious study is driven by one observation: There were surely any number of adults in my childhood who had a much more accurate picture! Weren't there? Who were they? Where were they? Why didn't they speak up? Did they speak up, and I did not have the ears to hear or eyes to see? I'm not sure. Was one a possibility that I was deliberately misled and lied to?

And to repeat the lesson from above, it is entirely possible for seemingly rational individuals to be absolutely certain about notions that have limited to no merit whatsoever. The less I knew, or understood, the easier it was to believe the story that was constructed. The number of facts that I could see was irrelevant; it was the story line that held them together. I began the believing and trusting course of action early, and it was strong.

Stories play a powerful role in our lives. I came to see that the culture, family, state, region into which I was born included a story about the Civil War, not the story, but a story. Over time a cultural story became internalized first as our story—meaning that of my family, my neighbors, my friends, my church—and finally it came to rest as my story. By young adulthood the story felt very personal. It was me. It was a big part of who I was. It was my story. I was literally "dancing with the one who brought me."

Human beings are capable of believing anything, no matter how absurd or ridiculous, when we are surrounded by other people who believe the same thing. It is a way to understand those who believe that the CIA was behind the assassination of President Kennedy, that walking on the moon was a hoax pulled off on a Hollywood movie set, that a man speaking for God could command hundreds of people at Jonestown to take cyanide as a way to please God, that people could sell earthly belongings, wear white robes on a hillside, and await the Rapture, that Black people are not really fully human.

A single incident in one's personal life could give rise to a full-scale narrative that directs the choices and behaviors of a lifetime. How else can I explain to myself how a single comment in a junior high school classroom in Lufkin, Texas, would haunt me for a lifetime?

For an assignment in art appreciation class in the eighth grade, I carefully constructed a geometrically designed four-pointed star, meticulously subdividing each point into identical reflections of each other. Going one step further, I painted each subdivision in bright colors to match the reflections. To my chagrin and embarrassment, it was held up before the class as an example of good lines and colors, "But this is not art," explained the teacher. For someone as guided as I by the desire and need to please others, particularly those in positions of authority, it was a blow to my emotional solar plexus.

In my best thirteen-year-old manner, I acted as if the teacher's comment was no big deal. As far as my classmates and friends could see, I laughed—or at least grinned—it off and went on with my school life. However, I would never again come near any classes having anything to do with art or creative activity. Neither would I ever use any word implying that creative or creativity was a possible characteristic, no matter how small the scale, of the kind of person I was. With this one single data point, "This is not art," I proceeded to create a narrative that in many ways I carry to this day. If anyone else, family or friend, had any other view of the star I had made, that is, representing another data point, it was completely lost in the fog of my teenage years.

When basic law and order are removed from a body of people, individuals and groups within the body respond with their most primitive drives and fears for their individual and collective survival, up to and including the most savage of actions. It took the most devastating war in the history of our country to settle the questions of slavery and that of remaining a Union. Guaranteeing the rights of the emancipated and the operation of a state as a part of a larger Union after the war required the use of huge numbers of Federal troops throughout the old Confederacy. As far as I can tell this twelve-year period of Reconstruction had the greatest impact on two distinct groups—those who had been in positions of political and economic power because of the system and those who were the most impoverished by that same system.

Spoiler Alert 9 - The Cornerstone Speech

At one extreme, there was the reasoning of many of the wealthy and powerful of the South as expressed by the Vice-President of the Confederacy, Alexander Stephens. In Savannah on March 21, 1861, near the outbreak of the Civil War, he declared:

> The prevailing ideas established by him (Thomas Jefferson) and by most of the leading statesmen at the time of the formation of the old Constitution, were that the enslavement of the African was in violation of the laws of nature; that it was wrong in principle, socially, morally and politically …. **Those ideas, however, were fundamentally wrong.** They rested on the assumption of the equality of the races. This was an error …. Our new government is founded upon exactly the opposite idea; its foundations are laid, its corner-stone rests, upon the great truth that the Negro is not equal to the White man; that slavery, subordination to the superior race, is his natural and normal condition. This, our new government, is the first in the history of the world, based upon this great physical, philosophical, and moral truth.

These comments of Stephens would be remembered as his *Cornerstone Speech*. On the other extreme was the reasoning of many within the impoverished White population. Although their living circumstances could be difficult, they shared an awareness that they were free and not slaves, leading to an oft-heard phrase, "I may be poor, but at least I'm not a nigger." In some incredible manner, a poor, uneducated White person could find some solace in believing that, though life was difficult, he or she was still better off—superior—to an entire race of other people. Frederick Douglass was known to say in abolitionist speeches, "Everyone in the South wants the privilege of whipping somebody else."

~ ~ ~

Neither the wealthy nor poor Whites were prepared for the profound changes that took place after the war in the South among the newly freed slaves. They were now free to own land and personal property, get an education, create businesses, accumulate wealth, sit on juries, vote, and hold public office. The removal of the Union Army from the defeated Southern states in 1877 curtailed many, if not all, of those rights and became the triggering point for the revival of the White supremacy movement. Both rich and poor Whites were then freer to act out their beliefs. The powerful Whites could use race to their personal advantage economically, politically, and religiously. Poor Whites could accept the division of the races because it gave them a sense of status that no colored person could take from them. The similarities of everyday life experienced by poor Whites and former slaves seemed to pass without much notice.

It gave birth to the Jim Crow era and the violence-based separation of the races that lingers to the present day. Slavery morphed into segregation in all aspects of Southern living. It also created a legal system that made it virtually impossible for a

White person to be held accountable for any harmful act against a Black person. **Some "historians" are more concerned with creating or protecting a certain view of history than with discovering what happened.** Reardon's book, *Pickett's Charge, In History and Memory*, explains this phenomenon as it relates one battle in the Civil War and the distortions around its retelling.

Pickett's Charge was the name given by early writers to an all-out infantry assault ordered by General Lee of the Confederacy against the Union positions of General Meade at Cemetery Ridge on July 3, 1863. It was the last day of the three-day Battle of Gettysburg, a small town in Pennsylvania. The charge was across open ground and uphill against Union fortifications. General George Pickett was one of several Confederate generals who led in the assault. Two others, James Longstreet of South Carolina and James Pettigrew of North Carolina, became of special interest to me. They, too, were among the Southern generals responsible for providing leadership for the attack, with Longstreet being the most senior in rank. Pickett's division was populated by Virginians, the other units had soldiers from several other states including Pettigrew's brigade, which had a large number of North Carolinians.

The farthest point reached by the attack has been referred to by some historians as the *high-water mark* for the Confederacy during the Civil War, the closest a Confederate army would ever come to threatening the Union capital of Washington, D.C. Approximately 12,500 men in nine infantry brigades advanced over open fields for three-quarters of a mile under heavy Union artillery and rifle fire. The attack was repulsed with over fifty percent Southern casualties.

The Southern war effort never fully recovered psychologically or physically from this defeat. The North, from this point on, held a commanding edge over the South that eventually culminated in General Lee surrendering his army to General Grant at Appomattox in April 1865. That's a rough, general history of the battle and day. How the day is remembered is another matter altogether, the ramifications of which haunt, provoke, and guide me to this present day.

The essence of the argument among historians revolves around two competing observations. The first argues that it was serious misjudgment and a mistake in leadership on Lee's part to order such an attack under such circumstances. The second is that Lee's judgment was both timely and accurate and if he had been adequately supported by his generals in the field, the day would have turned to the glory and triumph of the army of the Confederate States of America. The argument over those two views is the basis for the Reardon book. In some corners, the debate persists to the present day.

For all practical purposes, the second view overwhelmingly carried the day for decades. It best suited The Noble Cause narrative that emerged in the South immediately following the War. And no one conveyed the noble image so completely as did General Robert E. Lee specifically and Virginians generally. Some feel Pickett's name was attached to the charge because of the state his men represented. After all, there were other famous charges within the Gettysburg battle such as Devil's Den, Wheat Field, and Little Round Top, but none of them was assigned a general's name as a method of identification. The Noble Cause narrative helped us Southerners justify the impact of slavery and secession on our original ideas of, "We the people—all men are created equal—endowed by their creator—with inalienable rights;" that we had held while in the larger Union. Fighting for our states' rights and our Southern way of life against Northern invaders was key to our shift from larger to smaller loyalties. General Lee was the embodiment of that nobility, more so than any other Southern figure, including the President, Jefferson

Davis, and the guardian of that narrative. Protecting Lee's iconic image was serious business.

In my earliest readings about the Gettysburg battle, I was aware of General James Longstreet's strong objections to the strategy behind the charge. Most earlier battles fought by Lee's army—including several seen as great Confederate victories—had primarily been fought from a defensive position, in familiar territory, with short supply lines. First and Second Bull Run, Seven Days, and Fredericksburg are examples. Longstreet, perhaps the most important of Lee's corps commanders—though Stonewall Jackson, but for his untimely death, may have rivaled him—was a key part of each of these battles along with many others for the entire war. There were many references to Longstreet by Lee as his Old War Horse. Longstreet's suggestion, rather than attack, was to bypass the entrenched Union position, locate a more favorable defensive position between Gettysburg and Washington, D.C, and wait for the Union troops to do the attacking. Lee rejected the suggestion and insisted on the attack. In an after-battle report, and long before the Noble Cause narrative had titled the event as Pickett's Charge. General Pickett was harshly critical of Lee's decision and blamed him for the destruction of his division. His report was later destroyed!

General Longstreet, following Gettysburg, continued to play a key role in leadership for Lee and the South right up to the war's end. However, years later in his written memoirs, he was critical of Lee's wartime performance. By the time the memoirs were published, the Noble Cause narrative had taken such root that to speak disparagingly of Lee was totally unacceptable. Like Sam Houston earlier, Longstreet was branded as a traitor to the South. He became anathema, an apostate, to many of his former Confederate colleagues. Some of them went so far as to cite his reluctance to fully support Lee's decision as the primary reason for the battle's loss.

Much of Reardon's book is focused on the resistance put up by historians of North Carolina through the years to the theme that the Virginians were brave and noble and lacked only the support of others. Of interest to me was the documentation suggesting that it was a North Carolina unit that made the farthest advance up Cemetery Ridge on the fateful day.

During this rethinking of my original attitudes and beliefs about the Civil War in general, and Robert E. Lee in particular, I came across a very interesting quotation. It was attributed to historian James McPherson. The quote was in reference to the 1864 Battle of Cold Harbor, which was fought nearly one year after that of Gettysburg. It was a battle that was remembered by Grant as the worst decision of his entire war career. More than five thousand Union soldiers lost their lives while fewer than eight hundred Confederates lost theirs. It was a battlefield I visited in 2010 as a part of attending a Southern Historical Association meeting in Richmond. Grant's troops were attacking on the offense, Lee's were fighting from well-entrenched defensive positions. McPherson wrote: "... the high Union casualty rate at the 1864 Battle of Cold Harbor—where Union General Ulysses S. Grant's frontal attacks have led to charges that he was a butcher—was basically the same as at Pickett's Charge. Yet Pickett's Charge has been celebrated in legend and history as the ultimate act of Southern honor and courage against the Yankee Goliath, while Cold Harbor symbolizes callous stupidity—..." The Lee legend has indeed romanticized some harsh realities.

I have come a long way from the young boy who believed that if something was important my teacher would make it known to a senior adult who now understands that what conclusions I come to are up to me. And the validity or value of that conclusion is based on the amount of time and energy I am willing to invest in checking, questioning, and verifying.

Chapter 12

SOUTHERN CULTURE AND THE SOUTHERN BAPTIST CONVENTION

This final lesson learned from readings of the Civil War has proven to be the most impactful of them all. I say this realizing that, with time, even these thoughts might be further amended.

Spoiler Alert 10 - The Role of the Southern Baptist Convention and Its Shaping of My Southern Culture.

The bases for my early beliefs about the Civil War and my religion were essentially the same and came from a common source.

As my parents, friends, church, college, seminary, and denomination made up the micro-villages of my youth, so did the educational, legal, business, governmental, and social systems of my region form its macro-villages. My denomination had been an integral part of the shaping of that culture!

~ ~ ~

The first serious readings regarding Frederick Douglass, the namesake of the Black high school of my childhood, had the same impact on my curiosity regarding the treatment of the Black race as did Shaara's book on the Civil War in general.

I was hooked. Most of the comments regarding my enlarged understanding of the role and place of Africans and African Americans in the history of the South came from the readings by and about Douglass. I came to understand the role of my Convention of Southern Baptists in that same history.

Spoiler Alerts. The Spoiler Alerts throughout this account (the early work experiences with Harold E., the drinking fountains at the Sam Houston Museum, my grandfather's refusal to allow my mother to pursue nursing as a career, the numerous men and women of color as chapel speakers, the role of the SBC in the Civil War point to the formative role of religion in general and Southern Baptists specifically in the shaping of the foundational ideas of the Southern culture regarding the treatment of Black people in the South.

Basil Manly, Sr. (1798-1868)—Like Lewis Wigfall for my understanding of my Texas history and Frederick Douglass for my understanding of Black history, Basil Manly, Sr. would be the catalyst for my delving into the Southern Baptist Convention's history. In the course of my college, seminary, and early minister days, I learned of two other large Baptist bodies—American Baptists, with churches mostly located in the northern part of the U.S., and National Baptists, primarily an association of Black churches. I was also aware in my early minister days of considerable pride in the term *Southern*. After all, we were the largest protestant body in the country, and the largest church in most of the towns and cities of my youth was Southern Baptist. We must have been doing something right or God would not have blessed us so. But whatever the stimulus, it had to do with the Civil War, and one day I found myself searching the internet for any connections between the Baptists and the war. I was poorly prepared for what I was about to learn and experience.

Before offering an overview of Manly's life, an additional observation is important, particularly in support of my earlier claim that this area of inquiry has proven to be the most impactful of them all. Manly's life as a Southern Baptist preacher was the embodiment of his five tenets of a fundamentalist Christian. What makes him so significant was his formal elaboration of the ramifications of those tenets in one's everyday beliefs and actions. Those tenets are as follows:

• The volume of sacred writings commonly called the Bible, comprehending the Old and New Testaments, contains the unerring decisions of the word of God. [The Bible in its nature is infallible and literal].

• These decisions are of equal authority in both testaments, and that this authority is the essential veracity of God, who is truth itself. [All teachings in both the Old and New Testaments of the Bible are of equal value].

• Since there can be no prescription against the authority of God, whatever is declared in any part of the Holy Bible to be lawful or illicit, must be essentially so in its own nature, however repugnant such declaration may be to the current opinions of men during any period of time. [A restatement of number two though I saw no reference to an earth with four corners].

• As the supreme lawgiver and judge of man, God is infinitely just and wise in all decisions and is essentially irresponsible for the reasons of his conduct in the moral government of the world—so it is culpably audacious in us to question the rectitude of any of those decisions—merely because we do not apprehend the inscrutable principles of such wisdom and justice. [Any questions, variances, contradictions are but a part of the mystery

of God and ludicrous to be given any question whatsoever];
therefore:

• If one, or more decisions of the written word of God, sanction
the rectitude of any human acquisitions, for instance, the
acquisition of a servant by inheritance or purchase, whoever
believes that the written word of God is verity itself, must
consequently believe in the absolute rectitude of slaveholding. [In
sum, anything recorded in the Old and New Testaments of the
Bible is the absolute truth of the universe, and owning and using
Black men, women, and children is the unquestionable Will of
God].

The only acceptable response as a believer is, in the
Calvinistic theology of the times, that it is one's "duty to accept
God's divine plan for life," and get on with living it out.

As it turned out, these five statements with Manly's full
support and buy-in proved to be the most accurate description
of my earliest ideas regarding Christian religion. If it was in the
Bible, it was God's *Holy Word.* All that was left for me who had
been born again was to believe it, trust it, and do my best to live
it. And if you were a minister, to declare it, which, to the best
of my ability, is what I tried to do. What amazes me now is how
accurately the five statements describe my own experience. In my
mind, they were not the underpinnings of a carefully thought-out
view of Christian religion known as fundamentalism. This was
the Christian religion pure and simple! The only difference for
me, in the 1950s, was the specific references to slavery, which is
no longer applied.

Basil Manly, Sr. was born in 1798 on what was considered a
small plantation. The farm, requiring the service of six slaves,
was located near Pittsboro, in Chatham County, North Carolina.
Manly's older brother, Charles, became governor of North

Carolina. His younger brother, Matthias, became a justice of the Supreme Court in the same state. All were products of the Bingham School in neighboring Orange County, where I currently live. Their father, Captain Manly, a title he earned leading a militia group during the American Revolution, felt strongly that a solid education was the foundation for any man wanting to "make something of himself." Charles and Matthias followed Bingham by graduating from the University of North Carolina and continued their studies by studying law and being admitted to the North Carolina bar to launch their careers. Basil followed a considerably different path to distinction. Depending on one's values and viewpoint, a case could be made that Basil was the most distinguished of the three.

Following his mother's more religious mindset, Manly had his own born-again experience and was baptized at the Baptist Church of Christ in Rocky Springs, North Carolina, in 1814. Soon after his baptism, he believed he was "called to be a preacher" and, against his father's wishes, began immediately to fulfill that calling. He was licensed to preach by the Rocky Springs Church in 1818. His remarkable career as a Baptist preacher began.

From the start, there was something about his name, way, and manner that attracted the encouragement of Baptists in his area. Reverend W. T. Brantly invited and supported him financially to attend a small college in Beaufort, South Carolina, for further study. In December 1819, after eighteen months of study at Beaufort, he entered the junior class of South Carolina College, in Columbia. He graduated from the College in December 1821 as valedictorian and "honor man of his class." (In 1906, South Carolina College was re-chartered and became the University of South Carolina.) Immediately after graduation, Manly began what can only be described as an incredibly influential career as a Baptist minister in the South.

One year after graduation, he moved to Edgefield County, South Carolina, and became the pastor of a local church as well as a rural church, Little Stevens Creek Baptist. He was formally ordained at Stevens Creek in 1822. The four years he spent in Edgefield set the stage for the rest of an amazing career. He became the leader of what became known as the *Edgefield Revival*. Evidently, his youthful exuberance and passion and his strong writing and speaking skills set off a general spirit of revival in the region. It became a religious awakening that saw the conversion of so many people to the Christian (Baptist) faith that it caught the attention of the state as well as the Southern region. Many of his sermons and essays on various topics were published. At my first reading of this background, the similarities between his early years and those of Billy Graham went completely unnoticed. Now, the similarities are striking. They both became well known, and their influence on the beliefs and actions of others in their day was huge.

In 1823, Manly was elected secretary of the Baptist State Convention of South Carolina and was named to a five-man committee charged with selecting a site and completing all necessary arrangements connected with the founding of Furman Academy and Theological Institution, later to become Furman University, in Greenville. For the rest of his life, he devoted much of his time speaking and raising funds on behalf of this school. He was twenty-five years old. In 1824, he was invited to speak to the Georgia Baptist Convention to "spread the news" of the revival in Edgefield and his personal as well as his congregation's conversion experiences.

A quick word about Richard Furman for whom the institution in Greenville was named. For his day, late 1700s to early 1800s, he was perhaps the best-known Baptist in the U.S. In 1814, he was among the founders and the first president of the Triennial Convention, the first national organization of Baptists in the U.S.

In 1821, he helped create and lead a similar organization for his home state of South Carolina. A strong believer in literacy and education for all, he helped found Columbian University, later to be known as George Washington University. He was a slaveholder, and throughout his career, while pastor of the First Baptist Church of Charleston, he was an ardent apologist for the "peculiar institution." His most famous written support of slavery was an extended letter addressed to the governor on December 24, 1822, known as *The Exposition of the Views of the Baptists Relative to the Coloured Population*. The Bible was his source of defense for the institution.

Before Furman's death in 1825, he hand-picked Basil Manly as his successor. Manly was 28 years old. The church in Charleston was known as the oldest and wealthiest Baptist church in the South. Manly served as the church's pastor for the next eleven years, until 1837. During that period the congregation increased in size and influence. Establishing a Baptist newspaper for the region, Manly promoted the Baptist in the state and nation. He increasingly became what one writer called an ecclesiastical politician.

Because of his absolute belief in the Bible as the literal word of God, Manly, like Furman, was a staunch defender of slavery from the beginning and remained so throughout his life. I try to imagine what it must have felt like to be in the audience of an intelligent, passionate, well-spoken Baptist preacher advocating for slavery along with our need to be "saved and born again." When I recall how I felt as a seventeen-year-old listening for the first time to Billy Graham, I am even more provoked. I believed everything Billy Graham was saying! Would I have believed everything Basil Manly was saying? And more, could this have been the kind of things my grandfather heard throughout his developmental years? If so, I can see how he hardly could have had a different attitude toward his only daughter's interest in nursing than the one he took!

In 1832, Manly actively supported the states' rights position in South Carolina during the Nullification Crisis. He was reported as wanting to "further the cause of Christ through politics." Although he defended the institution of slavery, Manly believed the hardships of slavery should be tempered by Christian behavior. Again, using the authority of the *Word of God*, he preached that slaveowners should treat slaves fairly and provide for both their spiritual well-being and their physical needs. At the same time, he also believed in and practiced corporal punishment. After all, slaves were commanded by God to "obey their masters."

His life and career exemplified the complexity of slavery in the South. He invested his career reconciling support for slavery with Christian principles. That he would acknowledge and champion the humanity of enslaved Africans amazed me. On one hand, that put him on the side of abolitionists in the North who saw enslaved people as fellow human beings. On the other, it put him in direct odds with those Southern Fire-eaters, like Lewis Wigfall (who also had lived in Edgefield County). Wigfall saw Africans as sub-human, an inferior species. It was not unusual for some slaveowners to see evangelical preaching about slavery as a threat to the institution because if slaves were viewed as humans with souls, they deserved equal treatment under the law. For Manly, such tensions were resolved by trusting in *God's Word*, the Bible.

For Manly it was the duty of a Christian to accept and defend one's place, and the place of others, in God's divine plan. As far as I could tell, in the earliest days of these conflicts, he hoped for a peaceful secession of Southern states from the Union. Even so, as he was often heard to say, he was willing to lay down his life for his beliefs.

While in Charleston in 1835, he declined the invitation to be the president of South Carolina College. Largely because of his support for education, in 1837 he received an honorary Doctor of Divinity degree from the University of North Carolina. That same year he left First Baptist of Charleston to become the second president of the University of Alabama.

Manly served as the president of the University until 1855. While there, as in every place he had been before, his passion for what he believed, and his boundless energy, served him well. His public life expanded even more. He worked for social programs like prison reform and aid for the mentally ill. He promoted agricultural reform, including scientific methods of land management and crop production. In the area of education, always a passion, he helped found the Judson Female Institute, later to be named Judson College. He helped found the Alabama Historical Society. In 1853, he declined the presidency of Furman College.

In Tuscaloosa, interest in business showed itself for the first time. He invested in industrial ventures in hopes of diversifying the Southern economy while making a profit. In 1852, he showed interest in owning a farm. The interest led to his purchasing a 587-acre tract along the Black Warrior River in Alabama. In 1859, after leaving the University, serving as pastor of Wentworth Baptist Church in Charleston, and returning to Montgomery as pastor of First Baptist Church, he added another 427 acres to the original tract. Slaves on his Walnut Bluff Plantation, across this stretch of time, numbered between eighteen and forty. Manly believed that ministers had as much right to own slaves as anyone else. I could not locate information that he lived on his plantation for any length of time, except for a brief period near the end of his life. It was either run by an overseer under his direction or in his later years by two of his sons, James and Fuller. I will always wonder if Manly's father, who thought it a mistake for his son to become a preacher, lived long enough to know how wealthy this son became.

The Southern Baptist Convention, my Convention, officially came into being in Augusta, Georgia, in 1845. As observed earlier, until then state Baptist groups in the South had been aligned with the National Triennial Convention. Since the Triennial's beginning in 1814, issues and tensions around slavery had manifested themselves in a variety of forms, and in varying degrees of intensity. However, they had managed to hold together for thirty years. All that came to an end in Augusta.

No one played a more significant role in this Georgia meeting than Manly. A year before, in Tuscaloosa, in 1844, he had drafted what became known as the Alabama Resolutions. Written from his broadly known position regarding slavery and states' rights, the resolutions were originally presented to the annual meeting of the Alabama Baptist Convention (ABC). They were written in response to a general climate of disdain that many in the North held toward their brothers in the South, the ones who supported the "peculiar institution."

Resolution #2 was the only one I could locate. My guess is that it reflects the tone and tenor of the other four or five. "Resolved, That our duty at this crisis requires us to demand from the proper authorities in all those bodies to whose funds we have contributed, or with whom we have in any way been connected, the distinct, explicit, avowal that slaveholders are eligible, and entitled, equally with non-slaveholders, to all the privileges and immunities of their several unions; and especially to receive any agency, mission, or other appointment, which may run within the scope of their operation or duties."

The resolutions as presented to the ABC included the recommendation that they be immediately sent to the Acting Board of the Triennial Convention. It also recommended that copies be sent to the Baptist conventions in other slave-holding states. Manly later reported to his son, Basil Jr., "With deep conviction of the vast issues involved, the convention passed the resolutions standing, unanimously." The resolutions, however, failed to be adopted in Philadelphia. The National Convention claimed that it did not want to take sides in slavery issues and wanted to remain neutral.

Baptists in Georgia decided to test the claimed neutrality by recommending a slaveholder to the Home Mission Society as a missionary. The National Home Mission Society board refused to appoint him. In the Society's view, missionaries were not allowed to take servants with them. That automatically rejected slaves. Many Baptists in the South considered this an infringement of their right to determine their own candidates. At which point they decided to separate from the national organization and form a "Southern" Baptist convention, which they did at the meeting in Augusta. As far as I could tell, we Southern Baptists were known from the beginning as a pro-slavery denomination. Many of our founding leaders had consistently identified slavery as an institution created by God for His purpose. The North's attempts to abolish the institution left them no choice but to do whatever was necessary to preserve the Will of God for the races!

Realizing that the forebearers of the Convention that represented the religion of my childhood and young adulthood seceded from their national organization for religious reasons fifteen years before the Southern states seceded from the U.S. for states' rights reasons struck me as strange. It still does. Was religious belief as powerful and influential, if not more so, as political or economic beliefs? Were the political and economic beliefs more powerful because of the underlying religious support? Judging from many of the current social conflicts in the U.S. (e.g., abortion, LGBTQ issues including gay marriage) the question remains to this day. And as then, there are

fundamentalist Southern Baptist ministers admonishing their
followers to stay true to God's Word and Will.

For reasons that are not clear to me, Manly resigned the
presidency of the University of Alabama in 1855. His leaving
such a high-profile position, with both religious and political
influence, seems significant. He returned to Charleston for the
next three years. Thirty years earlier, he had served there as the
pastor of the First Baptist Church. This time it was to lead the
Wentworth Street Baptist Church.

For whatever reason, Baptists in South Carolina were glad
to have him back. In addition to pastoring Wentworth, he was
elected president of the South Carolina Baptist Convention
in 1856, 1857, and 1858. In 1858, he became the founding
chairman for the board of trustees of the Southern Baptist
Theological Seminary. In the beginning, it was affiliated with
Furman College in Greenville. Years later it would move to
Louisville, Kentucky, where it remains today.

At some point in the mid-1850s, he wrote and published
a widely read and distributed book, *The Bible Doctrine of
Inspiration Explained and Vindicated*. It embodied the bases of
all he believed and proclaimed as a minister. Later there were
questions raised regarding the book's title, but Manly was firm.
It wasn't the fundamentalist doctrine or the Baptist doctrine, it
was the Bible doctrine. There may have been other doctrines out
there, but this one was the Bible's!

In 1859, Manly returned to Tuscaloosa. He was hired as a
home missionary to be the State Evangelist for the Alabama
Baptist Convention. He continued his whole-hearted support of
the secession movement, and he expressed his ideas for a separate
Southern nation in sermons and public addresses and worked
tirelessly to bring those beliefs to reality. I can only assume that
his beliefs regarding slavery as a part of a divine plan were
well-known throughout the state. It would seem that his political

activism enhanced his reputation as an evangelist and minister. It obviously lent credence to the idea that secession was the right action to take for the South.

Soon after returning to Tuscaloosa, he was nominated to the State Convention of Alabama to help the state decide on secession. Within a year, in late November 1860, he moved to Montgomery to become the pastor of the First Baptist Church there. The election of Abraham Lincoln to the presidency of the United States had a huge impact on his actions. He stayed true to his belief that slavery was a part of God's Divine Plan. Before he left Tuscaloosa, he introduced a resolution supporting Alabama's secession from the United States to the state Baptist Convention meeting in Tuskegee. The Convention voted overwhelmingly to support the resolution. Many believe that the Baptist declaration and pledge to support secession was the catalyst for the secession movement in the state of Alabama.

The Secession Convention was held at the capitol building in Montgomery, beginning on January 7, 1861. Manly was elected to serve as chaplain and opened the convention with a prayer. Following the vote for secession, there was a call for all the seceded states to meet in Montgomery on February 4. At that meeting, he was chosen to serve as official chaplain of the new Provisional Congress of the Confederate States of America. When the Confederacy was formed, he saw it as God's Will and Plan for the South.

I was fascinated to see Manly's role unfold in the early Confederacy. Inauguration Day was February 18 in Montgomery. Jefferson Davis of Mississippi, newly elected president, and Vice-President Alexander Stephens of Georgia rode together in an open carriage for the official ceremony. The third person in the carriage was Dr. Basil Manly, pastor of the local First Baptist Church, and the newly elected Chaplain of the Congress of the Confederate States of America. In what must have been a day of incredible excitement for all, especially for Manly, he stepped to the podium to deliver the invocation.

The prayer was recorded in his diary for that day. I marvel at the carefully chosen words and can only imagine what the pace, manner, tone, and volume of the actual delivery must have been like. I was, and remain, awed by the claims made— the Confederacy had come about by God's providence via the wisdom he had given senators, and God had selected Jefferson Davis to lead. A religious supremacist was speaking to the Confederate nation and the Southern Baptist Convention!

> O Thou Great Spirit! Maker & Lord of all things!
> Who humblest Thyself to behold the things that are
> done on the earth; and before whom the splendor
> of human pageantry vanisheth into nothing! By
> Thee rulers bear sway; Thou teachest Senators
> wisdom. We own Thy kind providence, Thy Fatherly
> care, in the peaceful origin of the government of
> these "Confederate States of America." We thank
> Thee for the quiet considerate unanimity which
> has prevailed in our public councils; and for the
> hallowed auspices under which the government of
> our choice begins.
>
> Let this special blessing rest on the engagements
> and issues of this day. Thou has provided us a man
> to go in and out before us, and to lead Thy people.
> Oh vouchsafe Thy blessing, on this Thy servant! Let
> his life and health be precious in Thy sight. Grant
> him a sound mind, in a sound body. Let all his acts
> be done in Thy fear, under Thy guidance, with a
> single eye to Thy glory; and crown them all with
> Thy approbation and blessing! With the like favors,
> bless the Congress of the "Confederate States"; and

all who are, or may be, charged by lawful authority
with public cares and labors. Put Thy good Spirit
into our whole people, that they may faithfully do
all Thy fatherly pleasure. Let the administration of
this government be the reign of truth and peace;
let righteousness, which exalteth a nation, be the
stability of our times, and keep us from sin, which is
a reproach to any people; establish Thou the work of
our hands upon us; turn the counsel of our enemies
into foolishness; and grant us assured and continual
peace in all our borders! We ask all, through Jesus
our Lord. Amen

His prayer was described in the local press as "brief, fervent,
and patriotic." I will always wonder about the influence of
Manly on the Cornerstone Speech that would be delivered by
Vice-President Stephenson a short time later in Savannah.

I am also reminded of a speech, not a prayer, given eight
years earlier to a large crowd in Rochester, New York, with
slavery in the South as the backdrop. Frederick Douglass, forty-
three years old, was declaring that, "Churches were the bulwark
of American slavery" and that "Ministers were shamelessly
giving the sanction of religion and the Bible to the whole slave
system." He was referring to moments like these in Montgomery.

Manly remained in the chaplain's role until the national
capital moved to Richmond a few months later. Afterward, he
remained active in supporting his new country. His passion for
what he believed does not seem to have waned. He participated
by supporting the army with prayers, tracts, Bibles, and medical
supplies. He aided in funerals and comforted families of the
Confederate dead.

For reasons I could not locate, his time as pastor of First
Baptist in Montgomery was bumpy and brief. He resigned in

November 1862 and returned to Tuscaloosa to support his
son Charles, who had become the pastor of the First Baptist
Church. He helped in the creation of Alabama Central Female
College and took back some management of his Walnut Grove
Plantation. His sons James and Fuller, who had been running it,
had now become part of the Confederate military.

One of his last major contacts with the Southern Baptist
Convention as a governing body was at the biennial meeting,
again in Augusta, in June 1863. Since the last meeting of the
Convention in 1861, the South had suffered terrible losses of life,
especially at Antietam. Lincoln used that battle as a backdrop
for making public his Emancipation Proclamation. The losses
at Gettysburg and Vicksburg were less than a month away.
However, Manly's sense of duty to God and defiance of the
enemy remained as strong as ever. He urged all Baptists to "do
their duty and defend the South!"

Still in Tuscaloosa, on November 22, 1864, Manly suffered a
stroke that led to considerable paralysis. His health was further
complicated by rheumatism. He was forced to stop all activities
at Walnut Bluff and rent out the plantation. The Civil War
effectively ended five months later in April 1865 when Lee
surrendered to Grant.

On September 12, 1865, President Andrew Johnson signed
a full pardon of war-related offenses committed by Manly. The
inauguration prayer listed above was one of the offenses cited.
In addition, he had to take an oath of allegiance, pay any costs
owed from any proceeding, disclaim property, or proceeds from
the sale of confiscated property, and if he were to ever make
use of slave labor again, the pardon would be revoked. In 1867,
Basil and wife Sarah moved from Alabama to Greenville, South
Carolina. There they lived with another son, Basil Jr. who had
become a professor at Southern Baptist Theological Seminary.
Basel Sr. died in Greenville on December 21, 1868.

My curiosity is high regarding the last days and months of his life, especially during the early years of Reconstruction. At no time, to the extent that I could determine, did he ever back away from the belief that the Black race was meant to be, by the Will of God, enslaved and subservient to the White.

Below is a list of perplexing thoughts and questions that I experienced during the months spent trying to understand the impact of a religious supremacist like Basil Manly Sr. on the beginnings and evolution of the Southern Baptist Convention. Many of them linger today. I expect some will remain a mystery.

• What impact did the outcome of the war—the end of the Confederate States with the horrible loss of life, injuries, property damage, and emancipation—have on the cornerstone idea this is all the Will of God? Did Manly continue to see, and admonish others to join him in seeing, "acceptance" of the mysteries of God's Word as a Christians duty?

• Was the post-war status of Black people contrary to God's Will and to be condemned and resisted? What was the White Christian's stance toward a Black person who was no longer subservient or to the Northern military which was enforcing laws of the United States in the former Confederacy?

• If Manly had been alive when Reconstruction ended, what would have been his message to churches regarding the backlash against Black citizens, White supremacy, Jim Crow laws, and the Klu Klux Klan? Was the Klan's use of the fiery cross reflective of a deep tie between fundamentalist White Southern Christians and the belief that the subjugation of the Black race was the Will of God. By the time of my childhood and young adulthood, mainstream churches were among the most segregated of all the institutions of the South.

• What, if anything, could have led Manly to a place where he could recognize that it was a selective Biblical literalism regarding the Curse of Ham (Genesis 9) that had driven his support of Black slavery from the beginning?

• How much of the basic tenets of *The Bible Doctrine of Inspiration Explained and Vindicated* was incorporated into the Southern Baptist Convention's seminary education of young ministers from the time of its writing to my own time as a student?

• How, in my four years as a ministerial student at a college owned by the Southern Baptists and three years at one of its theological seminaries, could I have gone without once hearing about the incredible role played by slave-holding pastors and evangelists like Richard Furman and Basil Manly Sr. in the foundation of the Southern Baptist Convention and the run-up to the Civil War?

When I try to remember what I thought/felt/sensed was most important about the churches of my childhood, strong emotions are still stirred at several points. In this case, "important" simply means those ideas and issues that were most often spoken of, taught, preached, experienced.

One was that it was important to be a New Testament Church—as opposed to being one that was Bible or Old Testament. Was that a conscious effort over time to separate the denomination as much as possible from the Old Testament Curse of Ham claimed as God's original judgment of the Black race?

What then was the primary function of the Church as I knew it? It was to worship and serve God. One worshiped God by praying, singing praises, and studying his teachings through Bible readings. One served God by living a sin-free life as much as possible and proclaiming the Gospel everywhere through evangelism and missions. The basic goal was to avoid Hell and get ready for Heaven.

Using another model, the major emphasis was one's vertical relationship with God—getting right with Him by accepting Jesus as one's Eternal Savior (being born again) and serving Him as stated above. There was not much made of our horizontal relationships with all other human beings. The vertical emphasis rendered social issues touched by racism, segregation discrimination, education, and poverty to be of little or limited consequence.

The Youth-Led Revival program of which I was so proud was focused on all things vertical and, by cultural default, for *Whites Only*. The preferred church building style featured arched roofs, often including a steeple with a bell or clock in the front. If there was a steeple, it was commonly topped with a cross that extended even farther skyward. We were heaven focused!

In summary, the cultural Noble Cause narrative, or story if you will, of the Civil War and its interplay with the stories associated with Biblical literalism made several outcomes somewhat predictable. Whites were God's chosen people. Blacks were destined to forever be enslaved to God's chosen ones. Resistance to God's plan for humanity had led the North to start the war. At the very time that Black slavery was receding around the globe in the name of God's love for all people, *God's True Will* of racial subjugation on Earth had rested with the South. We were not only White supremacists, we were religious supremacists as well. Any religious groups who saw life and living in any other manner were simply wrong—and needed to be saved or *born again*.

CONCLUSION

There is no concluding this book. I still live each day, reacting, thinking, feeling, and evolving. No new births are anticipated; new insights are hoped for. I am less certain than ever, while being certain that certainty must be examined as a premature declaration in most cases, and more often either inaccurate or a data point along a continuum. And so, my story continues. Who knows what I might write in a year or five years from now? Hopefully, it would be to share new understandings about navigating the mysteries of being a human being. In all the roles we humans may be called upon to play—child, sibling, husband, parent, relative, friend, neighbor, citizen—from neighborhood to world, it now seems to me that living is more a mystery to be experienced than a problem to be solved or a dogma to be believed.

APPENDIX A

East Texas Baptist University
Chapel Remarks

Homecoming Week
By Harles Cone, October 9. 2002

"Then ... and Now"

If my memory serves, and that's an increasingly huge
assumption, this is the fifth time I have been asked to speak in
chapel since I graduated forty-five years ago. Every time I speak
it is with a great deal of anxiety and concern. The anxieties stem
from memories of how I felt as a student attending chapel—
especially how I felt when the chapel service was given over to
some person from out of the college's past—someone who was
going to tell us what it was like when he or she was here. It's not
always a pretty memory.

What I did to get ready this time was to ask myself two
questions. The first is what do I specifically remember from
chapel services I attended that are clearly with me to this
day? Generally, there were many memories ... of sermons,
instrumental music, choirs, solos and so forth. But holding
myself to something clear and specific was not so easy. What do I
specifically recall, over all these years?

Strangely, there were two memories that were highly specific.
One was of a member of the college's board of trustees, a
Baptist pastor from Shreveport who, using the topic of freedom
and hell, was making a point about how anyone can go to hell—
rich can, poor can, intelligent can, illiterate can, and in the midst
of his point said, "and even Dr. Bruce can go to hell." That got
my attention. Dr. H. D. Bruce was, at that time, the president
of the college, and I remember thinking the board member's
message was perhaps intended more for Dr. Bruce than it was for
the rest of us.

The other specific memory had to do with a verse of scripture
used by Ralph Langley, a Dallas pastor in those days. It's a verse

from the book of John to which I will refer in a moment. For now, though, the combination of the verse and Mr. Langley's forceful treatment of the concept involved has stayed with me all these years. The verse has never meant more though than it has the past five to ten years.

Before identifying the verse, I want to acknowledge the second question, that guided me as I prepared for today. This question has two parts. When I consider where I am at this point in my life, how I think, how I feel, what I do, and then ask if someone like me had come to speak at chapel when I was a student could I have a) had the vaguest idea of what he or she is taking about? and b) could I have given any serious consideration to it? In fairness, I feel the answer to both parts of the questions would have been a resounding no. I do not feel I would have been capable of either understanding or consideration.

Despite that clear conclusion, I plan to continue.

As you can see from the program, I asked that my remarks be titled *Then … and Now*. My intention is to discuss, in the briefest of terms, how I felt and thought about God, faith, and religion when I sat where you are sitting (not literally, since chapel for us was held in Scarborough Chapel) and how I feel and think about faith today, with two very important caveats—and please hear this, I will be careful not to use a phrase that suggests I have grown between then and now. Grown suggests smarter, wiser, more mature and to my knowledge none of those feelings are in my heart. I believe the best anyone can do is to live according to the light that he or she has. I am the same person—the light has changed. The other caveat, based on the experiences of my lifetime, if I should be invited back to address a chapel gathering five years from now, I would fully expect changes to have occurred with how I feel and think now and what I will be feeling and thinking then. Changing thoughts and feelings, though slow at times, fast at others—and always painful—seem to be the story of my spiritual journey.

The verse I alluded to earlier is in the third chapter of John, the eighth verse. In King James English it reads, "The wind bloweth where it listeth, and thou hearest the sound thereof, but canst not tell whence it cometh, and whither it goeth: So is every one that is born of the spirit." In more modern English it reads: "The wind blows wherever it pleases. You hear its sound, but you cannot tell where it comes from or where it is going. So it is with everyone born of the spirit."

When I was nine years old, with some prompting, I confessed that Jesus was my savior at the First Baptist Church in Lufkin, Texas. To my knowledge that was the first outward step I took that reflected my inward state—the beginnings of my grappling with being a person of Spirit.

In hindsight, I can see that I started this journey with a lot of beliefs ... but very little faith. I inherited, literally, "the faith of my fathers," though, in my case, the mediator was primarily my mother. And it was not so much being educated in faith as it was being indoctrinated into a view about faith—a lot like eating fruit that had already been chewed.

In my youthful exuberance, it seemed vitally important to hold the correct beliefs—and to convince others of their correctness. Believing in Jesus was absolutely crucial—and the phrase believing in Jesus meant primarily believing things about Jesus, things about his birth, his life, his baptism, his death, his resurrection, and his return and the Bible, in which these stories were told.

Believing things about Jesus and the Bible was easy then. It was what I was taught to believe and most of my relationships were with people who were reared and taught as I was. It seems strange to think of it now, but then, Bible study for me

was not study at all. It was a matter of searching the Bible's pages
for verses and passages that confirmed what I already believed.
That was then. This approach to being a Spirit person became
increasingly difficult as I grew older.

I have since come to believe that faith is not a belief at all. It
is more like trust—and hope.

It seems to me now that believing in Jesus has almost nothing
to do with believing doctrines, but rather it means to give, for
want of a better expression, one's heart, one's inner being, one's
soul, one's spirit, if you will, to an attitude, a style of living.
For me it was what I believe Jesus referred to as the Kingdom
of God: The way the world would be if God were in charge—
instead of the Romans, the priests, the rich, the men as they were
in Jesus's day. Kingdom that he said existed within us all, if we
could but see it, grasp it, and trust it—that is, "faith it."

For me now, there has come to be a sharp distinction between
the historical Jesus, who he was, what he said and did during
the brief period of his life—and what various groups within the
church began saying about him during the years that followed
his historical life. The faith (or spirit of the historical Jesus) has
become much more important to me than a belief about Jesus.
While Jesus talked about the Kingdom of God, within years his
followers began talking about Jesus. The messenger became the
message. What one believed about Jesus became more important
than the message of Jesus.

I have come to believe that the appeal of Jesus is traced to
what those who contacted him directly experienced by being in
his presence, observing, and practicing what he said and did.
Something about the way he was, what he said, his manner, his
way, the way he engaged them, accepted them, touched them—
in the deep places of their hearts—helped them experience
dimensions about themselves and the world that heretofore were
unknown to them. And further, this contact with him had such

impact on them, they were willing to leave their homes and their past way of living to stay near him—perhaps to keep the excitement alive, perhaps to learn and observe more. I don't think the earliest believers wondered much about what kind of divine person Jesus was, but what kind of man, human, he was.

To me, a powerful aside is the observation that his message was primarily recognized only by those who existed outside any systems where power, or wealth, or influence existed. His first audiences were those who were outside any religious, political, educational, gender, ethnic or family advantages. The movement was, in the beginning, as one writer put it, literally, "a kingdom of nobodies,"—and how could it have been otherwise? As far as I can tell, the historical Jesus condemned all forms of domination over the human spirit, including patriarchy, economic exploitation, hierarchical power arrangements that disadvantaged the weak while benefiting the strong, subversion of the law by the rich, religious purity rules that separated people from each other, racial superiority, ethnocentrism, and the entire sacrificial system that promoted sacral violence. And he envisioned a God that was non-violent and all-inclusive.

Who was there in his day that could have been open to such a message? Certainly not the Romans, nor the rich, nor the influential, nor those with religious beliefs that separated and condemned those who were different.

When I can grasp it, and I confess I am able to only in brief moments, the world in which I live seems very much like the one in which Jesus lived. In our world, we pay honor and do homage to power, wealth, education, gender, ethnicity, family ancestry, religiosity, and political preferences at the expense of and to the diminishment, if not destruction of anyone who falls outside these unquestioned parameters. I feel that what Jesus was saying and doing would be as generally unacceptable in the twenty-first century as it was in the first century.

But how about those first believers, those whose attitudes, whose experiences, and whose spirits were transformed by their contact with Jesus? I believe they experienced Jesus, and the Kingdom he spoke about, as empowering and life giving. In their world they were seen as women, Samaritans, lepers, harlots, tax collectors, gentiles, unclean, sinners—nobodies. In God's Kingdom they were citizens, distinct, valued, loved.

They came to believe, as he taught them, that they could experience what he had experienced. They could have what he had. They could meet and engage others the way he had met and engaged them. They too could bring healing to each other, and they could eat and drink together. They could live above and beyond the barriers that choked and oppressed them. Life, Jesus taught and demonstrated to them, was in their spirits, their hearts—not in their possessions, their ancestry, their gender, their wealth, or their religiosity. That is the Jesus and the faith I would like to know.

I said at the beginning of my comments that my faith or spirit trip began with an emphasis on how important it was for me to believe specific things about Jesus: his birth, his life, his death, his resurrection, his return, and how important it was for me to get others to agree with those beliefs as well. Faith for me now, finds none of those emphases within the historical Jesus nor the Kingdom he talked about.

As much as possible, I want my faith to be firsthand, not second hand. I want to have as much direct experience as possible with "the wind blowing wherever it pleases." With the utmost respect, I can say that I am more fascinated and challenged by what Jesus thought and taught about The Kingdom of God than I am about what Peter and Paul taught about Jesus. This commitment allows me to read about the faith of Paul without having to accept it as my faith or without having to believe that his view was God's view. The spirit of Jesus that was alive for Paul in the first century is the same spirit that is alive for me, and you, now.

This faith excites me, challenges me—and makes me fearful all at the same time. I know less than I have ever known, I have more hope and trust than I have ever had.

I want to end my comments by sharing a quotation sent me a few years ago by a friend. I wish I had written the words. While this is often attributed to Nelson Mandela, the author is Marianne Williamson.

> Our deepest fear is not that we are inadequate. Our deepest fear is that we are powerful beyond measure. It is our light, not our darkness, that most frightens us. We ask ourselves, Who am I to be brilliant, gorgeous, talented, fabulous? Actually, who are you not to be? You are a child of God. Your playing small does not serve the world. There is nothing enlightened about shrinking so that other people won't feel insecure around you. We were born to make manifest the glory of the God that is within us. It is not just in some of us, it is in everyone. And as we let our light shine, we unconsciously give other people permission to do the same. As we are liberated from our own fear, our presence automatically liberates others.

APPENDIX B

Reading Lists

BOOKS OF 1965

1. *The Prize*, Irving Wallace
2. *Screwtape Letters*, C. S. Lewis
3. *Easter is on Monday*, Douglas Stewart
4. *Willie Mae*, Elizabeth Kytle
5. *Man's Search for Meaning*, Victor Frankl
6. *The Meaning of Persons*, Paul Tournier
7. *The Kennedy Wit*, Bill Adler
8. *Man: In Whose Image,* William Henry Lazareth
9. *They Speak with Other Tongues,* John Sherrill
10. *The Gospel According to Peanuts,* Robert Short
11. *Call to Commitment,* Elizabeth O'Connor
12. *Pathways to Happiness,* Leonard Griffith
13. *A Man for Every Woman,* Richard Klemer
14. *The Beatitudes,* Hugh Martin
15. *To Change the World,* Ross Coggins
16. *For the Living,* Edgar Jackson
17. *The Meanings of Gifts,* Paul Tournier
18. *How to be a Jewish Mother,* Dan Greenburg
19. *Scripture and the Christian Response,* H. T. Kuist
20. *Teach Us to Pray,* Charles Whiston
21. *He Sent Leanness,* David Head
22. *Too Much, Too Soon,* Diane Barrymore
23. *Guilt and Grace,* Paul Tournier
24. *To Resist or to Surrender,* Paul Tournier
25. *Strengthening the Spiritual Life,* Nels FerrGe
26. *Protestant Christianity,* Dillenberger and Welch
27. *Beyond Reasonable Doubt,* Hugh Montifiore
28. *The All-Sufficient Christ,* William Barclay
29. *When the Cheering Stopped,* Gene Smith
30. *The Sons and the Daughters,* Patricia Gallagher
31. *The Three Sirens,* Irving Wallace

32. *A Time to be Born*, William Procter, Jr.
33. *Your Game and Mine*, Arnold Palmer
34. *Lilies of the Field*, William Barrett
35. *Shout for Joy*, David Head
36. *The Work of Christ*, P. T. Forsyth
37. *Christian Perfection*, P. T. Forsyth
38. *The Art of Loving*, Erich Fromm
39. *Edge of Wisdom*, Robert Wicks
40. *Life Together*, Dietrich Bonhoeffer
41. *Dangerous Fathers, Problem Mothers*, Carlyle Marney
42. *Leaves from the Notebook of a Tamed Cynic*, R. Niebuhr
43. *Dialogue in Romantic Love*, Prentiss Pemberton
44. *The Real God*, Alfred Starratt
45. *The Taste of New Wine*, Keith Miller
46. *Games People Play*, Eric Berne
47. *Living the Ten Commandments*, Carroll Simcox
48. *Foundations for Reconstruction*, Elton Trueblood
49. *Smoke on the Mountain*, Joy Davidman
50. *The 10 Commandments in Modern Perspective*, Weatherley
51. *The Power to See it Through*, H. E. Fosdick
52. *Goldfinger*, Ian Fleming

BOOKS OF 1966

1. *In Her Majesty's Secret Service*, Ian Fleming
2. *Here I Stand*, Roland Bainton
3. *Who Moved the Stone?*, Frank Morison
4. *Share My Devotions*, Catrina Whaley
5. *Pastoral Care in Historical Perspective*, Clebach & Jaekle
6. *The Living of these Days*, H. E. Fosdick
7. *Theology and Pastoral Counseling*, Ed Thornton
8. *The Miracle of Dialogue*, Reuel Howe
9. *Church Meetings That Matter*, Philip Anderson

10. *Dear Mr. Brown,* H. E. Fosdick
11. *The Hope of the World*, H. E. Fosdick
12. *Creative Brooding,* Robert Raines
13. *Good Grief,* Grainger Westberg
14. *Sex and the College Girl,* Gail Greene
15. *Ministering to the Alcoholic and His Family,* Tom Shipp
16. *Dr. No*, Ian Fleming
17. *The Secret of Victorious Christian Living*, H. E. Fosdick
18. *The Decision Maker,* Willard Wetzel
19. *The Wisdom of Insecurity,* Alan Watts
20. *Bonjour Tristease,* Françoise Sagan
21. *Suddenly Last Summer,* Tennessee Williams
22. *Return to Peyton Place,* Grace Metalious
23. *Casino Royale*, Ian Fleming
24. *One Hundred Dollar Misunderstanding,* Robert Gover
25. *Christ and Man's Dilemma,* George Buttrick
26. *The Last Temptation of Christ,* Nikos Kazantzakis
27. *Letters on Christian Living,* C. A. Roberts
28. *Thunderball,* Ian Fleming
29. *Hindu Art of Love,* Richard Burton
30. *The Meaning of Prayer,* H. E. Fosdick
31. *Room at the Top,* John Braine
32. *The Christian Agnostic,* Leslie Weatherhead
33. *The Witness of Kierkegaard,* Søren Kierkegaard
34. *Help! I'm a Layman,* Kenneth Chafin
35. *The Secular City,* Harvey Cox
36. *The Salty Tang,* Frederick Speakman
37. *Spencer's Mountain,* Earl Hammer, Jr
38. *Sermons and Soda Water,* John O'Hara
39. *Cry, the Beloved Country,* Alan Paton
40. *Living Under Tension*, H. E. Fosdick
41. *Between God and Satan,* Helmut Thielicke
42. *Campus Gods on Trial*, Chad Welsh

43. *Foundations of Education, Vol. I,* Stone & Schneider

44. *Religion as Creative Insecurity,* Peter Bertocci

45. *Are You Running With Me Jesus?,* Malcolm Boyd

46. *Playboy Philosophy, Vol. I,* Hugh Hefner

47. *Foundations of Education, Vol. II,* Stone & Schneider

48. *The Summing Up,* Somerset Maugham

49. *The Little Prince,* Antoine de Saint-Exupéry

50. *The Healing of Persons,* Paul Tournier

51. *Mirror for Man,* Clyde Kluchohn

52. *Summerhill, A Loving World*, Herb Snitzer

53. *Summerhill*, A. S. Neill

Harles Cone, PhD, licensed psychologist, completed his professional career as an executive coach hired by corporate boards to work with their key executive leader. Previously, he was a management trainer, licensed psychologist in private practice, college professor, and Southern Baptist youth evangelist, assistant pastor, and pastor. This book chronicles his journey from growing up in a small town in East Texas where he accepted without question his indoctrination into a Christian fundamentalist religion and a Southern White supremacy culture to living in Chapel Hill, North Carolina, as a happily retired "philosopher." He now views the world as an unending mystery to be experienced, not a problem to be solved, nor a dogma to be believed.

www.ingramcontent.com/pod-product-compliance
Lightning Source LLC
Chambersburg PA
CBHW060409130626
46555CB00005B/2014